To:
Rob Drieslein —
Best wishes —
And may all your
memories be great!
Keep up the
super work with
"Outdoor News!"

Netting **Reel** *Memories*

By

Merv Heitschmidt

Merv Heitschmidt
2-7-05

PREFACE

After having been a fishing guide for twenty-five years and a middle level English teacher and coach for thirty-five and a half years, I feel it is now time to finish the book I started some years back. The book was partially done, but left on the "back burner" so to speak, until more considerate attention could be given to accomplishing a means to a completed product.

The contents of this book are, for the most part, all factual (aside from a few names which were lost or forgotten) and focus on a central plan to attempt to entertain those who enjoy true life experiences and fishing adventures.

Being a transplanted farm boy from the wheat field plains of Kansas to the forests and lakes of northern Minnesota, in the mid-fifties, I quite readily took to the waters of Cass Lake, located on the Mississippi chain just downriver from Bemidji, Minnesota. My parents owned and operated Birch Villa Resort which had been located on Cass Lake for many years.

In 1957, our first year at Birch Villa, I was focused on helping my dad work on renewing and remodeling cabins, dock, and out-buildings along with keeping up the general maintenance of everything that needed attention whenever and where ever it required our services. My dad was a "jack of all trades" as he had worked at many different jobs over the years including, auto mechanic work, farm work, carpenter, plumber, electrician, painter, oil field work, heavy equipment operator and you name it. He loved all the different challenges of the resort because he could put all his experiences to work in this type of setting. I did not know it at the time, but I was getting educated in those areas too, as we worked side by side much of the time and I couldn't help but have a little bit of his expertise rub off on me. We added a two bedroom addition to the number eight single cabin located on the lake level that first summer. That addition, along with all the other little odd jobs around the resort kept us quite busy.

That spring I had pleaded with my dad to allow me to use one of the narrow sixteen foot resort rowboats in order to learn the lake and also have a chance at guiding fishing parties that came to the resort seeking guide service. There were already three established guides working their own independent service out of our resort and approximately ten or twelve other guides on the lake at that time. My dad gave in, and that is when and where my very enjoyable guiding career was launched. I did get several chances to go fishing on my own that first summer as dad would allow me to take my boat out almost every evening just to begin learning the lake and getting to know my way around, plus how to handle a boat. I didn't actually do any professional guiding that first summer, but I would usually end up with friends or relatives in the boat whom I did guide voluntarily without pay. It was a busy summer because I tried to spend every spare moment on the water, or at least whenever I had the chance, even if it meant only twenty minutes in front of the resort. By the end of summer I had learned a lot about that part of the lake within a mile of Birch Villa and was ready for the next year in order to expand my horizons and venture forth to areas I had not yet been too well acquainted with.

The chapters that follow will hopefully be of interest to those who enjoy a good true tale and will span the twenty-five years of guiding plus a few events beyond that time up to present-day experiences for obvious reasons to be brought out in the final chapters.

It seems strange, how fishing guides, after a long season on the water, usually look for other waters as a place to spend their vacation time. I guess the loving urge and enjoyment for fishing probably explains why they are fishing guides in the first place. This is probably the reason why I am not an exception to that theory myself, because I love to check out the fishing in other parts of the country while traveling with family and friends. Whether it be trout in southern Missouri or northern Arkansas, salmon and halibut in Alaska, red snapper in the gulf, catfish in Kansas, or just another new lake in Minnesota, I enjoy trying them all.

Most occupations carry with them some aspects that are not totally enjoyable; however, the guide's duties are many and in most cases, gratifying. It gives great satisfaction to catch lots of fish, but not until later do you fully realize where the deep gratification comes from. It lies in the personal relationships you build with the people. I am often asked what I miss most from the guiding days. My reply is, "the people." I do not recall too many things I disliked about guiding except for the fact I was away from my family much of the time, but unfortunately that goes without saying as is the case with many occupations. I believe my wife probably suffered more of those annoyances than I did. She was the one stuck at home with the kids, and outside of some quality time on the beach most days, her job was "full time Mom." I am sure my wife, Jan, put up with many annoying things during those guiding years, yet she never complained about my being on the water a lot. As a matter of fact, she is still putting up with a few of my fishing hang-ups as you will more than likely read about later. Jan "likes" to fish and enjoys going out in the boat, but me, I "love" to fish and she allows me that freedom, for which I am respectfully grateful. Thank you, Jan, I love you.

Perhaps my reasons for writing this book are two-fold: first, I dedicate it to my family whom I love very much. To mom and dad, Alyce and Alfred Heitschmidt, I owe a great deal of respect and thankfulness because they allowed me to make choices and provided positive encouragement. To Larry and Juanita Heitschmidt, my brother and sister-in-law, they were excellent role models and also influenced my life with their positive support. To Jan, my wife of thirty-seven years; Cristi Heitschmidt and Joel Komschlies, my daughter and son-in-law; Chad and Reg Heitschmidt, my son and daughter-in-law; Colton and Ashley, my grandchildren; plus close personal friends, all whom I love very much. It is important to mention some of the mentors who taught me practically everything I know about the structure, patterns, and methods of fishing the waters of Cass Lake and also a few surrounding lakes in the area. The late Cliff Riggles was a "guide's guide" as he helped with countless areas of my guiding education and the ability to relate to people during the hours spent with them in a boat on many trips on the water. Cliff was a lifetime resident of the Cass Lake area and his flare for telling stories of the early days of fishing were always of great interest. He knew the woods and the lake like the back of his hand and was an excellent hunter, fisherman and conservationalist. Having spent a lot of time with Cliff both in the woods and on the water, I can safely say, I owe him a great deal of gratitude for the opportunities and experiences I was fortunate to fulfill. The late Gerhardt "Kutsey" Nornberg was another big influence on my life as a fishing guide. "Kutsey," as we knew him, was a dedicated guide who provided a lot of wisdom to the sport of fishing, and even though he probably didn't realize it, he was a silent role model to many of us younger guides. The late Frank Studley was a guide and launch operator who knew the lake very well too. He gave us lots of expertise as to patterns of feeding times on various areas of the lake at different times of the day. These people were all so important to my guiding career that I wouldn't be able to say with the correct words the value of their influence on my life in any capacity. Without their concern, help and support, the inspiration of this book would not have been possible. Secondly, to all fishing friends, fishermen, and the many, many students who listened and helped me believe in these "fish stories," as they called them, as perhaps being something I should document. Many of these "fish stories" have been used over the years as "classroom rewards," for a job well done, and as a point of reference from time to time pertaining to life's experiences. A few have rather sad endings, others are funny, and yet many are just plain weird, but they are all true. It is my hope that you enjoy these stories as much as I enjoy sharing them with others.

Merv Heitschmidt

HISTORICAL SKETCH

As a bit of Cass Lake history, an old timer and long time resident to the Cass Lake area, Paul Smith, told my dad and I about some of the first landmarks on Cass Lake. The first resort or campground was located on the south shore of Star Island about half way between the two points. There is just an empty lot in that location today, but a trail leads from there back to Lake Windigo. I am told Windigo is a native American word meaning "hidden waters" and is located more toward the north central part of Star Island. Lake Windigo has been written about in Ripley's Believe It or Not as the only lake within a lake in the world, that has a different lake water level and temperature than the outer lake. It is not connected to the outer lake, but is accessible by a portage on the north side of the island. Birch Villa Resort is said to have been one of the first resorts on Cass Lake's mainland, so named about 1918, by a man called George Lydick. Mr. & Mrs. George Lydick owned the land on the west shore of Cass Lake where Birch Villa Resort and Sah-Kah-Tay Beach Resort are now located. Also known as Bug-Aee-Zoo-Wee- Ning Beach on the land records. They would allow one or two tourists (usually railroad men) to stay in their own private dwelling at Birch Villa. During the summer months of 1918, the Lydicks acquired the "Zella Mae," a side-wheeler boat that was one hundred forty feet long and forty feet wide, and beached it on shore at Birch Villa's present location. They renamed the beached boat "The Glykin House," as it had a deck that went all the way around the outside of the ten or twelve small cabins in the center of the boat. They rented these rooms out to people when they came to fish. During this time, George Lydick was close friends with G. L. Pennington of the Soo Line Railroad and Mr.Lydick promoted a lot of fishing for Soo Line officials. They would arrive by rail in Cass Lake and come out to Birch Villa to stay onboard "The Glykin House." Mr. Lydick would row them out to a raft in front of the resort and leave them there for an hour or two before returning to bring them back to shore, usually with their limits of walleyes. Mr. Lydick would also have minnows shipped in by rail so he could provide a bait service for the fishermen as well as the fishing time on the raft.

It is my understanding that the Lydicks had two daughters, so in 1922 they divided the land, which is now Birch Villa Resort and Sah-Kah-Tay Beach Resort equally between the girls. That is when Sah-Kah-Tay actually got its name, because of the division of the land that had been listed as Birch Villa Resort. I am told the name Sah-Kah-Tay means "sunshine home." The girls didn't do anything with the land except carry on the small business their parents had begun a few years earlier. In the mid to late twenties Sah-Kah-Tay Beach Resort was sold and improved to become one of the famous spots to visit in the area. Many big names and well known bands played and stayed there and I won't attempt to go into any kind of detail here, as it has already been given a much grander account of than I could ever offer. In 1937, Paul D. Smith, owner of Birch Wood Products in Cass Lake, bought Birch Villa Resort and developed it into a thriving resort with twelve non-modern cabins and a main lodge, plus the addition of several wooden cedar-strip rowboats and a twenty-four foot Chris Craft launch. Then in 1956, my mom and dad, Alyce and Alfred Heitschmidt, moved to Cass Lake from central Kansas and purchased Birch Villa Resort from Paul and Ruth Smith. Al and Alyce are responsible for a lot of the improvements to Birch Villa as they modernized, remodeled and expanded many of the cabins.

In 1973 Birch Villa was sold to the Marv Topper family who operated it for about four summers. Then in 1977 the Toppers sold to the Ed Hill and Ray Coss families, who owned and operated the resort for another five years until 1982. Then the Roger Morehart family along with his mother-in-law and father-in-law bought Birch Villa and operated it until 2001, when Mark and Kari Nelson and family came to the resort and are still operating it and replacing the old cabins and lodge with much needed new ones.

A picture of the old Star Island Lodge where the campground is now located on the SW corner of Star Island.

1957

In 1957, our first year at Birch Villa, I was focused on helping my dad work at renewing and remodeling cabins, dock and other out buildings along with upkeep and general maintenance of whatever needed attention. My dad had been an auto mechanic, farmer, carpenter, plumber, electrician, painter, oil field worker, heavy equipment operator and was self-taught at all those occupations. I guess that is where the term, "jack of all trades" would fit into his list of various job descriptions. He loved all the different challenges of the resort because he could put most of his experiences to work in that type of setting. Back then I did not realize it, but I was getting educated in those areas too, as we worked side by side much of the time, and I couldn't help but have a little of his expertise rub off on me. Early that summer, we added a two bedroom addition to the number eight cabin, located on the lake level. The addition, along with all other little odd jobs around the resort, kept us quite busy.

That spring I pleaded with my dad to let me use one of the narrow sixteen foot resort rowboats in order to learn the lake and also have a chance to guide fishing parties that came to the resort seeking guide service. There were already about fifteen guides working the waters of Cass Lake, including the three that used Birch Villa as their headquarters. My dad gave in, and that is when my very enjoyable guiding career was launched. I did get several chances to go fishing on my own, that first summer, as dad would allow me to take my boat out almost every evening just to begin learning the lake and getting to know my way around, plus how to handle a boat and motor. I didn't actually do any professional guiding that summer, but would usually end up with friends or relatives in the boat, whom I did guide voluntarily, without pay. It was a busy summer because I tried to spend every spare moment on the water, even if it meant only twenty minutes in front of the resort. By the end of summer I had learned a lot about that part of the lake which lies within a mile of Birch Villa, and was ready for the next year to be able to expand my horizons and venture forth into new areas.

An event which I shall never forget, took place at Birch Villa on September 5, 1957. I had been in school all day, and when I arrived home, there was a lot of activity around the boat dock. I dropped my books inside the front door of the lodge and went straight to where everyone was gathered. I found one of the guides, Cliff Riggles, and his customer from Chicago each holding big muskies for pictures being taken. Cliff was holding a forty-eight inch, forty-two pound musky, and his client held a forty-six inch, twenty-eight pounder. I stood there staring at these two knowing I wanted to catch a forty pound musky, so my goal was set. I had no idea when or where it would happen, but if it did, this book might reveal those details hopefully before it is finished. The muskies were a spectacular sight and I immediately enlisted myself into the conversation and questions being forced upon the two successful fishermen. "Where did you catch them?" "What lure did you catch them on?" "How long did it take to land them?" These were the questions most often asked when big fish had been caught. When the excitement had subsided and people had gone back to their cabins, I was asked if I wanted to go with Cliff and his fishing companion to town when they took their muskies to be officially weighed. Obviously my response was a big "yes," and we were on our way to have these two beautiful fish registered at LeRoy's Minnows. At that time, LeRoy Ellis was operating his live bait business at his home in south Cass Lake city limits. The fish were officially weighed and more pictures were taken by LeRoy's wife, Betty. We were about to leave when Art Lyons, a guide on Lake Winnibigoshish, near Bena, Minnesota, came in with a larger musky than Cliff's forty-two pounder! Art's fish weighed in at a hefty fifty-four pounds, and, I believe, was fifty-six inches in length. All I could think was, "Wow! What a day!" Here were two of the biggest muskies I had ever seen, all in one afternoon! What are the chances of that happening? We didn't know at the time, but later found out that Art Lyon's musky was a Minnesota state record and still stands today. The conversation on the way back to the resort was about how ironic for these two large muskies to be caught just twenty miles apart on separate lakes on the same day. At first we had visions of something like another Leech Lake rampage, which occurred only two years earlier, where many large muskies went on a feeding frenzy during a week long period. I've heard various rumors that there were over two hundred muskies caught during the rampage and approximately seventy some were registered at Federal Dam Landing on the east side of Portage Bay in the northeast corner of Leech Lake. I can remember that time, as my parents and I were vacationing at Cass Lake. We drove to Federal Dam to witness hundreds of vehicles and trailers parked along the road, on both sides, for two or three miles each way, leading to the Federal Dam Landing site. There were about thirty huge muskies hanging from a makeshift "A" frame wooden hanger for display and picture taking purposes. Another twelve to fifteen muskies were lying on the ground, waiting to be hung with the rest. It was a phenomenal sight as we just stood by watching in amazement, wondering why and how something like this could possibly happen at such a magnitude as this. There was utter chaos as people were hurrying around trying to figure out what to do with their fish. Some men were having problems getting their fish weighed and registered. To add to this confusion, there were those of us who were not helping matters, by standing around gawking in amazement, and being obstacles for those who were trying to get the job done in an orderly manner. I believe I was asked three or four times if I had a musky to weigh and register. After we had overstayed our visit, we made our way back to the car. As we drove away, all I could think was, I want to catch one of those big fish someday. I was only thirteen years old at the time, but it remains in my memory like a picture taken yesterday. We later heard some horror stories of boat fights, people getting mad at one another on the lake as they jockeyed for positions and locations along the good fishing areas during the time this rampage was going on. I am glad I wasn't out there with the hundreds of other boats, trying to get to the good spots, as they were all taken and backed up with many fishermen waiting their turn to give it a try. Cliff and I were having visions of another one of these rampages as we drove back to Birch Villa from LeRoy's Minnows. As we rounded the corner to drive down the hill into Birch Villa, we noticed once again, some sort of excitement near the dock area. I don't know why I mention this, but I still had not changed out of my school clothes, and after handling those muskies a few times, my trousers were soiled with dried musky slime, so I smelled of the pungent, musty, musky odor that comes with the handling of these fish. I ran to the dock again after Cliff had parked his old yellow, fifty-five Chevy pickup at the lodge in front of Birch Villa. My dad was there looking out at the lake with his binoculars, and he told me there was a large black bear swimming about a mile out from the resort. Every time a boat passed by, the bear would utter a rough gargling growl and tread water so that its body was half out of the water. I was told to go call the game warden, who at the time was, Swede Olson. I called Swede and told him about the black bear and asked if he wanted to do anything about it. He told me he had been after that bear because it was ransacking resort garbage cans in the area as well as scratching on the sides of cabins, destroying some of the siding and frightening the tourists. He hesitated and told me he had just received a call from near Bemidji, Minnesota and had to take care of some other pressing business first, but he didn't want to lose the bear either. Swede told me to load the high powered rifle and take my dad out in the boat and then destroy the animal. He cautioned to be careful and use our discretion as far as safety was concerned, and not to get too close to the bear as it was large enough to turn a small boat over in the water, which was something I did not wish to experience. After hanging up, I loaded two rifles, first our eight mm Mauser, and the old Springfield 45.70 caliber, then went to the dock to report to my dad. We took a small resort rowboat equipped with a ten horsepower Johnson outboard motor and left the harbor for the mile trip between us and the rogue bear. My dad was in the front, and I drove the motor as we approached. The bear growled that raspy, gurgling, throaty sound and treaded water, just as we had been told by the recent passers-by who reported this unusual occurrence to my dad earlier. We could see a great amount of vehement behavior as the bear continued to growl at us with violent thrusts of its body. I said a little prayer that the motor would not stall or quit running during this ordeal. We did approach with caution and tried to maintain a safe distance of at least thirty or forty feet between us and the bear. Thankfully there wasn't much of a breeze, so it was fairly easy to control the boat. My dad had the eight mm bolt action rifle, and I had the old single shot .45-70 nearby on my boat seat. Dad put two shots strategically in the front middle chest of the bear, but that seemed to make matters worse as the huge black mass of fur kept coming at us treading water and making those awful low growling noises. I backed the boat away safely, and dad told me to try with the .45-70, so after positioning the boat to get a good angle at the bear, I picked up the rifle, aimed carefully at the head and squeezed the trigger. At first I thought I had missed as the bear didn't seem affected by my shot, but within a few seconds its big body relaxed and slumped in the water, face down. We circled the floating bear several times wondering if it would come alive all of a sudden and charge us again, but it just lay there floating listlessly on the surface. At the time it seemed like a slaughter, but this critter had been harassing, ransacking and destroying property in the local area for weeks, and the authorities were concerned mainly with its mad like behavior. Not to mention the fact it could have brought danger to anyone who might have crossed its path. Swede Olson told us later that he had set several traps in an effort to capture the bear, but it was smart and wary, and would elude the traps only to go on raising havoc with whatever got in its way. He also told us it was not his practice to give this kind of responsibility to unauthorized personnel. But, under the circumstances, having known us and not having succeeded in catching the bear, he was willing to try almost anything for the safety of people vacationing or living in the area. Dad and I finally went close enough to the dead bear, floating on the surface, and jabbed it with it with an oar. There was no response, so we waited a bit longer and then tried again, but still no movement on the part of the bear. We used the anchor rope to tie around its head and front legs, and began towing it back to the resort dock. It proved quite a load for the ten horse Johnson outboard, but after about twenty minutes we arrived in the harbor with our furry cargo in tow. There was a good sized crowd that had gathered to view this creature. Some people were concerned about our shooting on or over the water and possibly across the lake, but we had thought of that, and lined the bear up with a large sandy bluff not far away, on the southwest corner of Star Island. If any bullet had missed its mark, it would more than likely have hit the sand bank of the island. It was during the fall season and the lake was not crowded with boats either. We probably wouldn't have fired a shot if there had been any boats nearby. Swede Olson would not have given us the order to destroy the bear if he thought we wouldn't exercise every possible means of safety. It was quite an ordeal and took six of us to hoist the huge bear out of the water up onto the dock. Of course the fur had soaked up a lot of water to add to the weight, so that, along with the awkwardly limp flexibility of the bear's body, made it difficult to raise it onto the dock. Swede Olson arrived shortly after the bear was out of the water and took pictures before calling the local butcher, Frank Jenskow, to come and pick the animal up for butchering. In those days they could still do that and sell the meat over the counter. I must say, after being given a small portion of the meat for tasting , I thought it was rather good. My mom had not cooked bear meat before, so she had a neighbor lady and her husband over the next day to help cook it so we could try it for the first time. I thought it tasted much like pork and have eaten it several times since. At the butcher shop the bear weighed in at five hundred twenty pounds after being hung and left to dry overnight. I was curious to know where I had hit the bear, and upon closer examination, my bullet had entered the nose and had gone into the front of the skull, so it was probably the final blow that killed the animal. This definitely had been a full day, and when all was said and done, darkness had settled in, supper was waiting and partially cold. I had still not changed out of my school clothes, a fact that my mom reminded me of many times because I almost ruined a perfectly good pair of trousers. I know I'll be dating myself, but the slacks were light tan in color and had one of those little Ivy League straps with a buckle in back. Mom had to wash them two times just to get them clean enough for me to wear to school again.

Fall gave way to getting the resort winterized and ready for our first Minnesota winter. I enjoyed most of the winter sports, especially the ice fishing, but having not ever ice skated, because Kansas didn't provide too much of a chance at that sport, I never was a very good ice skater, even though I tried. I concentrated on school work and playing basketball that year and enjoyed my first year as a sophomore at Cass Lake High School. It was a good chance to make many long lasting friends.

Postcard of Cliff Riggles in his guide boat.

Postcard of Cliff Riggles and passengers leaving Birch Villa Harbor for a walleye trip.

Cliff Riggles, standing on the bumper with his forty-eight inch, 42# musky. His client, (name not known), is standing next to the 28# musky he caught.

Cliff Riggles' forty-eight inch, 42# musky after being mounted.

Muskies from the "Leech Lake Rampage" of 1955.

Black bear that Alfred Heitschmidt and Merv shot in the lake. Guide Kutsey Nornberg helped pull the 520# bear out of the water, along with five other men.

The spring season came quickly once the frozen surface of Cass Lake began to thaw. The role of resort operators kept us busy getting all twelve cabins and boats prepared for the upcoming season. I was especially excited because it would be my first year at being an official guide. A man from the Minnesota State Department of Boiler Inspection had come to the high school in March to give me a test which I was told to take, to obtain a guide's license. It was a lengthy exam that contained questions pertaining to boiler run vessels of older times that I was not even acquainted with. Some questions did cover the handling of boats and how to approach docks or piers under different wind conditions, and I found it interesting as well as educational. I took the two hour test and passed, and was issued a license to operate boats on any Minnesota waters. Especially those under the jurisdiction of the U. S. Coast Guard, which included Cass Lake, since it is on the Mississippi River chain. I was now ready to negotiate the waters of Cass Lake and begin guiding as an official business.

Some of the earliest experiences in my guiding career began at that time. One of those memories came about when an elderly couple, Louie and Erma Milner came to our resort in northern Minnesota during June of 1958. Louie and Erma were on their way to Yellowstone National Park and happened to be going through Cass Lake late in the afternoon. They drove to our resort, inquiring about possibly renting a cabin, only wanting to spend the night and be on their way the next morning. It just so happened we had a small one bedroom cottage on the lake, and Louie said, "We'll take it!" As the evening progressed, Louie and Erma found themselves enjoying the company of other guests and my parents in the main lodge. We discovered that Louie was a fisherman, and Erma enjoyed being out in a boat, too. The conversation eventually turned to the good fishing everyone was enjoying at the time, and Louie became more interested in the lake. He started asking more questions about the kind of fishing and the guide services available. Since the fishing was good and in full swing, the older guides were all booked up and I was the only one available. I must explain here that I was fourteen years old, just learning the lake, and Louie was told that I was a capable young boy who could take him and Erma fishing the next morning, if he wanted to go. Louie looked at me and almost immediately decided that he would more than likely continue his trip to Yellowstone. As he and Erma said their goodbyes for the evening and left the lodge, I was disheartened. I thought to myself, "How can I become a guide if nobody hires me to take them fishing?" There was something I liked about Louie, I had a special "gut feeling" that if we could spend a little more time together, we just might become good friends. I said a little prayer as I watched them exit the front door of the lodge, hoping he would reconsider going fishing with me the next morning. Fortunately, God sometimes answers prayers quickly, because as I looked up, Louie came hurrying back into the lodge and asked if I would take him fishing the next day. I was so excited, I almost told him that I would take him for free, but my early beginnings at professionalism kicked in, and I agreed to take him and Erma the next morning at 8:00 am for the going rate of $12.00 for a four hour trip. I furnished the boat, gas, rods and bait.

The next morning I was up at 5:00 am and had my boat at the dock ready to go by 5:30. Louie and Erma didn't show until 8:00 am, so we rigged them up with proper fishing gear and headed out on the lake. The first sandbar or dropoff we tried produced only a few nice perch, so we continued on to another location only to find the same result. I could see Louie was getting a little restless by the time we reached the third spot, and he was probably thinking, "Why did I waste my money on this young rookie?" There were several other boats way out north of Cedar Island, but I chose to start in close and work my way out, trying to locate a few hungry walleyes. Within a few yards after beginning our initial drift, Louie hooked and landed a nice two pound walleye. Now things were looking up and Louie began to loosen up and began talking a little more. I had thrown out a marker buoy so we worked that area and began catching walleyes at a fairly good rate. Louie was really enjoying himself and the mid-morning walleye bite was kicking into high gear. A perfect breeze had come up and we were able to drift along the bar as we bounced the bottom with two ounce trolling sinkers and a three foot leader with a 2/0 hook dressed with a three inch shiner minnow. After we had fished about four hours, I announced that it would soon be time to go back to the resort. Louie, not wanting to get short-changed on his four hour trip, said questioningly, "One more time?" I agreed, "One more time." We reeled up our lines and went upwind, above the marker buoy I had thrown out to spot the area we had been catching the walleyes in. On that drift we caught three more walleyes and were two fish short of our limit of eighteen. We had now been fishing for four and a half hours, and it was past noon, but Louie said once again, "One more time?" I being young, energetic and gullible, was easily persuaded, so I answered, "One more time." Most of the time the guides were back at the dock around noon, and I had seen the Birch Villa guides going in about that time. It was now after 12:30 pm, but I wanted to make an impression on my first official customer, and Louie was really loosening up now and being much more friendly than before. We repeated the drifting process again and finally filled our limits of beautiful golden colored walleyes. On the way back to the dock I thought that I would give Louie a nickname, "one more time Louie." When we did reach the dock at 1:30 pm, the other guides were about to come looking for us, because they were worried that maybe we had motor problems or something similar. After telling the tale of "one more time Louie," they all laughed, and Louie's nickname stuck for the rest of his life. After that first fishing trip with Louie and Erma, they always requested to have me as their guide, and if I wasn't available, Louie would say, "I'll just wait for Merv." Both Louie and Erma had become so in love with the beauty of Cass Lake and its fishing, they never ever went to Yellowstone, because as Louie put it, "Why go way out there when we've got all this at Cass Lake?" Louie and Erma were from a small town in central Indiana and like many Midwesterners, they were very friendly people. As the years passed, Louie and Erma continued to return to Cass Lake each year for their two week vacation at Birch Villa, and we began to build a relationship that I will never forget. Not only did we fish a lot together, we ate out occasionally when they were at the resort, and visited by telephone often and sent Christmas letters to each other every year. In every correspondence I received from them, Louie would always close with, "I can't wait to get back to fish with you, 'one more time'!" We fished together the eight years that they came to our resort, and at Christmas time 1965 I received a call from Erma. She was crying, and she told me that Louie had just suffered a massive heart attack and had passed away that morning. As we talked, she told me how much Louie loved Cass Lake and how much he thought of me. Before she hung up, she said as Louie passed away she was holding his hand and he squeezed her hand and said, "If only I could go fishing with Merv, one more time." That was the last time I heard from Erma as we received a phone call from her daughter the next spring informing us of her mother's death, also due to a heart attack. Louie and Erma left behind many memories I shall always treasure.

Another recollection from those early guiding days was a time I was guiding three men, Randy, Phil and James, from Ottumwa, Iowa. We were fishing for walleyes and the bite was fairly slow on this particular occasion, but we did manage to catch a few walleyes early in the four hour trip. It was getting close to the time for us to head back to the resort when I looked down and Phil, who was in the front of the boat, was pulling in a tiny walleye about ten inches long. To my surprise I could see another huge walleye following the smaller fish he had hooked. As the fish came near the boat, the larger walleye took the small one in its mouth. I knew the big fish wasn't hooked, so I grabbed the net, but somehow the bag of the net was folded over itself, and as I tried to scoop the big walleye, it kept bouncing off the taut net like a gymnast on a trampoline. After about the fourth bounce, I had the big walleye more or less airborne and directed its bounce right into the boat. I looked at Phil and said, "You got a nice walleye." The fish was thirty inches long and weighed ten pounds on my DeLiar scale. James wanted a picture, so he told Phil to hold the fish up and he would snap his picture. Phil refused to take his picture with that walleye saying he didn't catch it, so it wasn't his. We did everything to try to get him to hold the fish for a picture, but he wouldn't do it. Upon closer examination, we could see that the right eye of the larger walleye had a hazy film over it, so it was blind in that eye. When the fish approached the boat, chasing the smaller hooked walleye, the blind eye was on our side, so the fish didn't see us or the boat and that allowed me to use the net and get the fish bounced into the boat. I told the men that if we simply told everyone Phil had caught the fish, people would believe the story before they would believe the bouncy net version. They all agreed (even Phil) and when we reached the dock, one lady saw the big walleye and exclaimed questioningly, "Where did you catch that big one?" Randy jokingly answered, "Right in the mouth!" Everyone laughed and we all pointed at Phil and said that he had caught it. I don't know if Phil was embarrassed or what, but he said he hadn't caught it, and that I netted the fish. Everyone started to exclaim, "A likely story, who caught it, really?" It took some ironing out and explaining, but we finally got the story straight for everyone, after about twenty minutes. Phil then realized that since it was his small hooked walleye that had caused this strange twist of events to occur, he probably should claim rights to the larger fish.

Since it was 1958 and Minnesota was celebrating its centennial, many of the men were sporting beards for the upcoming festivities and the beard contest to be held in August during the annual Cass Lake Water Carnival. My dad and Cliff Riggles were among those who were in the competition. I was only sixteen years old at the time and didn't have much of a whisker growth, but people would jokingly ask me why I wasn't sporting a beard. I would reply by saying, "I've been shaving for two years, and both times I cut myself!"

I have been asked many times if anything funny ever happened in my boat. There were many occasions that were funny to those of us in the boat, but this is one of those "you had to be there" situations. It happened one morning when I didn't have a guide trip. A good friend of mine, Joe Riggles, and I were out fishing for muskies in early July around 6:00 am. Joe was the son of Cliff Riggles, and we spent a lot of time together fishing, going to school, being in school plays, cleaning fish, and just plain hanging out together. This particular morning, Joe had somehow managed to get his line in the propeller of the five horsepower Johnson motor. In an effort to rescue his lure and salvage as much line as he could, Joe tipped the motor up so the prop was out of the water. He was leaning over it, untangling the whole mess when the old green Johnson decided to tip back down into the water! All I could see was arms, legs and a flailing fishing rod as Joe disappeared over the back of the boat and into the water with a huge splash! I rushed to his aide to help him back into the boat and see if he was OK. I'll never forget the look of surprise and shock on Joe's face as he came to the surface, treading water, weeds hanging over his head and face, paddling with one hand, holding his fishing pole in the other, sputtering and exclaiming, "Boy, this water is really cold!" Fortunately it was a July morning, but the temperature at that time of day can still be rather chilly. Together we did manage to get Joe back into the boat and the only thing hurt was his pride. He became quite cold on the ride home, but dry clothes and a good warm breakfast brought him back to normal. It was a long time before we let him forget that experience.

I recall a time when I was attempting to put a five horsepower motor on one of our resort rowboats tied to the dock. As I stepped from the dock into the narrow rental boat with the motor in my hands, the rope holding the boat came untied and the boat began to float to the side, away from the dock. I did a modified version of the splits and fell into the water with the motor in my lap, on top of me. There was no harm done
and Joe was on hand to help me get the motor back up onto the dock and re-secure the boat to its moorings. We put the motor on the boat and it started without a problem. I changed into some dry clothes, but not before almost everyone at the resort heard of the incident and was teasing me about my surefooted ability to prove my seamanship! I never heard the end of that little accident for a long time either.

Another time I was successful in getting into the boat with the motor and setting it in place on the boat's transom, but I forgot to tighten the securing screw type bolts which held the motor on tightly. As was usually the case, I tried the motor out by taking the boat out of the harbor "for a spin" to make sure everything was running properly. As I left the harbor entrance, I turned the motor sharply to the right and it gave an upward surge and came off the transom. I made a futile attempt to hang on to it, but it got away. Fortunately for me, I had fastened the safety chain, and the motor was still hanging onto it, attached to the boat, but underwater. Since it went into the water running, I spent most of that morning taking it apart and drying it out before running it again and saving a costly repair bill. Much to my dismay there were a few people at the dock who witnessed the little incident, and I didn't hear the end of the teasing for a long time. My dad thought the motor ran better after that, probably due to a good cleaning and rinsing out.

Another funny thing occurred one morning during that same month of July. I was guiding two men from Illinois, Russ Ord, and his son-in-law, Oliver Taube. We were musky fishing and had just drifted over and across a heavy weedbed on a so called sunken island in the middle of a bay on Cass Lake. I was motoring the boat back across the same weedbed in order to set up another drift. As we were running at top speed with the five horsepower motor, about six miles per hour, Oliver was dangling his line over the side of the boat allowing the Heddon Crazy Crawler lure to skip and bounce on the surface of the water. For some reason we had all fixed our gaze on his skipping lure when out of the weedbed, a musky apparently attracted by this flashy, fast moving bait, jumped out of the water grabbing and imbedding the lure well into its jaw. I immediately slowed the boat and the fight was on! For the next five minutes, Oliver had all he could handle as the fish, on a short leash, began to jump, splash, fight, dive and simply go crazy! Finally, Oliver was able to feed out enough line to make a decent fight out of a rather odd catch. When it was all over, we had a good laugh about the antics which took place both in the boat with Oliver, and in the water with the musky. It was fish vs. man and at first we weren't too sure who was going to win. Oliver did manage to conquer the forty-four inch beauty that weighed a hefty twenty-six pounds. The fish had a nice girth for that time of year and Oliver had just caught his first ever musky. The remainder of that trip did not prove to eventful, but that one experience was worth the gift of a memory for a lifetime. Those are the kinds of fishing experiences which help build, not only exciting tales, but relationships between friends and fishing companions.

That same summer, but on a different occasion, another fisherman whose name was Don Simmons, from Decorah, Iowa, was in my boat doing the same thing, dangling a bait over the side as we moved along with the five horsepower motor. His lure was a Heddon Meadow Mouse, and he let it skip on the surface. Out of nowhere, wham, a musky cleared the water with the lure in its mouth! As it turned out, this fish was not as large as the one Oliver Taube had landed, but it did prove quite interesting as the twelve
pound, thirty-six inch musky got very wild, very quickly on such a short length of line. We did manage to get the fish into the boat and there was another happy, first time musky catcher.

A rather strange thing happened in my boat one day, as I was transporting a telephone repair man across the lake to service a telephone line for a private party on Star Island. We received several calls from the telephone company back then to transport workmen to the island. There were over a hundred summer homes on Star Island, and many of them had telephone service, provided by an underwater cable. On this particular service call I was bringing the repair man back to the mainland where his truck was parked at our resort. About halfway between the island and our resort a small northern pike jumped out of the water and landed in my boat. I am not sure if the fish was near the surface and had been startled by our boat passing by, or if it was just jumping for some other reason, but it ended up flopping on the bottom of the boat. I gave the four pound pike to the telephone man and he was elated. He told me later, on another trip to the island, he had taken the fish home that evening, cleaned it, and his family enjoyed a fresh fish dinner.

A neat memory from 1958 was a musky fishing trip we made, without a net, that turned out to be successful. In those days we usually carried a devise called a "gaff hook" to land, or boat the bigger fish that wouldn't fit into our regular good sized walleye nets. My customer was a good friend from Holyrood, Kansas, my birthplace. His name was Bob Schlessiger, and he had never fished for muskies before that time. Bob was a good fisherman and had caught many large catfish back in Kansas, but this was a new and different experience for him. I had been guiding professionally for a year and a half at this point, but I had never yet caught a musky myself. By now I knew where to go and how to fish for these freshwater monsters. I had been watching and practicing what the other more experienced guides were doing, and listening carefully to their stories and experiences. I had guided a few fishermen to muskies during this time, and when asked if I had caught a musky or what my biggest musky was, I sheepishly replied, "I haven't caught a musky yet." It was embarrassing to say the least. Oh, there had been many "follows" as we called them, when the huge fish would be curious enough to swim after the lure and follow it back to the boat where we could see its size and gracefulness in the water. I presume the musky either thought it was chasing this foreign contraption away from its lair, or habitat, or it was just curious enough to follow the lure to see just where it had come from or where it was going. At least that was my theory, and it still is, after many years of chasing and hunting this elusive beast of the underwater world. Anyway, it was Bob's first musky trip, and we headed for an area on Cass Lake known as Allen's Bay (I never learned how it came to be known by that name), where we began to fish a weedline off a large sunken island of foliage. The weeds were submergent vegetation (under the surface) that we refer to as "cabbage" because of the wide flat leaf form. In some lakes, this cabbage seems to be good habitat for holding muskies and other smaller fish which probably become prey for the musky. Please do not misunderstand this bit of information, as the muskies do also inhabit other forms of structure in various lakes as well. Certain times of the year and water temperature can also make a difference where you are likely to find these toothy creatures. As Bob and I trolled slowly parallel to the weedline, we would cast our musky lures from the deeper water up to and over the cabbage weeds at the edge of the drop-off in hopes to attract a musky. Bob was having some problems with backlashes occurring much too frequently. He was using a short, four and a half foot steel rod with an old style Pflueger bait casting reel spooled with thirty pound test nylon line. His rod left something to be desired as two of the line guides were loose and would slide up and down the line with every cast and retrieve. The line was very poor, and I could see several frays in it as Bob would cast out and reel in. On one occasion, his reel backlashed, and I watched as the lure settled to the bottom among the weeds. It wasn't a difficult problem for Bob as he quickly corrected the line and began to reel and lift the lure up out of the weeds. Upon raising the lure, a red bucktail inline spinner, a huge musky swam from the seclusion of the cabbage weeds, and literally inhaled it. Bob, looking down at his reel, didn't see the fish as I yelled, "Set the hook!" Bob uttered, "Huh?" Again I shouted, "Set the hook!" Bob still had not seen the fish, but fortunately he did set the hook with a sudden jerk upward on the rod. To his surprise, the fight was on! After what seemed like an eternity and a number of times counting the frayed bits of line as they moved in and out while Bob played the fish carefully, he brought the musky near the boat. I cautioned him not to put too mush resistance on the line or it would break. Finally, Bob had the fish played down and along side the boat, ready for landing. Of course, being the guide, I had the gaff hook ready. I carefully slipped the point of the gaff into the fish's gills from behind the gill covers and began to hoist the heavy mass of fighting fury over the side and into the boat. "Whoops!" I said, as the musky flipped itself free and fell back into the water. Bob had to fight it all over again, and the second try ended with the same outcome as the first. I've heard this term a lot, "the third time is a charm" and it was, as I was able to boat the flopping monster. It was the largest musky I had attempted to land, and Bob and I were both shaking so bad we had to sit down to let our nerves calm a bit. I carried a small scale called a De-Liar in my boat, and have found over the years that it is quite accurate to within a pound or two. When we put the fish on it, it bottomed out at twenty-eight pounds and measured fifty inches. The ride back to the resort was quite a celebration. Bob would let out a loud yell and I, in turn, would retaliate with a whoop and holler of my own, all the way back to the dock! In those days we kept almost everything we caught, even the muskies of all sizes (a fact that I am not particularly proud of today) and the idea of "catch and release" wasn't even a consideration. Everyone wanted to "show off" and have "bragging rights" to celebrate their rare catch. We even carried special little flags in our boats to fasten to our fishing rods and we would "fly the musky flag" as it were, to alert everyone that a big fish was caught as we returned back across the lake. Needless to say, the flag attracted a lot of attention, and people would rush to the dock to see the great catch! I even had other boats follow from halfway across the lake just to get a peek at a big fish. Bob's fish was a chunky one and was officially weighed at thirty-three pounds. He was a proud fisherman who immediately had become hooked on muskies. The very next day, Bob and I went to Bemidji, Minnesota, where he purchased a new musky outfit and several more lures. His new fiberglass rod was a five and a half footer equipped with a new Pflueger Rocket bait cast reel and one hundred yards of fifty pound test nylon line. I hesitate telling this part of the story, but Bob never caught another musky. He did fish for muskies after that for a couple years, but he passed away before he was able to land another one. As I stated earlier, this was not a netting memory, but rather a memory for the lack of a net. I was very relieved with the birth of the "musky net" because I never felt a mastery in the use of a gaff hook. Nor was it my favorite tool to use in landing a trophy musky because of the damage it could do.

That summer quickly came to a close, and during the winter of 1958 and into the spring of 1959, I ordered a new guide boat from the Cass Lake Boat Works, which was owned by the Larson family who lived in Cass Lake. Their factory was located in the heart of the village of Cass Lake and was just across the street from the high school I attended. My reason for mentioning this is the fact that I had made a deal with Arnie Larson, the CEO of the boat works and father to Corky and Conrad "Connie" Larson, who also helped with the family-run business. The boat I ordered was a sixteen foot oversized (extra wide, extra deep) cedar strip with extra heavy duty bracing made of thick solid oak. It was priced out to me at a cost of $525.00 finished. Being a student in high school, I didn't have that kind of money. My parents were strapped with resort payments and were working winter jobs to help make ends meet. For that reason, I did not want to ask them to put the extra burden on themselves just for my benefit. My dad worked at the local Deep Rock station as a mechanic, and my mother was working as a cook just down the street and around the corner from the Deep Rock station at a place called Craig's Café. Craig's was located across the street from the old Teal's Super Value grocery store next to Elmer's Gamble Store. After talking to Arnie Larson about my hardship, he allowed me to come into the boat works after school evenings, when I wasn't practicing or playing sports, to help work on and build my boat. The Larsons were kind enough to allow me to work off some of the expense of the boat to make it more affordable, for my meager budget. It was an experience I'll never forget and in the end, the boat only cost $300.00 out-of-pocket expense. At the time I also owned a nifty orange colored 1957 Cushman Eagle motor bike, and in the spring of 1959, I traded it for two new Johnson outboards. One was an eighteen horsepower and the other was a five and a half horse. Now I was set to begin another year of guiding in a new and larger boat.

Louie and Erma Milner with friend Lucy Mills and Merv.

Another stringer of walleyes Louie and Erma Milner had.

The big blind walleye and remainder of the catch.

Cliff Riggles & Al Heitschmidt sporting their centennial beards.

1959

As the spring 1959 season came, I was anticipating a great fishing opener in my new outfit complete with boat, motor, cushions (which were also legal personal floatation devises at that time,) and all the other equipment which came with the boat. Unfortunately, since I was the freshman guide, I was scheduled to navigate the resort's twenty-four foot launch on opening day of the fishing season. As it had turned out, all three of the other guides had booked smaller fishing parties in their own personal boats, so I was stuck with the three larger parties that had been booked onto the launch. I was very disappointed, needless to say, that I couldn't use my new boat for that first day of the 1959 season. What happened that opening day, however; greatly overshadowed my frustrations with the unchangeable launch schedule. We had an unwritten policy at the resort that required a chain of command. Kutsey Nornberg and I were the only two guides that would navigate the resort's launch. When Kutsey, who was the senior guide, was available to drive the lunch, he had first choice, which left me to take whatever I could muster up. Also when Kutsey had a guide trip scheduled in his own boat, then I was on deck to operate the launch. That's exactly what happened on this particular opener in 1959.

On that opening Saturday I was to take three different parties out fishing for walleye, and the first trip was to leave the dock at 8:00 am and return around noon. The second excursion was to leave the dock at 1:00 pm and return at 5:00 pm and the third to leave at 5:30 pm and return at 9:30 pm. Yes, it would be a long day on the water. As the day started, everything was on schedule, and we departed with the first group of six people (all men) at 8:00 am. Upon arriving at the mouth of Turtle River at the far north end of Cass Lake, we anchored in ten feet of water approximately one hundred yards straight out from the river entrance. Even before the boat had a chance to secure itself with a solid holding anchor, I was netting two, nice, two pound walleyes simultaneously, and within about fifteen minutes, we had four walleyes on the stringer and three more flopping around on the floor of the launch, waiting to join their captive friends. To my surprise we had a limit of thirty-six walleyes on the stringer within two hours after anchoring! We did stay another half hour to try for some jumbo perch, but only the walleyes were cooperating that morning, and after releasing another six or seven, we headed back to the resort with a happy group of fishermen and their limits of walleyes. What I hadn't mentioned before was that I was also one of two fish cleaners at the resort, and we had an unwritten policy that we would make every effort to clean fish while they were fresh. As it turned out, we cleaned fish from about 11:00 am until 12:30 pm (the other guides had limits too), and I was scheduled to leave the dock with the launch again at 1:00. My mom packed a lunch, which I ate on the second trip back up to the mouth of Turtle River. The walleye bite had not slowed as the new group of six people (four men and two women) began to catch fish immediately after the anchor was in the water. We were fishing with what I think is an obsolete rig nowadays. It included a two ounce trolling sinker attached to the end of our line with a three foot, twenty pound test "gut" leader and a plain #2/0 hook at the end. The "gut" leader was actually an early type of heavy, stiff monofilament that makes me wonder how we were able to catch anything with that style of rigging. Again, as it turned out, we were on our way back to the dock with a handsome stringer of thirty-six walleyes, after about two hours of fishing. These folks were grateful for the opportunity to catch limits and to practice an early form of catch and release which was a term we had not been too well acquainted with at that point in time. We arrived at the resort around 4:00 pm and my fish cleaning partner, Joe Riggles, and I began cleaning fish (and again all other guides had done well.) It was 5:30 pm when I was on my way back to Turtle River entrance, and my crew of six (three men and their wives) were anticipating a big haul of walleyes. This time things were a little different as the area of the river had quickly become a famous spot for all the fisherpersons in the world, or so it seemed. We did not get the usual spot that had been so successful for us on the two previous occasions that day, but I was able to maneuver the launch as close as I could. It took about ten minutes for the first fish to be netted and landed, a seven pound beauty, much fatter than I had thought it should be, considering the time of year, after a recent spawning run. We began catching walleyes at the rate of about one per every five minutes which was not as fast as the two previous bites, but it did improve after we were able to move and position the launch closer to "the spot"! It took three hours this time to catch our limit, and we were on our way back to shore at around 9:30 pm. By the time I had cleaned out the launch and gassed it up and put it back in the docking stall where it was kept, it was about 10:30 pm. Joe had already taken all the fish to the fish cleaning house and had started the task of filleting walleyes. We finished cleaning that night just before midnight. The next day was to bring more of the same, except I had only two guide trips with the launch, and, yes, we did fill out limits again. I have to say that it doesn't happen that way every season. Some years, depending usually on whether there is a late or early spring warm up, the walleyes will spawn a little earlier which means they might be moving back down river and into the lakes earlier too. It also means they might be putting on the feedbags earlier as well. If the season warmup occurs later, then the walleyes may or may not feed quite as heavily as one would expect. The problem with early warmup is that the fish will be back in the lakes and scattered before the opening season, and then it requires a bit more finesse on the part of the fisherman to properly locate and catch with any consistency. We happened to hit it just right during that spring of 1959 and even though I didn't get to use my new boat on opening weekend, I did have a remarkable experience with the great people with whom I was able to fish, and the fun we shared as the walleyes cooperated. In the launch that weekend we brought in one hundred eighty walleyes, and Joe Riggles and I cleaned over five hundred walleyes all together, not counting a few northern pike and perch also.

Things did work out for me later as I was finally able to "break-in" my new boat and motors, as time went on. I had just completed my junior year in high school and during the first week of June, my brother, Larry, his wife's grandfather, Karl Kobler, and a friend of our family, Delmar Huck, all three drove up to Cass Lake together to do some early season walleye fishing. The first day out with them in my boat, the wind was fairly strong out of the south, and we were trying to locate a school of walleyes on what we call the West Cedar Bar. It is a drop-off obviously located to the west of Cedar Island in Cass Lake, and it has various degrees of gradual to sharp forming edges which run perpendicular to the island itself and consists of a series of underwater curves and cuts that have a tendency to attract and hold fish for extended periods of time. My brother, at the time, was a speech clinician for the Scott County School District located in the western Kansas town of Scott City, Delmar Huck was a farmer in Scott County who loved to fish, and Karl Kobler, "Grandad," as we called him, was from Hays, Kansas where I later attended college, played basketball, and lived with "Grandad" for four years. We were fighting the brisk wind on West Cedar when Delmar managed to catch a nice walleye as we drifted up on the corner of a part of the sandbar. I immediately threw a marker bouy out onto the shallow side of the bar, from where the fish was hooked, and we took the boat back upwind above the marked spot. As we drifted back over the area, we had several bites, but the boat was moving too fast for us to provide any kind of slow presentation with bait. We were using shiner minnows on a plain #2/0 hook again, as before. I told the men to reel up and we would try to make our anchor hold on the sand as it came up the drop-off. The twenty-five pound navy type anchor did take hold on the third try, and we began to cast our minnow rigs out over the drop-off. We would retrieve the minnow very slowly and work it up the drop from about fifteen feet of water to about ten or twelve feet. It seemed that when the bait got to the ten foot point that's where the walleyes would be. We had a great time and actually forgot about the wind because the bite was exciting enough to keep our minds occupied with the walleyes. It took us four hours to get our limit, but it worked out that Grandad, who was eighty-eight years young at the time, caught the largest walleye, an eight pounder. I'll never forget the proud look on his face as we took his picture with the fish, he was in his glory! As I remember, that spring and summer proved to be one of the best in my record- ed memory of walleye fishing. There were many guide trips between the opening day launch trips and this last mentioned walleye trip to West Cedar, but these memories seem to fill that area of my mind as I recall some of the "good times" of those early guiding years.

A very unusual situation came up in the middle of June that summer as I was heading out across the lake one morning at eight o'clock. I had three men in my boat and we were on our way to check out some new areas or areas that we hadn't been fishing up to that point yet this fairly new season. As we left the harbor I noticed a dark object in the water about a quarter mile straight out from the resort and directly in our path, so I thought I would veer off to the left side of this object, but close enough to see what it was. Usually if a piece of driftwood or a log hap- pened to come loose from its mooring on shore and end up drifting somewhere in the lake, we would tie on to it and tow it back to shore and leave it in some safe place so it wouldn't present a safety risk or hazard to other boats on the lake. On this particular occasion the object drifting in the lake turned out to be a deer swim- ming in circles and seeming to be a bit disoriented in its behavior. We came close and circled the animal noticing it was a doe with blood on its head and we circled the deer again this time seeing that apparently someone had taken a shot at it earli- er. There was an open wound which only grazed the skull of the doe and split the hide open exposing a bleeding crease over its right eye. We were going to leave the animal to fend for itself and not annoy it more than it had been already, but as we began to motor away the deer continued to swim in circles and act like it was going to give up as it leaned to one side with a listlessness of defeat. I swung the boat back toward the deer and as we approached she didn't seem to fight back or even try to swim away to avoid us. I took the anchor rope from the bow of the boat and made a makeshift lasso and threw it over the doe's head tying the other end to the back of the boat. Then I swung the boat back toward the dock and began the slow arduous task of towing her in to shore, but letting her swim enough to keep her balance and maintain a feeling of her own self control. She did not fight the rope around her neck until we got close enough to shore where she could touch the bottom, and then she began to get a bit unmanageable. My first intention was to bring her to shore on the beach at Birch Villa, release the rope from her neck, let her get her bearings and watch as she trotted off over the hill between the cabins. As we experienced her antics in the shallow water, I knew there was no way I wanted to contend with this now excited doe at the end of my anchor rope. I knew what one swipe of one of her flailing front hooves would accomplish if it made contact with any part of our body, after all a deer will use its hooves to protect itself. Now I turned the boat back out away from shore and managed to get the deer into deeper water where she settled down and began to swim again. This time I altered the plan a bit and took the deer into the harbor where the water was deeper and the doe wouldn't be able to touch bottom and fight back. As we entered the harbor where the water gets shallower for a few yards the doe felt the bottom and began to get wildly active again until I drug her into the deep water of the boat harbor itself. She calmed down again and swam behind the boat until we reached the dock. Several people had gathered to see the deer and to witness what we were going to do with her. At this point it was a matter of "making up the rules as you go" type of situation and we weren't too sure just what we were going to do yet either. My dad surveyed the problem of the still bleeding open wound of the doe and he ran to the main lodge to get some BFI powder, a powdery substance which we used to put on an open wound to stop the bleeding. While dad was gone I untied the rope from the boat, crawled out onto the dock and just tried to help the deer maintain some sort of composure so as not to go to wildly crazy. At that point I believe the doe must have felt some form of endless restraint and began to bend or curl its legs up under its body and force its own head under water. I honestly feel the doe had given up any hope of being freed at that time and she was attempting her own form of euthanasia in order to put an end to something she didn't feel she was going to escape from. I worked very hard at pulling her up with the rope still around her neck and each time I was able to get her head out of the water she was making a snorting, breathing noise like she was forcing herself to breathe in water. Dad finally arrived back with the BFI powder and as I held her head up he liberally applied it to the open wound of the deer. She was still fighting the confinements of the rope, but we managed to lead her back to the end of the dock where we could loosen the lasso and set her free. The one big problem was, we had to get her into shallow water again in order to loosen the rope. When her feet touched the bottom at the end of the dock she stood up on her hind legs and fought with her front hooves much like a boxer would do only with stiffer movements of the upper extremities. As she came down, one of her hooves struck the end of the dock with such a force it chipped a good half inch piece of wood out of the two by twelve plank. I was fortunate as I had just jumped back out of the way of her flailing feet. I led the doe back to deeper water and lying down on the dock, managed to relax and release the rope around her neck. I then turned her around in the water by handling her with both hands around or on her neck and she swam toward the shallower water at the end of the dock, under her own power. Cameras were clicking and snapping as the doe reached hoof deep water, shook the water off herself, staggered a few steps, stopped again and shook, then bounded off between the cabins and out of sight over the hill. It was a sad story turned good and we'll never know whether that doe would have survived if we had just left her there swimming in circles and bleeding badly from the near miss of an illegal, out of season bullet. I would like to think we made a difference that day in the life of the deer. The game warden got wind of the story and tried to make a big deal of the rescue of the doe and even wrote articles for the local papers with pictures and the whole bit, but I think and still believe that any person left in the same situation would have done something to help the creature survive. I didn't see it as an heroic act, but more of a gesture of kindness and responsibility to help conservation.

Probably one of the most memorable, if not the most memorable event in my guiding and fishing career was my first musky. It happened during the mid-summer month of July and I was guiding a man named Alvin Lilly from Kansas. Al, as everyone called him, was a novice musky fisherman and wasn't too sure he wanted one of those big fish in the same boat he was fishing in. After Al's first mid-sized follow, he was even more convinced that he didn't relish the thought of sharing space with one of these large fish he had just seen in the water swimming after his lure. As it turned out, Al didn't have another follow, because the attention turned to my end of the boat as I set the hooks on a nice solid strike. It was a musky! I held my breath as the big fish took line and then relinquished under my retrieve time and time again. Eventually the musky gave in and I brought it along side the boat, attempting to single-handedly hold the rod tip up with the left hand while slipping the gaff hook into its gills with my right. It was a painful feeling as the fish flopped off the gaff and landed back in the water only to run and be played in again. All this time, Al was sitting as far up in the bow of my boat as he could get, and when I asked if he would help he responded by telling me he thought I was doing just fine (nice guy.) as it turned out, I managed to boat the fish on the second attempt and it was one of the greatest feelings of accomplishment I can remember. After all the shaking and excitement I put the fish on a stringer and checked the weight on my De-Liar scale. It bottomed out at twenty-eight pounds, so I knew it was a nice musky. Al was ready to go in, but I convinced him that the muskies seemed to be active, so we continued casting. We went right back to the same place and I had another strike! This was another good sized musky and as I attempted to put pressure on the pole, the line broke! I guess it was really poetic justice for my being so greedy, but remember, I was still a greenhorn at this sport, because I had just landed my first musky not twenty minutes before. I was upset at myself because it is my theory that when a fish breaks my line, I'm probably to blame and in this case, I was. Al and I casted for another hour without anymore action and then headed back toward the resort, yelling, celebrating and flying the musky flag! The musky officially tipped the scale in the bait shop at twenty-eight pounds, fourteen ounces and measured forty-eight inches. Now the pressure was off and I could tell my clients I had, in fact, caught a musky. I had the fish mounted for the expensive price of $40.00 and it still hangs in my shop today. I'm not sure about the fish that got away that day, but I'd like to think it was the forty-seven incher I caught two months later in the same location. When I lost the fish, I remarked to Al that it looked like a twin to the first one I had caught. Actually, after two and a half summers of hard musky fishing, I wondered if the big day would ever present itself and after that experience, I have been an avid musky fisherman for the past forty-five years now.

An early group experience proved to be both successful and supportive to my young guiding career as one day there six men from the Fargo, North Dakota area who came to Birch Villa inquiring about guide service. It seems they were interested in a northern pike trip on the Mississippi River above the power dam between Lake Bemidji and Wolf Lake. As it turned out, Cliff Riggles, our oldest and most experienced resident guide and myself, the youngest and least experienced, took these men to the destination they wanted to fish. Our time together was not only successful, (we caught our limits of pike that day, twenty-four) but we had a great time learning about each other and getting to know each other's back-grounds. It was a complete lesson in human relations for me, as each man had his own story to tell and each came from different occupational backgrounds, not to mention the unique diversity of ethnical histories every man shared. It was a busy time for me, netting fish, catching fish, stringing fish and visiting when the situation arose. I was teased a lot, being the freshman guide and trying my best to please the customers. Upon returning to the resort, I overheard Cliff telling my dad I had done a great job relating to and yet respecting the men we were guiding that day. He told my dad if I was able to handle that group with their kidding and fun intentions, then I could handle any guide situation. I wasn't supposed to hear those complimentary remarks, and I didn't let on like I had, but I can tell you , it catapulted me into a state of guiding oblivion. As I stated earlier, the fishing was fantastic as we landed our limits of northern pike ranging from four pounds up to twelve pounds. The neatest thing about the entire day was two of the men in my boat had never landed a northern pike before and the largest fish either of them had ever caught was a small sunfish less than a half pound. It's times like that which make a guide's day.

During the summer months, in our spare time, my dad and I built a new cabin on the lake level. It was our number nine cabin, which still stands, and it replaced a smaller single bedroom cabin which we moved to another location to continue its usefulness. The new cabin was a deluxe two bedroom with full bath, kitchen and dining area to complement its location and a good view of the lake.

The musky bite had been good that summer as was the early season walleye success. My record shows we boated thirty-six muskies ranging from seven pounds up to a couple thirty pounders. One of those muskies was a loner story, as I tried one hot day in mid-July to get someone to go with me, because I had a "feeling" there was a musky out there just waiting to be caught. Cliff thought it was too hot, Larry, my brother, was resting, the dock boy, Tim Monda, wasn't interested, and Kutsey thought it was too hot and still. It seemed like no one was even the least bit excited about a free ride, not to mention a free guide trip for a couple hours, just to see if my "feeling" was only that. I got in my boat and headed out alone, telling the dock boy, Tim, that I would be back by noon for lunch. It was a very hot, still day with temperatures in the low to mid-nineties and just cruising across the water seemed to feel like a refreshing dose of air conditioning. My destination was Allen's Bay, a well known area for muskies, and as I approached a nice weedbed between the two Potato Islands, my thoughts went back to the day before, when I had raised a nice musky just at the edge of the weedline near a finger of bull rushes that jutted out from a rocky shore. I started a few yards back from the scene that disclosed the fish a day earlier and began casting toward the weeds with a yellow Marathon Musky Houn bucktail in-line spinner. After about five casts in the hot stillness of the day, I was asking myself why I ever thought it would be fun to come out here and face this torture, in this oven of a place. No sooner had that thought crossed my mind when I felt a surge on the end of my line and saw a swirl of water on the surface and realized I had a fish on while instinctively setting the hook. The battle was on and here I was, alone in the boat, with an overly aggressive mid-sized musky, jumping, twisting, doing cartwheels and giving me a fantastic fight. I wasn't sure yet just how large the fish was, but I did know it was of keepable size and I wanted to take it home to show those lazy people what they had missed. The fight lasted for what seemed like an hour, but probably was only five minutes in all reality. It was a beautifully proportioned fish and its spotted sides stood out against the silvery background of its girth as it jumped and dove in every attempt to free itself from the captivating hooks in its jaw. As the musky began to slow and play itself out, I was faced with another obstacle, landing the beauty with the gaff hook! The thought had not entered my mind, so I really wasn't prepared for this ritual, but the tired fish cooperated fully and I was able to pull this monster into the boat on the first try. By now I was sweating heavily, but not realizing it due to the excitement with the forty-five inch, twenty-four pound fish that was now lying in the bottom of my boat. Again I'll remind you, we hadn't even thought about or heard the term "catch and release" so our mind set and mentality wasn't headed in that direction, just the opposite, take the musky home, show it off, brag about it, clean and eat it. I did just that, took it home and after several pictures and many explanations as to where, how and with what I caught the musky, I filleted it and we ate it at the fish fry we hosted weekly for the guests at Birch Villa Resort. I had some fun with that story as I didn't let any of the people who chose not to join me that day forget about what they had missed and every chance I got, I would "rub it in" just to torment them a bit.

You will remember as I stated earlier, I didn't like the "gaff hook" for several reasons. First, I felt it was harmful to the fish's gills and it could easily destroy a musky with very little effort due in part to the sharp point which tore at the flesh and gills of a fish. Secondly, the gaff was wrongfully handled by many fishermen who became frustrated by not being able to successfully land a large fish, so they would use the back side of the gaff to hit or club the fish on the head in order to stun it so they could insert the hook of the gaff in the gills to bring the fish into the boat without further difficulty. I was guilty of this myself, but on the one and only occasion it paid off and we kept the musky. I never clubbed a fish to stun it, but one day I was guiding a man named Hank Bosse from somewhere in Illinois. It was Hank's first time at musky fishing and as luck would have it, he hooked into a monster within the first half hour of casting. It was a large, lazy, powerful musky, but not very aggressive as the fish never attempted to jump or roll or even roll on the line. It just swam back and forth around the boat about three or four times occasionally giving a quick burst of speed with its powerful tail when we attempted to bring it along side the boat to get it ready for the gaff. After what seemed like a long battle with the musky, Hank was able to get it to stop along side the boat and I slipped the gaff into its gills. Upon feeling the gaff this creature went ballistic right there beside the boat with me at the handle end of the gaff holding on for dear life. As the fish thrashed and twisted, I managed to get the gaff hook completely through the gills at the base of its throat and with some tremendous thrusts the heavyweight musky twisted free of the gaff, came off the lure, and slipped silently back to the depths of the weedbed. As the monster fish swam slowly away, I noticed it was bleeding profusely and I hoped that I had succeeded in doing what I had attempted before losing the fish, sever the juggler artery. If that happened, I had heard of attempts like this before, by other guides, to rescue what was probably going to be a dying or dead musky. There were stories of others who had severed the main artery of a large fish and it would bleed to death and float to the surface in most cases, because it would die before having a chance to expel all the air from its flotation sac thus leaving enough buoyancy to bring the fish back to the surface. All we could do was wait, hope and pray we could be fortunate enough to salvage a musky that would otherwise be a waste of mother nature's resource. We fished around the area for some time, casting half heartedly and watching for any telltale signs of some unordinary action on the surface of the water. Nothing happened for a long while and after about an hour of waiting, we decided our mission was not going to prove successful so we would move on, try another area and return to check it out, on our way back to the resort. As I was starting the motor I thought I saw something out of the corner of my eye, some abnormal movement on the surface just behind the boat. I turned the boat to get a better look when Hank yelled, "There it is!" We saw it at the same time, the big musky had floated to the surface, belly up, and we could see the gaff had done its damage by tearing through the main artery at the base of the gill. As we lifted the almost dead fish into the boat and after a few thank-yous for answered prayer, we went back to the resort. It had been an exciting adventure, as we knew it was a big fish, but when it officially tipped the scale at thirty-two pounds, eight ounces and measured fifty-one inches in length, it became the largest musky so far that season to be brought in to Birch Villa. Hank was a very happy trooper that day and he had the fish mounted with plans to hand it over the mantle above his fireplace back home in Illinois. I was a very happy guide for several obvious reasons, but now as I look back on the entire story and think how it played out, I believe the most important thing was the fish did not go to waste. Hank got the meat back from the taxidermist before he left the resort and his musky was finished in time to be shipped back to him in Illinois before Christmas that year, what a beautiful and fitting gift to end this story.

I recall another launch trip I had to take that summer, and for some odd reason it seems like mother nature usually has a way of humbling a person when they think they know better. In this case I tried every excuse I could think of to discourage the six people who wanted to go fishing, that conditions were very poor. It was the middle of July, a hot, still day, and the sky was clear with an unusually bright shining sun. All species of fish seemed to have turned off their feeding habits for about a week. I had been "skunked" so to speak, on the last two or three guide trips and it just wasn't any fun to go out knowing you're going to catch "zero." If you have ever been out on a lake during ninety degree days with no wind and obviously no shade, at least in an open boat, it is genuine torture. So, as I said, I tried every excuse possible to cancel or postpone a walleye guide trip with the launch. The customers had a different perspective of this situation and since they had driven over a thousand miles to fish Minnesota waters, they were convinced they would fish. Reluctantly I conceded and prepared the launch for what I thought would be a "fishless excursion." We usually left the dock at 4:00 PM for most afternoon fishing trips, but on this occasion, due to the extreme heat, we set the departure time for 5:00 PM. This would have us returning to the resort dock about 9:00 PM which would hopefully give a bit of relief from the hot sun. We ventured out at the newly scheduled time and after approximately three hours of trolling with minnows there was one small fifteen inch walleye on the stringer accompanied by a twelve inch jumbo perch, not much to show for three hours of intense fishing. I say intense, because it seems as though we tried harder to catch fish when conditions were tough, at least more so than when the fish were biting good, because we didn't have to work as hard for what we caught when the fish cooperated. The twenty-four foot Chris Craft launch was equipped with two-way radio communication to the resort lodge, and after three hours of tough fishing, I radioed back to let them know we weren't doing too well, and we would be back at the dock at the scheduled time. With that I signed off and we tried another "hot spot" called North Cedar Bar. Yes, it is north of Cedar Island and extends far out into the larger part of Cass Lake basically running in a northerly direction. Probably the greatest part of guiding is meeting many different people and getting to know them very well. I used to believe that catching the fish was the best part, and at this particular time with only two small fish on the stringer I was enjoying only the cool taste of an occasional bottle of pop and of course the company of the people who were on the launch with me. These folks were really genuine human beings, because they were laughing, joking, poking fun on occasion, and just having a great time, making the best of a rather boring situation. As we pulled up onto the sandbar on North Cedar Island we were about a half mile from the island and the drop-off had a very gradual slope and incline as it inched away from the ten to twelve foot depth we were fishing to a depth of thirty some feet. It also sloped up the other way to the shallower water of about five to six foot depths. It was along this drop-off or breakline that we would maneuver the boat parallel to the edge keeping the craft in about twelve feet of water. This depth changed frequently as the feeding habits of the walleyes also changed, so we had to keep current with those habits in order to maintain some degree of stable consistency in our guiding routine. We were slow trolling along the drop-off when two of the ladies tangled their lines and needed some assistance from the guide, so I let go of the steering wheel and went to the stern of the boat to help undo the tangles. As this was taking place, the launch for some unknown reason, began to curve slightly toward the left or portside and up onto shallower water. We were turning into about six feet of water and I could see the bottom, but I allowed the boat to continue its turn thinking it would come about and we would continue on up the breakline. I was wrong, because all of a sudden one of the men yelled, "I've got one on!" I looked up and sure enough, his fish pole was bent right over the boat, bouncing up and down with the rhythm of the antics of a fighting walleye. I reached for the landing net and brought the four pound walleye into the boat. Shouts of joy filled the air as everyone had to get a good look at the beautiful golden sided walleye while I added it to the stringer. What happened in the next half hour was indeed a miracle, because at that time the other two men in the boat yelled, telling me they had fish on their lines too. We were still up on top of the sand bar in only six feet of water, and try as we might, we could see bottom, but we couldn't see the fish, yet they still continued to bite. I tossed a marker bouy out away from the area about forty feet to the east and we continued to let the launch slowly circle the area near that marker. Fish were being caught and netted two or three at a time and I could not keep up with the stringing of them, so we had flopping walleyes on the floor of the boat most of that thirty minute bite. The biting seemed to slow gradually and as I caught up with the stringing process I began to count, so as not to exceed the limit and remain within the legal limit. There were forty-one walleyes on the stringer and as I told the people we would have to quit, one lady caught the last of the forty-two to even out our limit! Needless to say it was a fun trip back to the dock and the chatter never stopped. As we pulled up to the dock there were several people waiting to welcome us back and my dad said, "you're early, did you give up on those lazy critters?" At that time someone on the dock got a glimpse of our catch on the floor of the launch and gasped, "Oh, my gosh!" That drew attention from everyone and those that had been around the resort for a week or two were amazed at such a huge catch. Out of those forty-two walleyes, one was a seven pounder, one a five pounder, there were two four pounders and the rest ranged from one to two pounds. Ironically the first small walleye of the evening was the smallest of them all. We had quite a celebration after the fish cleaning was over and there were lots of mini-stories surrounding the memories of that four hour trip. The one I remember most was that the two ladies who had tangled lines and who I left without untangling, said that after I netted that first North Cedar walleye they looked down and their lines were free and unknotted on the bottom of the boat. I know positively that I had not finished with the untangling of those lines, yet there they were, free of entanglement and ready to be fished with again. Those two ladies were the recipients of the seven and five pound walleyes. As I stated earlier, it was a good lesson in being humbled as I was continuing to learn very valuable lessons in life and what the true grace of God is all about. These are the kinds of experiences that help mold character and even though, as a young man I probably wasn't aware of that fact, yet it did play an important part in my life and the maturing process I was blessed to have. Those strangers who came a thousand miles to fish Minnesota waters quickly became lifelong friends as they continued to come back to Birch Villa Resort and take part in their yearly fishing excursions together on the launch. The days that followed that phenomenal catch in mid-July were not as successful, but we did catch a few more walleyes at that location late in the evening hours. The habits of that particular bite seemed to be short lived as the walleyes more than likely moved on and we caught less and less each day until nothing could be caught there, so we moved on too, looking and hoping for another fantastic find of equal or greater reward.

That summer of 1959 seemed to pass so quickly that before I knew it I was forced to begin thinking of the up-coming school year that was to be my senior year. It was difficult, because I remember thinking that I didn't want the summer to end, yet I was quite anxious for my last year of high school to get under way too. It was another lesson in life I look back on now, as I have had many occasions to have to "let go" of some things, so to speak, to make way for others. The old saying "life goes on" pretty well sums it all up. We need to learn to be able to accept that fact and live our lives to the fullest extent that God will allow. Near the end of that summer, I was wanting to go musky fishing one day when things were slow, and as luck would have it, a man from Grand Forks, North Dakota drove in looking for a musky guide to take him out. He said his name was Paul Bornhoff, he was on his way home, but wanted to muskie fish. I told him I would take him out if none of the other guides would and I mentioned that I had this funny "gut feeling" there was a musky out there just waiting for us. He laughed and after the other guides gave way to my desires, we loaded his gear into my boat at 9:15 AM and we were on our way. I motored the boat toward the north to a place called Allen's Bay, where there are several weed beds, which offer a good habitat for muskies, as well as northern pike and walleyes. There was a particular spot in the middle portion of Allen's Bay, where I had seen a nice sized musky just two days earlier, in the middle of a small sunken island weed bed. She had followed a buck-tail spinner bait that a customer of mine was using at the time. We commented on how nicely proportioned the body of the fish appeared as it swam lazily by the boat, but we were unable to get another rise after many more casting attempts, following the sighting. As I slowed the boat to make preparations and proper adjustments to allow for windage, I still had that same "gut feeling" about this being the right time and place. It didn't take long to prove my theory, as the huge body of swimming flesh slammed the yellow bucktail spinner bait Paul was retrieving, after only two casts! There it was, not ten feet from where we had spotted the fish just two days earlier! Another wild fight ensued, as this musky was a prime specimen of lasting endurance. In what seemed to be an hour, but was probably only five or six minutes, the huge fish jumped three times completely clearing the water. It made four dives for deeper water and rolled itself up in the line connected to the lure. Paul managed to hold on, with rod-tip up, keeping a taut line, letting the fish play out and reel line in when it would relinquish under the steady strain of its opponent. As the fish began to play out and slow its shorter than normal runs, my mind went to the process of landing this critter with the gaff hook that was lying on the bottom of the boat. I could tell Paul was an experienced fisherman as he was keeping a secure rein on the fish. As fate would have it, the moment the gaff touched the water, the fish made a terrific surge and rush to get free, but the line stayed tight and the gaff found its way under the gill plate. Upon turning the fish back toward the boat she was brought aboard with hardly any resistance. I was one happy guide as I cranked up the eighteen horse Johnson and headed for home. It was now 10:00 AM and we had just left the dock only forty-five minutes earlier. It was a little before 10:15 AM when we floated into the harbor at the resort, with the musky flag flying, and people began to gather on the dock, at the sight of the red "musky" flag tied to the tip of my fishing pole. There was quite a commotion around the dock for awhile as the sight of a musky was always a special treat, regardless of size. This particular musky measured forty-eight inches in length and weighed thirty-one pounds. It was a very well proportioned fish with a nice girthy body. We never used to measure girth back then, in fact, we never used to measure length very much either, because the weight was always the big factor in determining whether it was a big fish or not. After the pictures were taken and the story retold many times, it was off to the taxidermist to see about getting the fish mounted. The first price quoted was fifty-five dollars, but after some negotiating the taxidermist let us get by for forty dollars, the same as I had paid for a musky I had mounted earlier that summer. My client was given the meat from the musky after the taxidermist skinned it out, and he was able to take it home.

I believe that was one of the last big memories I had that season as summer turned into fall and school started, thus having to turn my thoughts to schoolwork and helping my parents make resort preparations for the winter. There was water to be turned off and lines to be drained, cabin plumbing to be winterized, boats to be dry docked, and many other chores to be tended before the snow came. It had been a great summer filled with lots of terrific memories. Memories that I'll never forget.

New 16' Cass Lake boat.

Postcard pic of new 16' Cass Lake boat.

String of walleyes from opening weekend.

Opening day walleye caught on a launch trip in Cass Lake.
This was the third trip of the day and was the result of an
evening trip.

String of walleyes caught by Grandad Kobler, Larry H.,
Demar Huck and guide Merv.

Grandad Kobler and Vincent Heitschmidt with a string of fish.

Deer Merv saved from lake with grazed head from gunshot
wound.

Merv's 1st musky.

Some northern pike caught on the Misssissippi R. near the power dam.

Merv with 45" musky caught alone on a very hot day.

Merv and Hank Bosse holding Hank's 32½ # musky.

Some of the walleyes caught on a launch trip.

Merv with a 37½ # musky he caught in Cass Lake.

Paul Bornhoff with a 48" musky.

1960

The winter of 1959-60 passed as quickly as the previous summer. It was a great year for me as I had been elected one of the senior class officers, was appointed captain of the fire team, served as editor of the yearbook, earned all-conference honors in basketball, sang in a boys' quartet and choir, played one of the leading roles in the three act play, and had a good spring baseball season. It was an inspiring time for me, and I thank God for a loving family, plus their support and attendance at all my activities. What more could a boy of eighteen want as the spring came and brought with it the new fishing season ?

There were big plans for 1960 as we moved the resort's fish cleaning house from on top of the hill, down to lake level, to prevent having to carry large stringers of fish to be cleaned all the way up the hill each time cleaning needed to be done. It was a huge improvement and saved time for those who did most of the fish cleaning. We also built one more new, three bedroom cabin on the lower level with a great view of the lake. These projects were done during the tourist season, and sometimes became an added burden with all the normal obligations there were in operating a resort. To add to this, we built forms and ran concrete for a new boat launch, something we had done without, but seriously needed, over time, with the increase of customers bringing their own boats.

It was another blockbuster opening season that year as I was faced with the challenge of three fishing trips with the launch on opening day. That was followed with two more launch trips on Sunday, which also included a baccalaureate service for our senior class that evening. Opening day was fantastic, as there were six people on each of the three launch trips, and we repeated with limits of walleyes each time out. It seemed like this was getting to be a common occurrence, since we had experienced the same result only a year before. On the first and third trips that day, our parties of six managed to limit out within two hours. The second trip took longer as we were only able to catch limits in three hours, instead of two, probably because it was mid-day with a bright sun. When Sunday morning arrived I was very tired in view of the late night before and the cleaning of many, many walleyes. Everyone was on the dock and ready to go at 8:00 am, so, again we ventured out to what had become our favorite spot, the mouth of Turtle River. It was over for us in short order as the walleyes were cooperating with the enthusiasm of a bunch of hungry sharks. We could barely get the minnow near the sandy bottom before a walleye would have it eaten. Back at the dock at 10:00 am, we took pic tures and cleaned fish. I was supposed to have another trip early that afternoon, so I could make it to my baccalaureate service that evening. As it turned out, we decided to eat and leave the dock at 12:00 noon in order to have time and not be rushed at the last minute. Again, as we arrived at the mouth of the river, the walleyes were eager and energetic, and within three hours we had limited out and were making preparations to return to the resort. After clearing the floor of the launch of dead partially squished discarded smelly minnows, we began our return trip and found several people waiting to see our catch. It was rather impressive because we had managed to land three walleyes weighing seven pounds, four that weighed five and a half pounds, and thirteen weighing in at four to four and a half pounds each. It seemed like a huge school of big ones was swimming right under our launch the whole time. I think that was probably the most impressive bunch of walleyes in my personal guiding career. I have caught bigger walleyes, but never that many or of that size and overall average. It was a great way to finish off a super weekend of walleye fishing, but I still had a commitment at the high school, so my day wasn't over. I am sure it was a nice service, but I think my mind must have still been out on the lake, because I can't recall anything about the evening's events at the school. I was there and I did attend. That weekend we caught one hundred eighty walleyes and, needless to say, there were a lot of happy fishermen and women.

As I think back about those times and all the fish we kept, I can't help but feel a little bit of remorse for not knowing or realizing what the outcome might lead to. We did not think or know of the true meaning of "catch and release" back then, and our mindset was to catch as many "big ones" as we could. It wasn't until later years and greater fishing pressure began to become more and more evident that we as a society realized something must be done to help the fishery. In a way, it was probably already a little too late, as I feel we are suffering somewhat from the repercussion of that earlier mentality. We would keep the larger fish and throw back the smaller ones. We thought it was good, because we were leaving those little ones for seed so they could grow big and be caught again. What we didn't realize was that we were taking all those nice big "brood stock" fish out of the waters and leaving only those little guys to reproduce. Think about it, if those little ones reproduce with other little ones, all you're going to end up with is, little ones, for the most part. I think it adds up to a logical theory and for the past twenty years, I have been releasing the larger fish to reproduce another time or more.

In June of 1960 I had another repeat of the previous year only in another location on the lake. It was the tenth of June, and some people from Chicago, who were staying at another resort on the lake, called and booked reservations on our launch for an afternoon walleye trip. I was the only guide available, so I agreed to take them out, and we were to leave the dock at four pm. They arrived early and we were able to depart at around three thirty heading out to try our luck on some sandbars, (which we had not been having much luck on at the time.) As I remember, the day was hot and still again with a bright sun in a clear blue sky. We tried several different spots and even used minnows, leeches, night crawlers and artificial lures of various shapes, sizes and colors. It seemed useless; the walleyes just would not cooperate, and we talked about giving up and going in early. I called back to the resort and reported that we weren't having luck, but we were going to try one more area east of Cedar Island along a steep, sharp drop-off, and if nothing happened there, we would be in early. The lake was like glass as we sailed across the water leaving a v-shaped wake to spread from side to side and continue until it dispersed into a slick, smooth, mirror-like image. We arrived at the spot, but much too soon, as the breeze from the moving launch felt like a cool refreshing breath of spring air. As I brought the launch to a slow troll, the customers began muttering among themselves about having to fish again. Before I was actually able to straighten the launch parallel to the drop-off, one of the ladies on the boat yelled, "I've got a snag!" I knew better because I had fished this area many times before.

It was nothing more than a clean sandbar with maybe a few small bottom dwelling weeds. As it turned out, the lady had hooked into a nice two pound walleye, which was the beginning of a thirty minute barrage that landed us thirty-six beautiful walleyes. We were in about twenty feet of water which was surprising to me, as we weren't usually accustomed to finding walleyes in that deep of pattern, at this time summer. Later in the year they would go deeper, and by mid-October we would catch walleyes in sixty to seventy feet of water, fishing right down on the bottom. This time of year, however; we caught fish in ten to twelve feet of water. Every fish came out of twenty to twenty-five feet of water that day, and I can only assume that there was some source of food at that location which attracted their feeding intentions. It sure was fun to pull into the harbor with a nice limit of walleyes, as there were quite a few people waiting to see and hear the result of our pre-determined fishless trip, but they were as surprised as we had been, upon catching those limits of fish. Everyone wanted to know where we had caught the fish, as they were anxious to do some catching of their own during this slow time we had been experiencing.

That "dry spell," as we called it, probably wasn't such a bad thing, nor did it come at a bad time. You see, we had just been introduced to a new electronic technological devise that came to be known as the infamous "green box." It was manufactured by a company called Lowrance Electronics and started a new revolution in the fishing industry, at least in our area, at that time. I was so excited about this unique invention that I'd been hearing about that I bought one sight unseen. It cost me around a hundred dollars, and I ordered it from the Lowrance company in Joplin, Missouri. Each unit came with a one year warranty, which was good, because there were a lot of "bugs" which needed to be worked out. It seems like my "green box" was in shipping transit more than it was in my boat, and all the other guides were having the same problems with their "green boxes" as well. We actually realized that despite the early development and defects, these "green boxes" were still a very valuable tool, and helped us as guides to save a lot of time on the water. It turned some of our lost fishing time into more valuable time since we were now able to spend more time "on the fish" rather than in too deep or too shallow water. I wrote a letter to the Lowrance company asking them if we purchased several of these "green boxes," would they give us a break on the cost of each unit. I also explained these units were very valuable tools to us as guides, and it was annoying to have to send them back so often. Our plan was to equip each guide with an extra "green box" to allow the guides an opportunity to fish with these newly found Electronics, and not have to be waiting for shipment, repair and return of the "Fish-Lo- Kator," as it was called. The company not only wrote, but also called back and told me we could purchase as many of the depth finders as we wanted for sixty dollars each, plus shipping. We immediately ordered another six "green boxes" to go with the six we already had. That pretty well solved our problem as we usually could use one unit while waiting for the backup unit to be repaired and returned. It did seem at first like we had a unit in shipping most of the time during that first year or so. The problems we found most common were burned out bulbs, over heated transistors, (which shut everything down) and malfunctioning or inaccurate readings and blinky on and off bulbs. Each time we sent a unit back, we added an explanation about its behavior. The company thought this was helpful and referred to us as some of their field testers. So I can't help but feel we were a part of the whole process of making better and more quality electronic equipment available to the consumers. I felt that Lowrance made vast strides of improvement in their business as those old depth finders soon became better pieces of equipment that needed very little attention and lasted for years, not just days as we first experienced. What a blessing to be able to watch our well memorized landmarks, and to see when we lost the bottom because of a sudden change in depth along a drop-off. Once we gained confidence, and believed those little lines to be the fish they really were, we began producing more fish. It was difficult for some guides, however; who hadn't learned the many landmarks of the lake and how to mark a spot by using those landmarks. The depth finder actually became a bit of a hindrance to them as they would find themselves watching the "green box" and quickly ending up in deep or shallow water because a certain bar or drop-off had turned or bent a little bit one way or the other. I witnessed many of the newer guides on the lake having this problem and I'm not sure they ever really ironed them out. I was only glad that I had spent a few years learning the lake with the use of a two ounce sinker and those unchangeable landmarks. It helped when using the depth finder because we knew when we were coming to one of those bends or turns and we could be prepared for it. I am reminded of how quickly those first depth finders used up the batteries and grew dead without much warning. Then with the help of improved transistors and a few other small electronic devises we were able to go weeks on one set of batteries and now even months without having to change them. What an amazing advancement! Back in 1960 another guide, who was a bit old fashioned, told me these depth finders would not make it. "They are too expensive," he said. "They don't last," he told me. I just shrugged and said to him, "I think they are here to stay." If forty plus years means anything, "They are here to stay." I look back on all the changes and additions to electronic technology, just in the fishing industry over the past forty plus years, and I am amazed at how far we've come. The fact still remains that these were improvements and refine-ments because of God given gifts and talents to some individuals who helped us have a better future, and we are thankful for that.

I am reminded of a day in July that same summer when I took a couple fishing for northern pike. Bill and Gladys Cunningham were from Oak Park, Illinois, at the time and we went by car to a place on the Mississippi River above Cass Lake where there is a power dam. Just up river from the dam was a widening area that we referred to as "Stump Lake," and it was a prime hangout for northerns. It appeared that after the dam was put in and the water level rose, someone harvested the top half of the trees that were now standing in water. Because the stumps were left under water, one had to be careful to negotiate a boat in and around them. The water at that point was consistently fifteen feet deep. We used eight inch sucker minnows and a large slip bobber which allowed the bait to get down to about three feet off the bottom and let the it swim around. A northern would take the minnow and swim off a short distance, then gobble the bait and swim a bit more and con-tinue this process. After about two full minutes of time or when we felt the north-ern had eaten the minnow enough to get the hook in its mouth, we would "set the hook." It was tricky with all the stumps to contend with, but we didn't lose very much tackle, because the northern didn't really use the stumps to their advantage either. Bill and Gladys had each caught two northern, and the stringer was beginning to look quite impressive. There were two five pounders, a ten pounder, plus another twelve pounder, and we weren't finished yet. At that time Gladys' bobber began acting very strange. It would tip over sideways for a bit and then back upright and commence to slowly go down just about five or six inches under the surface of the water. It continued to do this for the better part of five minutes when finally it disappeared for about two minutes, but the line wasn't moving or paying out. I told Gladys that she could try to set the hook, but it was her decision when she wanted to do it. She decided the fish had played around long enough and jerked the pole in an upward thrust. We could tell by the bend in her sturdy northern rod that there was a nice fish on the hook. As she reeled the fish to the surface, all I could see was a huge open mouth. When the fish turned, we could tell it was a nice walleye with the bright white spot on the tip of its tail, glowing like a light in the dark. I reached for the landing net and things were happening pretty fast as Gladys had the walleye's head out of the water. Without looking, I made a dip to get under the fish's body, but the net was wrapped over itself and acted as a trampoline. When I came up with the walleye on top, it bounced and flipped with all its might. Bill was yelling, "Get it in the boat, get it in!" Gladys was just hanging on to her fishing pole for dear life. In the process the fish began to bounce higher each time it hit and finally flipped and flew up off the net, and in the process, Bill kept yelling the same thing over and over. Finally I was able to divert the fish with a glancing bounce of the net back toward the boat, and here it came, sailing right toward me in the air out of control and off the hook! I backed off quickly and let the fish bounce off my chest and into the bottom of the boat where it continued its antics for another minute or so before coming to rest at our feet. "Wow," was Bill's comment as we eyed the golden sided beauty. The fish, fat and girthy, measured twenty-nine inches and weighed almost ten pounds. We stayed and caught two more northern to fill out Bill and Gladys' limit and headed back to the resort for some more bragging time. The Cunninghams became close friends over the years, Bill and his brother Frank would even make a fall deer hunting trip every year to Cass Lake, stay at Birch Villa Resort and hire Merv as their guide. Their families continued to spend two weeks each summer at Birch Villa to enjoy the beauty of the area. Bill and Gladys became repeat customers of mine and we talked about the "bouncing ten pound walleye" every time we got together; another experience I'll never forget.

That summer of 1960 proved to be a good musky year, too, as I recorded forty- one muskies boated and twenty-one of those kept. As stated before, even though we didn't know "catch and release," we did release smaller muskies when ever we could, according to the customer's wishes. There was no minimum size limit for muskies on Cass Lake until 1961 when the minimum length was set at thirty inches. In 1986 the thirty-six inch minimum length limit went into effect, and in 1994 it was increased to forty inches minimum for a keeper musky. I personally believe the enforcement of these regulations drastically helped the future of musky fishing and helped to improve the size and numbers of those fish being caught over the years since. Having been on the lake every day during the mid-fifties through the late seventies and even into present time (during the summer months) I have observed a steady increase of musky fishing pressure. Meaning there are an increasing number of musky fisherpersons each year as the sport builds interest and respect. The fact still remains that in my estimation, musky fishing on Cass Lake and statewide, for that matter, has improved even more steadily than the fishing pressure.

The late summer and fall of 1960 brought with it some longer periods of consistent weather patterns, which can sometimes make it difficult to catch fish with the same consistency. This particular fall was an exception to that theory, as the walleye bite continued throughout the months of late August, September and October. In early September, I hit a stretch of guide trips during which we would catch one big walleye each time out, but we could never get more than one. We caught other nice sized fish and usually came in with close to a limit of walleyes, but only one big walleye per trip. The strange thing was, we usually caught a big walleye in exactly the same place every time. I had positioned a marker bouy in shallower water just up from the drop- off; we would slow troll along in that area, with orange Brooks Reefers (a small plastic jointed three inch lure with a unique wiggle.) Every big walleye was caught within twenty feet of that marker each day and many others too, as stated previously.

I was attending Bemidji State College as a freshman that fall and my classes were over by one o'clock each afternoon, so I would drive the fifteen miles home and take a guide trip in the late part of the day, when the walleyes seemed to be biting best. In seven trips out we caught seven walleyes that each measured close to thirty inches and weighed from seven and a half pounds up to ten pounds. My customers kept most of those fish, but I had one generous client that allowed me to keep a ten pounder that I caught late in the week. It was the nicest looking and most well proportioned of them all. I had it mounted at the taxidermist's shop for a mere twenty-five dollars. That was an impressive stretch of time on Cass Lake that relinquished some nice sized walleyes. After that I did a lot of late fall musky fishing and caught several mid-forty inch muskies in shallow water, in and around the bulrushes. As summer blended into fall I was on the varsity basketball team at Bemidji State and that began taking up a lot of my extra time, plus the studies that had to be maintained too, so the fishing took a back seat to other priorities in my life. At this time I could only dabble in ice fishing on occasion and wait patiently for another spring to roll around and bring with it a new fishing season.

Some walleyes and northern pike from opening weekend on launch.

Mrs. Harlow and the Goodyears with some walleyes taken on a mid-summer launch trip.

One of the big walleyes, a 10 pounder caught during a week long series of trips. One big walleye each trip.

A 37¹/₂ # musky caught by Merv.

Another 50" musky caught by Merv.

Dock boy Tim Monda and Merv with a small musky.

1961

The spring of 1961 finally arrived, and all the resort jobs were finished in order for the opening season to begin. It was not as impressive as the two years prior to this opener. All of us guides spent the better part of the weekend looking for and trying to locate the walleyes, but with very little consistent success. We all blamed the high water. It had snowed excessively that spring and a huge melting run-off of water had made the lakes in our area rise to about thirty inches above normal. It was only logical that this contributed to a different lake effect. The thing that made it difficult, was the fact that we had most of the same people back to fish that had been there the two previous years. They, as well as we, were expecting to go directly to the mouth of Turtle River and catch fish without a lot of effort. That did not happen, as it was an early spring and most of the spawning had been over for at least two or three weeks. We fished every area, backed by every conceivable theory and philosophy we could muster, but try as we may, there was no consistent catch. The lake just wasn't the same. Some of us thought the walleyes were still scattered and attempting to get back to their original habitat or relocate to other areas. Others felt that there might have been a poor hatch in the fishery some years previous, while still others decided that due to the heavy fishing pressure and tremendous walleye harvest the two years prior, there were no walleyes left. Most of us didn't go along with the latter of these theories. Eventually, over the next few weeks, fishing improved tremendously, and we were able to locate and catch many walleyes, but the post-spawn bite came earlier than normal and didn't last as long as usual.

It was early June when Grandad Kobler came from western Kansas to fish Cass Lake again. At the time, "Grandad," as we called him, was now ninty years young, sharp as a tack, alert to modern trends and still able to drive his own car. He, my brother Larry, and friend, Delmar Huck, had made another journey to Birch Villa for some walleye fishing. On one particular occasion, we were fishing the edge of a drop-off on the north side of Star Island in an area we referred to as Anderson Point. We were catching walleyes in a very small concentrated area that had a small bend or dip in the drop-off. Most of the fish averaged one and a half to two pounds. Grandad was having the time of his life outfishing the rest of us by about three to one. As we started to turn around for another troll through this productive spot, Grandad had a bite, so we just let the boat drift, and he set the hook on yet another walleye. Before he got it to the boat his line broke, leaving him with nothing, not even the trolling sinker or part of the leader. He didn't want to admit to not having checked the strength of his line beforehand, so he diverted our attention by exclaiming that this fish was much larger than any of the others he had caught. He knew it because he could feel the weight of this huge walleye. He was devastated by the loss of the fish and his hook, leader and trolling sinker. When it was time to go in, he didn't want to leave, as he thought we could still catch this monster fish. We were able to convince him that we would come back to this spot the next time out, and then the fish might be ready to bite again. As I said, Grandad had a very sharp mind and an even sharper memory because the next time we headed out on the lake he was asking if we were going back to Anderson Point.

We did go back to that spot many times during the week Grandad was there, but we never caught his huge walleye.

The story doesn't end here, however; because the following week, I was guiding a young couple, husband and wife, and we just happened to stop at Anderson Point during our half day fishing trip. There was a slight breeze, just enough to set up a good drift along the famed drop-off where Grandad lost his giant walleye the week before. I had shared the story with this young couple, and we laughed at the thought of the walleye with a hook in its mouth even biting for awhile, not to mention still being in the same area or even possibly being alive. After a couple drifts and a few walleyes, the lady in the boat had a bite and set the hook on what was another routine walleye catch. Upon reeling in the line and bringing the fish to the boat, all I could see down in the water was her trolling sinker and leader and hook with minnow still in tact. Not having paid any attention to her rod tip, I figured the walleye had come off the hook before I could see it, so I relaxed a bit and began to put the net down when I looked up and saw that she was still playing a fish on her line. My thoughts were that the fish had gotten off the hook, but was still hungry and came back for the minnow again. Upon closer investigation, we could see that there was indeed a walleye at the end of the line, but not her line! She had snagged someone else's line that had been broken before and it was Grandad's! Apparently, the lady's hook had found its way into the small eyelet of the trolling sinker that apparently was lying on the bottom. As she picked the rod tip up, there was this drag that felt like and was a walleye. As we landed the fish, which was still in pretty fair condition, we began to laugh again; Grandad's monster walleye was none other than a fifteen incher that weighed barely a pound and a quarter. How did we know it was Grandad's walleye ? He was using one of my half ounce trolling sinkers, which I had scratched my initials in before using. He was also using one of my hand tied leaders, which carried a trademark, so to speak, recognizable by the specific knot I used to tie it with. That fact, plus all the other factors tying this information together was proof enough for me to believe it was Grandad's fish. I'm not so sure, however; I would have so easily believed the "hook through the small eyelet" miracle if I had not seen it for myself. I think that is the prime reason I remembered this particular story along with the fact that I dearly loved Grandad and enjoyed his fantastic ability to paint vivid word pictures of the past.

It wasn't long after the incident with Grandad that I had another phenomenal occurrence on the water. It was now mid-June, and the short lived walleye bite had begun to taper off. as walleye fishing was experiencing some ups and downs. One trip out we might do fantastically well and the next trip might prove a disaster with little or no success. People kept wanting to fish regardless of that fact.

There came a day early in my guiding career that I started becoming a philosopher. It actually happened on two successive guide trips. The first trip included a mom, dad and young daughter about the age of ten or eleven. We were slow trolling with the same walleye rigs, a half ounce trolling sinker with a three foot gut leader and a 2/0 Eagle Claw hook dressed with a shiner minnow. I repeated the fact that they had to keep their sinkers bouncing on and off the bottom as this would entice a bite or a strike. Walleyes back then were not known for any type of aggressiveness so we slow trolled, creeping along a well known drop-off, in hopes of locating a hungry school or two. The mom and dad were doing very well in keeping their bait "on the bottom," where walleyes do most of their feeding, or so we thought, back then. Mom had caught one small walleye and dad had three so far, but the young daughter, who was strategically placed near me in the boat, by mom and dad, was having a difficult time keeping her bait in the water let alone on the bottom. I told the little girl many times to "let out more line," but she continued to ignore me, so I began to ignore her too. As fate would have it, during my time of ignoring, I think it was during my time of ignorance, this little girl caught a nice two pound walleye, just inches from the boat and inches under the water! Who said those walleyes only bite on the bottom ? Who told me those walleyes are only "bottom feeders" ? I must have really been brainwashed by some influential fisherperson along the way. Again, as fate would have it, the little girl caught another nice two pounder, now I could have maybe believed a perch, northern or a small aggressive musky, but no, these were honest to goodness nice sized walleyes. When it happened again, my thick skull finally became soft and penetrable. I netted her third walleye and added it to the stringer, which I had not yet donated to, on this particular trip. I tried to keep my line up near the surface like the little girl was doing, as I could see her minnow under the surface of the water at all times. The interesting thing was, I couldn't see any fish. When the little girl caught another walleye, and I had a bite at the same time, I told mom and dad to bring their lines up near the surface. Within minutes we all began landing walleyes and even an occasional perch. We didn't catch our limit that morning, but we did manage to bring fourteen walleyes and ten jumbo perch back with us. After that day I established a philosophy, "Never try to out-fish children," and it has proven me correct more times than I want to remember.

That same mid-June I was fishing with a middle aged husband and his wife from Nebraska, and we were trolling parallel to a drop-off along the south side of Cass Lake in an area known as the "Kettle." I kept telling the lady just to put her line over the side of the boat and let it down until it hit the bottom, but she was afraid her line was going to get caught in the motor, so she would cast it out to the side, which put her bait into the weeds in about four feet of water. Every time this happened, she thought she had a bite because the weeds felt somewhat like a fish to her, but when she reeled the line in, all she had were weeds on her bait and hook. Each time I would tell her to let the line down just over the side of the boat, and each time she would cast it out into the weeds. Even her husband tried to tell her what she was doing wrong; needless to say, that didn't go over too well. One time she fooled us, though, and reeled in a walleye! After that occurred three or four times in succession, I moved the boat up into shallower, weedier water, and we all caught walleyes, fifteen all together, in fact. I don't think this lady had any idea that there were hungry fish in the weeds, but she sure showed me that I didn't know it all, yet. Thus, I added to my previous bit of philosophy, "Never try to out-fish women or children," and I've been able to prove the truth in that theory many times over.

There was another time that summer when I had my "eyes opened." I was guiding two middle aged school teachers, both ladies, and they loved to fish for walleyes, especially the style of slow trolling or drifting that we were doing at the time. We were north of Cedar Island again, and fishing was slow to say the least; there just weren't any cooperative walleyes to be had that day, or so I thought. It was a little boring, to say the least, but it was a "bluebird day," and luckily the two ladies enjoyed nature as well as fishing. One of the ladies caught sight of the beautiful deep green bulrushes that grow abundantly along the north side of Cedar Island, and she asked if we could go in closer so they could get a good look at the rushes. I thought and said out loud, "Why not! There isn't anything else too interesting going on out here in fifteen feet of water." As we trolled more closely to the bulrushes, I watched as the depth changed gradually on my depth finder, and soon we were in four feet of water. I could see the bottom and noticed an occasional perch swim in and out of the thick rushes. As we trolled the edge of those bulrushes, the ladies both commented on how we, as human beings, tend to take so many of God's gracious gifts for granted and we don't take time to really appreciate these wonders of nature enough. A combination of the beautiful clear blue sky day and being mesmerized by these two very intellectual women and their spiritual thoughts of nature made me lazy, and not caring whether the fish would bite at all. As we were deep in thought of all the beauty that surrounded us, one of the ladies screamed, " I've got a fish!" Much to my surprise, she actually did have a fish, a walleye, and it was a nice one! It was a very nice one because it was the first one of the day! We netted and landed this eighteen inch beauty and even before getting it on the stringer, the other lady had one, too. In the hour and a half that followed, we caught eleven very pretty walleyes. No, the bite was not fast and furious, but we did end our outing with a very respectable catch and enjoyed a bit of nature, too. These ladies were forever grateful for that experience and came back to Birch Villa to fish Cass Lake many more times. I couldn't help but think again about my newly formed philosophy, "Never try to out-fish women or children." Since then, time after time, I've seen women out- fish men and I've been out-fished by them, too! I do believe the high water that summer had something to do with these extraordinary catches, but that still didn't exempt the fact that we professionals don't know everything.

I am reminded of another couple that came to Birch Villa two or three times every year while we owned the resort, and they continued coming for a few years even after we sold to the next owner. I'm sure they visited Birch Villa and Cass Lake at least twenty-five years and grew to know many of the area's residents. Elsie and Ed Jensen were from St. Paul and would ride the bus from the Cities to Cass Lake, where we would pick them up and take them out to the lake for their vacation or long weekend retreat. Elsie was blind at birth, and Ed was declared legally blind as his sight was greatly impaired; he could see only with blurred vision. We always remarked that Ed could see just well enough to enable them to get around and go places together. Elsie worked at Lutheran Brotherhood and would ride the bus from their St. Paul apartment to downtown Minneapolis every day to her work site where she typed dictations for other people in the company. Elsie acquired a "seeing eye" dog a few years after I first knew her. What a tremendous support that was for her! Ed worked full-time for the Society for the Blind. These two would take their vacations and mini vacations to visit Cass Lake at least two times each year, and sometimes three. They tried to visit Birch Villa on Memorial Day weekend, two weeks the last of June and first of July, and finish out their summer with a long weekend over Labor Day. Each time they came, they would fish, swim when the climate allowed, take several walks to town, and visit with everyone. Elsie would play piano for us in the lodge each evening. They enjoyed all their times together; you never saw one without the other, and they were always happy and enjoyed life more than most of us can imagine. Elsie was a fantastic fisherperson! She was probably the best fisherperson I've ever had the pleasure of fishing with in my entire life, bar none. Obviously she couldn't do or see some of the things we other fishermen could, but fish for fish, bite for bite, touch for touch, she possessed an excellent gift of other senses which allowed her to be a great catcher of fish. Elsie and Ed even tried their hand at casting for muskies! I don't recall either of them ever catching a musky, but they did land their share of northern pike. Elsie would feel every little touch on her line and know immediately whether it was a fish or a false alarm. One time, I remember, we were trolling along, and a dragonfly lit on her monofilament line between the rod tip and the water. She said to me, "Something must have touched my line. Did you touch my line, Merv?" I mentioned to her that it was a dragonfly, and she became so interested in it that I had to describe the insect to her in complete detail and vivid color speculation. On occasion I would purposely grip her line between my thumb and forefinger and give light tugs as a walleye or perch might do. Elsie would immediately raise her hand toward me and say, "Now, Merv, you leave my line alone!" I couldn't fool her even once in all the times I tried. Elsie and Ed and I had a close relationship as they did with all the guides. They did not play favorites and wanted to fish with each of the four of us guides whenever it was possible. Another time I had Ed and Elsie out fishing northern on Pike Bay, a portion of Cass Lake so named by Governor Pike many years back. It lies almost as a separate body of water, only connected by a canal or navigable boat channel. While fishing in the late afternoon or early evening, we saw the sun setting on us and our less than a limit of northern pike, before we wanted it to. As twilight began to show creeping signs of the coming the darkness, my thoughts went to negotiating the boat back through the narrow channel and into Cass Lake proper. I felt we had better be heading back to the resort. Before I realized it, our lines had crossed, twisted, and left an amazingly unforgivable mess of monofilament to be cut and replaced or retied. We had been trolling with spoons and Brooks Refers, and sometimes the latter would take a notion to veer off sideways and become entangled in another person's line for no explainable reason at all. That is exactly what had happened in this instance, and I hauled all three of the twisted lines into the boat together and left them on the floor between Elsie's feet and mine. I told them it was pretty dark, and we'd better go in. I would cut and fix the lines in the morning. Elsie told me that the dark didn't bother her, and we didn't have to go in for her sake. She was always ready with a quick wit and good sense of humor. The trip in took a little longer because of the darkness and my needing to be a bit more careful in negotiating the narrow, shallow, slabwood infested channel. Years before there had been an old box factory along the channel at the northwest corner of Pike Bay near that entrance. It is now the site of a park and picnic area for the public to use. As we traveled from Pike Bay to Cass Lake, Elsie reached down and began to untangle what was an unsalvageable mess of lines. I told her not to bother because it was useless to attempt that entanglement in the dark, but she assured me that it didn't bother her. I am not sure of the exact amount of time it took us to get across Pike Bay from the southwest corner and through the canal and then across the west portion of Cass Lake back to Birch Villa, but when we entered the harbor and began pulling up to the dock Elsie said, "I think I've got it!" I looked down and in the light of the electrical fixtures around the dock, there in the bottom of the boat were three separate, neatly formed circles of monofilament line, ready to be wound back onto their respective reels. As Elsie and I reeled the lines back without a flaw of any kind, I couldn't help but think, what an amazing gift this lady has. I honestly don't think I could have untangled those lines with my excellent vision in daylight without having to cut at least one or two of them. I told her how I felt. "Elsie, you are an amazing lady, and I owe you one, because I don't think I could have accomplished what you just did." Her reply was, "Oh, there was nothing to it." Oh, yes, there was! Elsie proved that many times over as we fished probably about twenty years together, and enjoyed every minute of it. Not too many people outfished Elsie, but on occasion Ed would luck out and catch more fish than she would. Ed was a good fisherman, too, as he was the quiet type who would have a fish hooked before anyone else in the boat would realize it. He enjoyed the surprise effect it had on all the others in the boat. As you can tell, I had a great deal of respect for this couple as they displayed affection for each other as well as people around them. They were genuinely good friends who gave so much to the lives of others through their gift of thoughtfulness and love. I'll never forget them and the good times we had in the boat.

Throughout that summer, we had to contend with the high water. Most of the time we had elevated planks running all around the dock area and lawn at Birch Villa. Most resorts around the lake that had lower level access were battling the same problem. I believe this same condition occurred ten years earlier in 1951. We had to walk on planks to get to the cabins, our boats and even to the main lodge as the high water continued and just wouldn't seem to recede. Most of the guests on the lake level could motor their boats over the lawn right up near their cabin. We didn't have to tie boats to the dock; they rested on top of it, where we usually walked! It wasn't good for the lawn, but we didn't have nearly the amount of grass to cut as usual. The high water presented other problems, too. We could boat a little faster through the channel connecting Cass Lake and Pike Bay; however, we had to slow down when passing under the railroad bridge. Because of the high water the boat rode too high to make an easy pass under the bridge. We would have to stop and push down on the bow and stern of the boat in order to make it squeeze under the trestle so we could continue on. At one point we even had to stop going to Pike Bay because the boats didn't have clearance. Those trips had to wait until the lake level receded.

During the latter days of July there was a group of campers called the "Wally Byam Caravan" attending a campers' convention at the fairgrounds in the neighboring town of Bemidji, Minnesota. Several of the campers had made many short trips to Cass Lake to fish with the guides at Birch Villa. Their unique trademark was that they spent only two dollar bills when buying or paying for something. At the time, the northern pike bite was hot in Pike Bay, and the walleye bite was not! Most people wanted some of the pike action and we spent a lot of time on Pike Bay for about two or three weeks during that stretch. I think almost every trip I had was made up of someone connected with the Wally Byam Caravan. At the end of this "Pike Bay Folly" as we referred to it, I counted up all the two dollar bills that had been given to me by the Wally Byam people, and I had two hundred seventy-five, two dollar bills saved! Yes, a total of five hundred fifty dollars! That amounted to about twenty guide trips, plus tips, give or take a trip or two just with Wally Byam, not to mention a few trips thrown in for our guests at Birch Villa, who had first priority. In that "Pike Bay Folly" of late July 1961, we were catching the northern pike on a tiny little spinner bait called a "Shyster." It was approximately two and a half inches long and weighed one quarter ounce. The lure had an orange plastic body with a small treble hook at the back dressed with short, orange, buck-tail type hair. It had a brass plated willow leaf type spinner at the front, and when trolled over the weedbeds at about three miles per hour, it maintained a depth which allowed it to ride just above those submergent cabbage weeds. It drove the northern crazy. I don't know if the lure made a particular noise or whether the blade gave off a unique flash of some kind, but it literally drove the northern wild, as they attacked the simple little inexpensive lure with great gusto. If I recall correctly, the Shyster lures only cost thirty-five cents each, so we all bought them by the card. The northern pike we caught ranged in size from the little "hammer handles," (we called them that, I suppose, because they do resemble a hammer handle in shape and sometimes in size, weighing a pound or two), up to the ten and twelve pound class. We didn't keep the smaller "hammer handles," but we did keep three pounders and up. Most catches that came into the dock during that three week stint averaged about four or five pounds per fish. There was an occasional fifteen to eighteen pounder caught, but those were usually the exception. The odd reality to the whole picture was the fact that these large fish were attracted by those little tiny lures which they attacked with aggression. This "hot" pike action played out as usual, and we had to go experimenting for other means of luring the fish.

That summer gave us many fish and many wonderful memories. During the month of August the musky action grew hot once again, and during one two week stretch in mid-August the four of us guides combined for thirty-four muskies. One day during that time we brought ten muskies into the boat one morning, a pretty phenomenal morning of musky fishing in that day and age. The largest of those ten was a thirty-seven pounder, followed by a thirty-four and a thirty-one pounder. I believe there were a couple of ten pounders which were released to be caught another day.

The fall fishing was fair to good that year. Once again in October we had some good, deep walleye fishing. We were catching nice two pound average walleyes on the bottom in sixty-five feet of water with minnows. The bite didn't allow limits in most of our catches, but it did allow for an occasional eight to ten pounder. There is a problem with fishing at that depth; when the fish is brought to the surface too quickly, the change in pressure causes the air-sac to expand and push or force the stomach out of the mouth of the fish. So, if it is a smaller walleye, it won't work to release it because the fish will probably not survive. Most of the time, however; if you work or play the fish up to the surface more slowly, it will adjust to the change in pressure and will be able to be released without harm.

One weird memory I have from that fall of 1961 happened during the early November deer season. Cliff Riggles, his son Joe and I were deer hunting to the south and east of Pike Bay. As I recall the temperature was almost seventy degrees that day. At noon we all met and commented on the heat and how sweaty we got just walking slowly through the woods, and I jokingly said, "We could go fishing!" With that, Cliff got up, picked up his emptied lunch bag and headed for the pickup saying, "What are we wasting our time here for ? Let's go catch some walleyes!" We unloaded the rifles, put all the hunting gear away and drove back to the resort where we had to turn a larger eighteen foot rowboat over and off its winter storage blocks and slide or skid the boat back to the water. Yes, we forgot about hunting that quickly, and because of the extreme heat we didn't want the experience of hanging a deer not knowing when the temperatures would allow for a better cure for meat. It didn't take long to scrounge up an eighteen horsepower Johnson outboard motor and a five and a half horse to troll with, along with our tackle and some bait we had purchased as we drove past Leroy's Minnows on the way home from hunting. The trip over to Pike Bay by boat was different, as the leaves were gone from all the trees and the entire landscape had changed drastically from the way it had looked just a few short weeks earlier when we were still in the guiding mode. Cliff was the guide on this particular occasion, and I was along for the ride and yet another learning experience at increasing my fishing knowledge in the surrounding waters of the area. We pulled up to a rather steep drop-off near the south end of Pike Bay and began to bait up as we trolled out to about a thirty to thirty-five foot depth. We allowed our lines to play out and watch the minnow disappear into the dark depths below, and we could only hope that our decision to quit hunting deer and come fishing for walleye would pay off. It did! In a matter of minutes, Cliff had the first bite and set the hook on what we later found to be our largest walleye of the twelve we would catch. It was a nine pound beauty and as fat as any walleye I'd ever seen. In approximately two hours, Cliff and I had our limits of walleyes that ranged in size from two pounds up to the nine pounder Cliff caught at first. My largest was a nice chunky seven pounder; we had five fish in the three to four pound range, plus a couple of beautiful five pounders as well. All in all the stringer was made up of a pretty satisfying catch of walleyes, to say the least. Word got around, and a few other local fishermen took advantage of the same weather conditions which lasted for only about three days before the next cold snap and we had to put the boat and motors away for the winter. They stayed there this time! I have thought about that time in November when the temperatures allowed us some unique late fall or early winter, open water, lake fishing. We did continue our deer hunting that fall the last few days of a nine day season, and if I remember correctly, Cliff shot a nice twelve point buck, and I shot my first ten point buck, the only deer I saw close enough to shoot. I recall that deer being the biggest I'd seen in the woods and it looked like a monster when it first appeared. Then the snows came and brought a winter that allowed the fish a break from all the pressures of the fishermen for at least a few months.

High water surrounding Birch Villa an Sah-Kah-Try resorts
in 1951.

High water at Birch Villa dock in 1951

High water around Birch Villa dock in 1961.

High water at Birch Villa dock in 1961.

Larry Heitschmidt, Grandad Kobler, Grandson Kobler, Merv, the guide, and Arden Kobler with a successful catch off the Birch Villa Launch.

Small girl with Merv and a nice string of walleyes.

Elsie and Ed Jensen pictured with Merv holding some
walleyes caught in Cass Lake

Northern pike and walleyes during the Wally Byam
campaign.

Northern pike from the Wally Byam campaign.

A 37# musky caught by Merv in
August.

Merv holding a 48" musky weighing
30#.

Merv's first ten point buck.

1962

The 1962 resort and fishing season opened as usual and with the same result as the 1961 season, at least on Cass Lake. The fishing was spotty, to say the least, as the spring had been earlier than normal again. This left the walleyes more or less scattered and not yet schooled up. The guides were having their problems because there just wasn't a good consistent bite. It did eventually improve with the settling down of weather patterns and the time allowance for fish to get back into their normal early summer patterns. We had our usual amount of customers to guide, and the general daily routine fast became a blur of events with catching, cleaning and packaging the fish caught by our customers. After having cleaned fish for the better part of six summers at Birch Villa Resort, as well as three other resorts in close proximity to our location, we had kept a running tally of numbers of fish we cleaned. It seemed unbelievable, but we had averaged between nine and ten thousand fish cleaned each summer. A few summers we managed close to twelve thousand fish. Most of the time there were two of us that cleaned fish, but on occasion we would enlist the services of a third friend to help us out, especially during those times when the bite was heavy and lots of fish were being caught. I personally cleaned fish at the resort for twenty-five summers, so it was becoming an art as well as a good source of spending money. Those of us who cleaned fish for the resort over the years obtained a level of expertise that attracted much attention from those who chose to stand by and watch. We would consistently boneless fillet both sides of a walleye in twenty seconds. Now the northern pike, on the other hand, was a different story, as they do take a little more time due to the different body shape and bone structure, which is obviously different than the walleye's. There were a lot of stories told around the fish cleaning house. Most of the fishermen and spectators would gather there in the evenings to expound on their fishing experiences and knowledge in hopes of hearing and/or obtaining some small bit of information they could use another day and time on the water. For the life of me, I'll never understand why they wanted to gather by that stinky smelling old fish cleaning house! We tried to keep the pungent odors to a minimum, but it was a daily chore. If you can imagine the scent of decaying, discarded fish parts mixed with a strong dosage of Pine-Sol, then you are experiencing the wonderful aroma of the proverbial old fish cleaning house. We fish cleaners had a common bond and a special comradeship, that literally connected us to a special feeling of importance around the resort. There were lots of names of fellow fish cleaners over the years like: Mike Studley, Joe Riggles, Kenny Riggles, Tim Monda, cousin Tom Horn from Tulsa, Mark Pound (from Cass Lake, who we nicknamed Half Pound, because of his size), brother Larry and a few others who often came to lend a helping hand, as we sometimes were bogged down by too many fish. In the early years we were required to "gut and gill" all the fish, which was a state law allowing for easy identification. We would simply make a slice up the stomach and two small cuts in and around the gills. Then in one twisting pull, the gills and guts were removed, the fish was washed and then wrapped or packed on wet ice. The fish were then kept in the ice house until the guests would leave. We would wrap and box the fish and pack ice around them for their journey home with the customer. In those early days we purchased wooden boxes of various shapes and sizes from Larry and Diane Polries who operated the old box factory located on the northwest corner of Pike Bay in conjunction with Frank's Mill, a lumber company owned and operated by Larry's dad, Frank Polries, just south of the railroad tracks on Highway 371 in the town of Cass Lake. Those rough sawed, wooden boxes were used to pack the fish that were sent home with the many guests. Our customers then had to finish skinning or filleting the fish in preparation for eating. It was a hassle for everyone involved in the process, and we were overjoyed when the law was changed, allowing people the chance to fillet their fish and take them home frozen and ready to thaw and eat. It made things easier for us all, and I'm sure there was little or no spoilage of fish like we had heard of before.

Ed and Elsie Jensen visited Cass Lake again in 1962 during Memorial Day weekend and again in July for their two week vacation. I distinctly remember that particular year, because there was a man named Merle Sussdorf and his wife who came to Birch Villa pulling a big new runabout boat with a fifty horsepower motor on it. They were looking for a place to stay for two weeks, and it just happened that we had a cancellation from a family who had been involved in an accident and couldn't make their reservation a reality. No one was fatally injured, but a couple of the family members were still in the hospital recovering, and the others didn't want to leave them for the sake of a vacation. The Sussdorfs were fortunate as July is usually a tough month to find a vacancy at any resort. We helped them unload their boat and get settled in their cabin. It didn't take long to see that Merle had not experienced driving a boat before. After bouncing and careening off several other boats tied to the dock around the harbor, he was able to turn off the motor and paddle his way into a vacant spot and tie the boat to the convenient posts equipped with ropes for securing his vessel. It was a ritual for Merle each and every time he got into that boat as, I believe, he was half afraid to operate it, and yet half way wanted to master the ability to at least drive it safely out of the harbor. Safe was not a word that ever even seemed remotely close to being possible the entire time Merle and his wife were with us. He had more crashes which fortunately, didn't hurt anything or anyone else, but did cause a great deal of concern for those of us who had boats parked anywhere in the harbor. I truly believe Merle managed to run into every boat parked in the harbor at least twice if not more during his time at Birch Villa those two weeks. Elsie and Ed, hearing the sounds of the crashes as Merle maneuvered his boat around the harbor, did not let this daily ritual go unnoticed. One day while I was guiding Elsie and Ed and the fishing was slow, Elsie and I began composing a song, both the lyrics and music, about Merle and his antics with a boat he hadn't yet mastered. I wouldn't want to bore you with the musical notes, but here is a part of the song lyrics we came up with called, "Mariner Merle":

"Mariner Merle"

Mariner Merle, guns his motor 'cross the harbor,
Mariner Merle, a mighty man is he.
Mariner Merle, aims his boat across the harbor,
Gosh, Oh gee, Oh golly, hope he doesn't hit me!

There were a few more choice lines that we added along the way, but you get the idea of how most people felt about Merle, and most were happy to see him go, not because they didn't like him, but because they knew that once again their boats were safe. I took Merle and his wife fishing a few times during their stay at Cass Lake because, as he put it, he wanted to learn the "hotspots" on the lake. Did I have news for him! Anyway, after a few trips out, Merle took it upon himself to guide his wife in their boat, but every time I saw them on the lake, they were either shallow trolling in ninety feet of water or stopping and looking at a lake map wondering where they were. It seems that Merle was having a difficult time remembering not only where he was, but also where he had been! Believe me when I say I don't make it a practice of poking fun at others, but Merle just seemed to create his own problems. One time while jig-fishing for walleyes, Merle and his wife and I were drifting with a slight breeze at our backs and my boat was positioned sideways to the drop-off. We were casting the quarter ounce jigs out to the side ahead of us and retrieving them along the drop. I had warned both Merle and his wife about the dangers of casting sidearm, or from side to side with an overhead method, so as not to catch one another or hit each other with their hooks. We were doing fine and picking up an occasional walleye as we drifted along the drop-off when Merle decided he was going to try something different. Without saying anything he turned to the side and let fly a cast with a lot of force. On the backswing he managed to hit or bounce the leadhead jig off the top of his wife's head. She immediately dropped her fishing pole on the bottom of the boat, fell to her knees, and began to cry from the pain. It would be like getting hit on the head by a rock someone had thrown. Merle didn't even know he had hit her, as his back was toward her and so he went on fishing. I scrambled past Merle to the bow of the boat where she was kneeling and helped her back up onto a seat. Merle asked what was wrong, and when I told him he sort of shrugged it off and went on fishing. I knew his wife was in pain, not because of the tears, but because she didn't want to fish anymore and she kept holding her head as if she were suffering an accute migrane. I asked if they wanted to go in, but Merle said they would stay out and she would be all right in a little bit. She wasn't all right after awhile, and I finally did convince Merle to let me take her in to shore so she could rest in the cabin. I promised him I'd bring him back out to finish our time of fishing. It all turned out fine except for a knot that developed on top of his wife's head. We were able to finish our trip, but Merle didn't think he had done anything wrong, and I don't think he ever apologized to his wife for what had happened. I felt badly for her, but the next day she was back to her old self again and acted as if nothing had happened. Another time I had taken Merle and his wife out musky fishing on an evening trip. We were probably half through our evening of casting when a huge musky came out of nowhere and grabbed my bucktail spinner bait. It was near the mouth of the Mississippi River in Cass Lake, and the musky was big. It had come from under the boat and attacked my bait straight up from the bottom, so all I saw to begin with was a huge bucket- sized open mouth. I played the big fish around and under the boat several times and it never once tried to jump as most muskies do. Upon seeing the fish, Merle went right to the front of my boat with his wife, and he said he didn't want a big fish like that in the same boat with him. As I continued to play the big fish around the boat I could see it wasn't hooked as well as I'd have liked, so I asked Merle to reach down and hand me the gaff. He was stone solid frozen as he watched the huge musky take another turn around the boat. Merle was not about to move any closer or even try to help me with the landing of this fish. I had been in this predicament before and knew what I had to do, but I didn't like taking my eyes off the fish for even an instant while reaching for the gaff. I knew about where the gaff was, but by fumbling around and trying to feel for it, I was more vulnerable. As I glanced away from the fish to the gaff lying on the floor, sure enough the big musky decided to get aggressive again and shook its head and rolled over in the water shaking my hook out in the process. I threw my rod and reel down and made one last lurching attempt at gaffing the big fish. The gaff caught but did not penetrate the skin on the side of the fish, and I rolled her over one last time as I watched her swim slowly away under the boat down into the weeds. Merle was happy because he really didn't want that fish in the same boat as he was. I estimated the musky at forty pounds plus, and was convinced it was one of the largest I had seen up to that time. After we returned to the dock that evening, Merle told everyone that I had screwed up, as if I didn't already feel badly enough about losing the fish. He really emphasized how much I didn't know about muskies and musky fishing. Merle had just taken his first musky trip, and he was telling everyone how much I didn't know about the sport itself. It just didn't seem to make sense to me, but I did suffer a little from the sting and the hurt both from the loss of the great fish and from Merle's cutting remarks. As I thought about it later I think Merle was trying to direct attention to me in order to hide or cover up his own shortcomings as I'm sure he didn't want people to know he was afraid to have a musky in the boat. I don't think Merle ever went musky fishing after that. It was at this point in my young guiding career that I almost gave up on musky fishing myself. There had been a stretch of two weeks that followed the loss of that big musky where I couldn't get a rise or a follow no matter how hard I tried. Musky fishing was seemingly hopeless and I felt as though I probably wasn't cut out to be a successful guide for those big critters. After two and a half rather blank weeks of musky fishing, I came in one day and remarked to Cliff, one of our veteran guides, that I was considering giving up on musky fishing and concentrating more on the walleye and northern species, since I hadn't even seen a musky in two and a half weeks. Cliff looked at me and shook his head and then began to tell me to look around outside of myself, and tell him how many muskies had been brought in during that time span by anyone else. I thought about that idea for a while and couldn't recall any muskies caught by anyone else in the past two weeks. Then Cliff told me if I quit musky fishing, it would probably cut my guide trips by at least a third, and during the late summer months when musky fishing was more popular, it might even cut into my guide trips by more than that. He also told me to lay off the muskies for a few days and try some evening walleye fishing and think about it before making my decision final. I took his advice as I respected his word, and I did feel a bit more encouraged when thinking about the fact that I wasn't the only one who was not having any luck with muskies. It put my thoughts into a different perspective by looking at the whole picture. I did take a few walleye trips, which didn't prove too successful either, and I began to think that maybe our poor fishing was due mainly in part to the fact that our weather pattern had been sitting on a beautiful stagnant high pressure center which had produced nothing but nice, clear, blue skies and beautiful weather over the past two to three weeks. We were enjoying a beautiful fishless era in our mid-summertime exposure to what was usually thought of as the "dog days of summer," and due to the nice weather pattern we weren't complaining, except for the poor fishing conditions. As those days passed and, as usual, the weather patterns gradually changed, we found ourselves in the midst of another decent bite on the part of all the fish. It wasn't long after this change that I decided to give musky fishing another chance. By now we were well into the month of July when my brother and his family came to Birch Villa from their home in Kansas. I took brother Larry out musky fishing one evening; we were fishing in the Allen's Bay area just off the south side of West Potato Island along the drop-off and weedline running parallel to the shore and adjacent to the bulrushes. Larry was in the front of my boat, and so he was getting first crack at the fish as we slow trolled along and cast to the rushes and retrieved our lures over the submergent weeds. Larry had a "follow" as we called it, where the big musky came to the boat about two feet beneath the surface following his lure, a Marathon Musky Houn with a yellow bucktail on the trailing treble hooks. As the big fish began to turn away from the boat, Larry gave a quick figure eight motion on top of the water with the lure. That musky about faced and came charging back at Larry's lure. It surprised Larry so, that he impulsively jerked the lure up and out of the water a bit prematurely for a set of the hooks into the musky's jaw. As he pulled the lure up, the huge fish jumped right up after it, but Larry had already begun to recover from the surprise attack and was quickly dropping the lure back toward the water to allow the fish to eat it. Upon seeing this, the fish did a flip in mid-air beside the boat, getting us both wet, and began its descent downward into the water trying to catch up with the bait. Again, Larry pulled the lure up and the fish followed suit, flying out of the water after the bait at the end of his line. These antics went up and down like a yoyo out of control as Larry tried to let the fish have the lure, but each time the big musky would miss its mark and end up chasing the bait just a split second too late. My eyes were jumping up and down following every move and attempt of the fish trying to catch up with Larry's yoyo lure, but it just didn't happen. All this action took place within about ten seconds' time, and the huge fish decided it had had enough and was gone as quickly as it had appeared. All we had to show for this action was our wet clothes and a good laugh after having a chance to think about what we had just experienced. This big fella wanted the bait, but Larry was unable to deliver or present it to the fish for the taking. The story doesn't end here either, as the following morning I was guiding my brother again and a friend, Steve Stetz, who was staying at our resort with his parents from Oakley, Kansas. We were fishing the same area of Allen's Bay, and as we came around the corner of West Potato Island, Larry was explaining to Steve about where the big musky had followed his lure the evening before, and also trying to describe the action from that event. Again, Larry was in the front of my boat, and Steve was in the center, as we all cast our lures up toward the bulrushes and over the submergent weeds. On one particular retrieve, exactly where the musky had been the evening before, Steve let out a gasp. As we all looked toward his lure, we could see this same big, wide, thick musky following lazily behind his Jointed Creek Chub Pikie Minnow. As the huge fish approached the boat, it began to swing its fifty inch plus body parallel to the boat and continue to swim by without paying much attention to us. Steve lifted his Pikie Minnow up and out of the water and placed it down on the musky's back, which was breaking the surface of the water, as the fish swam by. The lure rode on the back of the fish for over half the length of the sixteen foot boat we were in, and that musky didn't even dash quickly away or act as if it were being threatened. It just swam silently back toward the weedbed from which it had emerged. I fished hard for that musky the rest of the summer, but it never showed itself to me again. I have wondered if just by chance someone might have caught it without anyone's knowledge. Usually, though, when a larger sized fish like that is caught, the word gets around the lake about it having been caught. I never fish by that area, but what I think of those two short lived events.

Another strange event happened during the early part of August 1962, and it proved to be quite a time delaying situation. I had two men in my boat from North Dakota and we were on our way across the lake to Allen's Bay again for an early morning attempt at musky fishing. This particular morning we had left the dock at six a.m. and were rounding a rather wide point on the west shoreline just opposite the west side of Star Island when I spotted a man in another small fishing boat waving a hand as high as he could reach. His other hand was positioned down in his boat. My first thought was that he had accidentally put a hook in the hand which was not free. I slowed my boat and turned toward the man signaling. As we approached his boat, he was yelling, "Help, I got me a loon! I hooked a loon!" He was pretty distraught over his predicament. The man had been fishing with minnows for bait, and the loon had swum underwater and took the minnow hooking itself in the process. I'm still not sure how he got the loon into the boat, but here he was sitting down on the back boat seat, his jacket pinned down with both feet and one hand over the loon and waving to us for help. The loon was frantically struggling to get free, but the man was determined to get the hook out first before releasing the frenzied bird. I had the two men with me hold the boats together while I climbed aboard the other man's boat to hopefully assist him in a successful release of the loon. This other man was then able to use both feet and hands to hold the loon while I grabbed its head and began to extract the hook from its mouth. The flesh of that loon was tough, and the hook would not slip out backward, so I had to climb back into my own boat to get a small pair of side- cutters, which I could use to snip off the barb end of the hook and free the poor, unfortunate creature. All this took time and even though I tried to hurry carefully from boat to boat and back to boat again, the loon was fighting the man continually not wanting to give in, and definitely not understanding we were only trying to help it out of a tough situation. In the course of this time, the bird had almost slipped free several times, but with the help of an extra set of hands, the man holding the loon was once again in control. Finally my attempt proved successful as I nipped the barbed point off the hook, and we allowed the loon to slip out from under the coat and over the side of the boat. It squawked frantically away across the lake to its freedom. The man was thankful for our help and told us the loon had literally attacked him when he first pulled it into his boat. I didn't see any blood on his hands, but he claimed the loon pecked at his hands and actually bit him hard enough to hurt considerably. He was staying at a nearby campground and was just out trying some early morning fishing before the rest of his clan had risen from their sleep. He also told us that he was from Kansas and had only seen pictures of loons before this up close and personal encounter with the one we had just freed. He thought it was better to see the pictures than have a loon in his lap! After that forty-five minute delay, my crew and I were on our way to the musky beds. Regretfully, the loon story was the only highlight of our morning fishing trip. The weather was nice, and we witnessed a beautiful sunrise, but the muskies just weren't too active that morning, so all we returned to the dock with was a peculiar story about the catch and release of an over greedy and over active loon.

Later in mid-August that summer, we were blessed with the presence of a man and his wife from Alton, Illinois. Tom and Monte Harlow came to Birch Villa for their usual two week vacation. They were usually joined by another couple, Mr. and Mrs. John Goodyear, not associated with the tire company. Tom Harlow's favorite hobby was to vacation at different places around the United States and film 16mm movies complete with soundtrack. He usually developed an educational and professional documentary format about some form of activity that occurred near the places he visited. I recall seeing a wonderful movie he made in Mexico depicting the history and explaining the various aspects of bullfighting in that country. Another film he made was centered around a fly-in trophy brook trout fishing trip to an area of Canada north of Quebec. Tom researched this area and the city and gave a complete description of life in and around that part of the province, as he did with all the films he made. I felt fortunate because he asked me if I'd be willing to take him out musky fishing for as many trips as it took to capture a musky catch on film. After some brief consideration, I accepted the challenge and the plans were then set into motion for Tom to begin this new documentary called, "The Story of the Musky." The very next morning Tom and I began our attempt to catch a musky, which I found out later, would be used to highlight and give support to a fantastic story. As we went from spot to spot, Tom would sit on the bow of my boat facing toward me at the back, filming every cast and retrieve I made, in order to catch the hit, the set, and the fight, all on camera. The 16mm camera he used weighed sixteen pounds, so you can imagine in a three to four hour stint, at the rate of approximately one hundred fifty casts per hour, I was making about five hundred casts per shoot. I would like to reiterate; Tom was holding the camera and filming every cast and retrieve! We were not doing too well with the musky action as the timing seemed to be against us, in as much as we were again experiencing bluebird weather. The few muskies we saw were either not too interested or just plain lazy in their actions. The first day went by with only two small follows, and the second day wasn't much better as we were only able to raise three fish, but one of those was a fairly nice sized musky. Unfortunately, Tom was not able to capture the follow-ups on film. I began to feel as though I was letting Tom down as we were not experiencing very much action, but he insisted that we continue with our plan and try not to be dejected and most of all not to give up. So the third day came and we left the dock at our usual six am departure and stopped to try each and every weed bed and drop off we thought might be able to produce a musky for filming. We were a little over three hours into this third morning when it happened. At this point on the film Tom says, "This is it! He's got one on!" and the background music begins to add interest to the battle with the musky. It was a small fish by today's standard, but it was a musky and that's what we were there for, the size didn't matter. I was able to do battle with the thirty-six inch fish as it jumped a few times, and for the first time I was able to use the new musky sized net that I had recently purchased. It worked well as Tom had to continue filming and I was left alone to do my own landing of this fish. We let out a few whoops and hollers as we journeyed back to the dock with our prize, and for the most part, my obligation to the film was over and the rest was left for Tom to pull together. I must say, I was more than anxious to see the finished product, but it wasn't until mid-winter that we received a copy of the film, and a beautiful note from Tom and Monte, thanking us for helping to make his film complete. I hadn't realized when we were filming that summer, but Tom was reading several books about musky fishing in order to add an educational experience to his documentary. That along with his endless interviews featuring all the guides around Birch Villa, seemed like a tireless process for him, and I wondered if he found time to relax during his vacation. He included a history of the Cass Lake area as well as the lake itself and Birch Villa Resort, plus all the people connected with the resort. Most importantly, he did a fine job and presentation about the great fish itself, the musky! Again, this was another one of those many memories that I shall always hold dear to my heart, as it wasn't just about getting on film and catching a musky. It was also about a bonding relationship I was able to enjoy, and a generation gap that I was able to bridge with Tom, his wife Monte and the Goodyears, as they were more than twice my age.

It seems that the summer of 1962 drew to a close much faster than I would have liked. This fall I was to transfer south to the state of Kansas where I would begin to enjoy a four year basketball scholarship that would take me, along with the team at Fort Hays State, to two conference titles and two national NAIA championship tournaments. I was excited about this transfer and I left Cass Lake that fall in early September.

Merv with "Marine Merle" Sussdorf and his wife and a stringer full of walleyes and northern pike.

Another bunch of walleyes with "Marine Merle" Sussdorf and his wife.

A launch trip with the Mondas. Art, Tom, Tim and guide Merv.

Tom Harlow and Merv with the 36"
musky caught while filming a move,
The Story of the Musky.

Merv with a 27# musky.

Kutsen Nornberg with a client and a 20# musky caught in
Cass Lake.

1963

As each year and opening season came we found ourselves trying new and different techniques to approach the walleyes which were quickly becoming more and more wary of particular hooks or lures. In the mid to late fifties, we used a simple rig, which most people now, would consider archaic and obsolete. The rig was a four and a half to five foot steel rod with an old style bait casting reel like the Shakespeare True Blue, Bronson 1890, Langley Lakecast or Pflueger Summit. If you could afford the more expensive twenty dollar reel, you could invest in a nice Pflueger Supreme. These outfits would be strung with twenty-five to thirty pound braided nylon or silk fishing line. There were no dacron or super lines, and we didn't have monofilament yet either. Oh, it was out there on the market, but we didn't have it yet, and it was called "gut" or "cat gut" fishing line. It was made of some sort of plastic, very crude in shape and size, uneven diameters throughout a spool and was very stiff and springy. We actually didn't have spinning reels of our own until 1963. As I remember it was that spring when a couple of us guides around the resort purchased a close-faced spin cast reel on a six foot medium light spin cast rod equipped with fifteen pound monofilament. The entire outfit cost us twenty dollars! Nowadays some people pay that much just for the line. I remember a major problem we had with those new outfits and that was with the knots we tied to secure a hook or lure on the end of the line. It seems that we began losing a lot of fish because the line came untied or broke very easily. As it turned out, we had to educate ourselves to something other than just a simple through the loop knot. It was rather funny at the time because all the guides sat around during their spare time, between trips, experimenting and trying to tie different knots with this new monofilament line. It looked as though these men were back in school trying to learn some things that up until now, they had been able to get along without, like using knots more sophisticated than the old "simple knot." After seemingly endless tries we finally figured out a knot that was similar to the now, well known, clinch knot, and it seemed to hold and not break as easily. In later years we found out that the simple knot, as we called it, was actually cutting into itself when a heavy strain was pulling on it, thus giving up only half the amount of pound test. So, if you used a fifteen pound test monofilament and tied a simple knot, you would only get about seven pounds of strain on the line before it broke. With the discovery of this newer knot, we were able to get the maximum amount of strength from the line which resulted in fewer lost fish. We could get by with a simple knot when using the braided line as it didn't seem to cut into itself as easily as monofilament. I know it sounds strange, but it was a major discovery for us guides, and it gave us a whole new perspective and renewed confidence in our fish catching ability.

My winter was spent in Kansas at Fort Hays Kansas State College, Hays, Kansas. That institution is now known as Fort Hays State University. The winter of 1962-63 passed very quickly, and even though I missed the late fall and early spring fishing in Minnesota at Cass Lake, I enjoyed a successful basketball season at Fort Hays which more or less kept my mind off my other life, fishing! Our team enjoyed a 19-4 season and placed sixth in the nation among the smaller NAIA colleges. It was an exciting time in my life; I was allowed the privilege of enjoying both my loves, basketball and fishing.

The summer of 1963 also provided some unbelievable experiences and relationships with fishing companions and friends. I would be remiss if I didn't say that one of the greatest friends I had over these past four years at the resort was Tim Monda. Tim was a sturdy hockey player from Grand Forks, North Dakota and his family used to vacation at our resort every summer. As a young boy, Tim fell in love with the lake and resort work, and as a result, landed the job as dock boy for four years. I felt like Tim became a brother, and we worked together at the resort laughing and enjoying the experiences and the people with whom we were becoming acquainted. Tim and I cleaned most of the fish that came into the resort during those years, and we kept an unofficial record which revealed an average of ten thousand to twelve thousand fish per year. We would start at Highland Inn Resort early in the evening, which was about a half mile down the shore to the south of Birch Villa. After cleaning fish there, we would stop at Cass Lake Lodge to clean their fish and continue back to Sah-Kah-Tay Resort before finishing up our fish cleaning job at Birch Villa Resort. Sometimes there were only a few fish at each resort, but sometimes we didn't finish cleaning until two or three o'clock in the morning, and those times made for very long days and nights. It didn't seem to affect us too much as we were young and energetic, and we were making some extra money which was our main goal at the time. Just think, we were getting a nickel a fish and we were making good money, or so we thought at the time. Anyway, Tim and I spent a lot of time together, in and out of the fish cleaning house, and we have some fantastic stories of our own which we should probably keep to ourselves. I recall a time when the lake water was high, and we had to walk around the dock on planks and we also had to stand on planks in the fish cleaning house to keep our feet dry. Somehow, one evening, Tim cut his hand, and my dad had to take him to the hospital emergency room for stitches and to repair a damaged tendon. I won't explain here how it all happened, but I felt responsible and down deep, I really felt sorry for Tim. I jokingly accused him of doing that to get out of cleaning the rest of the fish. As I say, we were like brothers, and it was tough to say good-bye at the end of that summer when we both headed back to school. Tim was and still is a very good friend whom I shall always remember and respect. We still keep in touch by e-mail, and almost every summer we meet at Cass Lake and that's always a special time for me. Tim was in the Air Force as a pilot, and after serving, he came home and did some crop dusting in North Dakota. He took instruction for his commercial pilot's license after the crop dusting days, and is looking at retirement now from Southwest Airlines where he has piloted for some sixteen or seventeen years.

Some great highlights from the summer of 1963 were the various musky successes. One in particular that comes to mind happened one morning in mid-July when Cliff Riggles and I were guiding fathers and sons. Cliff had the dads in his boat, and I was guiding the sons. The men with Cliff were Steve Stetz, Sr. (a renowned musky man,) Harry Enyart, and Dick Smith (Mr. Radio of KMBC in Kansas City). In my boat were, Steve Stetz, Jr., and Harry Enyart, Jr. We were fishing that area known as Allen's Bay of Cass Lake; the action and bite was good.

The first day Cliff's boat produced three muskies and two nice northern pike, and my boat produced two muskies and three nice northern pike. As my record reflects, the muskies in Cliff's boat were 29, 22 and 16 pounds respectively. The northern weighed 15 and 12 pounds. In my boat the two muskies weighed 24 and 14 pounds, and the three northern were 12, 11 and 8 pounds. The second day we caught six muskies; Cliff had three which weighed 34, 21 and 19 pounds, in his boat, and my boat produced 30, 29 and 25 pound fish! There were no keepable northern caught during the second day. It was a two-day musky surge that attracted lots of attention around the community and had us excitedly pumped for musky action in the weeks to come.

In late August that season, I was guiding two men from Scott City, Kansas; Dick Holister and Roger Strickert. We fished three days together and caught six muskies ranging in size from 12 pounds up to 31 pounds.

Then in early September I guided a father and two sons from Chicago. They were the Baldwin family, and we made two early morning musky trips which both proved to be fruitful. The first morning we had several follows and caught two small muskies, 14 and 16 pounds, plus a nice 14 pound northern. The second morning mother nature delivered us a change in the weather. There was a strong southwest wind with occasional driving rain and intermittent mist along with a temperature of around 40 degrees. It was cold and wet! I decided to fish an area we call Buck Lake, situated just off the north part of Cass Lake and connected by a small shallow entrance to the lake itself. As we entered Buck Lake, we noticed that the weather conditions were much more adequate there than out on the big lake, so we began our casting near the entrance of the lake. There is a very nice weedbed, near the entrance, which contains lots of beautiful submergent cabbage weeds. On the third cast, I connected with a fifty-three inch musky that later tipped the scales at thirty-nine pounds. This fish hit so violently that we could hear the sucking sound as she inhaled the in-line bucktail spinner I was throwing. It took longer to get the hooks out of her throat than the whole process of catching her. We then hit another corner pocket of weeds, where on the first cast, one of the Baldwin boys hooked and landed a twenty-four pound fish. While I was removing the hooks from that fish, Mr. Baldwin (the dad) kept casting and hooked into a fifty-one inch thirty-seven pound musky! I believe he had only made two casts after we landed his son's fish. Now, with three muskies on the stringers, we only needed one more for our limit, and we continued to fish. You must remember that we still had not been introduced to "catch and release" so our greedy mentality told us to go for the limit, which was a rare occurrence for us during this era of musky hunting. We proceeded to the next "hot spot," as I called it, because I had seen these fish several times during that summer, and I knew that when they turned on, it was a time to stay and have some fun! No sooner than we reached the next weedbed, number two Baldwin son made his first cast and experienced an explosion of water, as the big fish blew up on the surface and inhaled his Jointed Pike Minnow. It was a skinny forty-seven inch fish that weighed only twenty-nine pounds. While we were getting the hooks out of this fish, Mr. Baldwin continued to cast and caught another musky (which we released) that was forty-four inches. We didn't even take time to weigh it, but I estimated it to be around twenty- four or twenty-five pounds.

With four nice muskies on the stringers, we felt like we had done enough damage for that day and headed back to the resort. We fought a rough, choppy lake as we boated home, but none of us even thought about how rough it was with those four muskies in the bottom of the boat. Wow, what a catch, and it only took two and a half hours from the time we left the dock until we returned. The boat ride one way took about fifteen minutes. I forgot to mention that one of the boys had another musky on for about two minutes, but lost it when the big fish jumped and threw the hook. That is one musky encounter that I shall never forget.

The season ended with forty-seven muskies caught in my boat producing one of the best summers I had ever experienced.

Two days after that musky rampage on Buck Lake, I had to pack my things for another college year and head back to Fort Hays in western Kansas where I was blessed with another successful 17 - 6 basketball season and a repeat trip to the National NAIA tourney where 32 teams competed for the number one spot in the nation. We finished in fourth place that season and it was one of the greatest highlights of my life at that time.

The father/son musky trip.

Merv with dad John Baldwin and son Mark Baldwin. Muskies weighing 39# and 24#.

1964

As this season approached, I was still a college student at Fort Hays and I remember getting all jittery and nervous at school during the first few days of May. It was near the opening fishing season, and I knew I couldn't be there to enjoy it. I called my parents two or three times during that opening weekend just to find out how the other guides were doing and how good the fishing was. The other reason for calling was to find out how the progress on the new eighteen foot guide boat I had ordered the previous fall was coming. My dad assured me it would be ready by the first of June when I would return to the resort for the summer. I was as excited about getting home as I had ever remembered, but first I had to focus attention on my studies to try to earn the best marks I could.

The things I remember most about the summer of 1964 were not only that I had a new boat to come home to, but also that my cousin, Tom Horn, from Tulsa, Oklahoma, was going to be living with us for the summer filling the duties of being our number one dock boy and helping me clean fish. Tom was like another brother to me. I also remember the walleye action was super that year during the month of June, and held up very well, through the months of July and August. The musky action was good, too, and I finished the season that year with thirty-eight muskies caught in my boat (one more than the season before!)

The first and probably the earliest musky trip I guided that summer came before mid-June, and even though we didn't catch a musky, we did have some excitement with one fish in particular. I had my new guide boat, a beautiful eighteen foot, open fishing style with four bench seats. The boat was extra wide and extra deep which allowed the guide and passengers plenty of room to stand and walk around jumping, cartwheeling and thrashing vigorously around on the surface in a few short seconds before lodging itself between the two motors at the stern of the boat with one of the treble hooks snagging and holding to a part of the five and a half horse motor ! The musky continued to thrash and fight to free itself from the hooks, which it did in short order, but it stayed there between the motors long enough for me to get the net and put it over the back half of the fish's lengthy body. When the musky finally realized it had ripped the hooks free, it took a dive under the boat, and out of my net and swam away to its own underwater realm to heal and come back to fight another day. It was the only action we had that early June day, and I guess down deep, I was really surprised that we had any action at all because Cass Lake at that time was not known as an early season musky lake.

About three weeks after the episode of the musky between the motors, I was guiding a man and wife from somewhere in southern Wisconsin. It was just after the Fourth of July week, and we were fishing muskies out on the far side of the lake from the resort, in an area we called the "girls' camp" as there was a girls' camp located in a slight bay between Cass Lake and what was then called Shramm Lake. The name of the camp was Camp Cassaway, and it was more or less a landmark to identify the area of the lake near which we were fishing. The man from Wisconsin (I believe his name was Alan Barnes,) was throwing a red, in-line, bucktail spinner of the six inch musky size. A nice forty inch plus musky hit the lure near the surface just after the bait hit the water, and the fight was on ! This was a wild fish, as it jumped about four or five times completely out of the water in an attempt to throw the lure, but Alan held on and really did a nice job of working the rod and the fish. As he fought the fish around the boat the second time, I realized it was a forty inch plus, plus fish, a little bigger than I had first estimated. It swam out and away from the boat, turned and then accelerated itself withlightening quickness right at the side of the boat, hitting it with a bang ! We actually felt the large eighteen foot boat get the jolt from the fish. Later we agreed it was like someone had dropped a large anchor in the bottom of the boat from about four or five feet up. The musky just lay there for a few seconds quivering and dazed from the collision, but still well hooked in the side of the jaw. I reached for the net, not taking my eye off the fish, for fear it might come to and get really wild and aggressive. Luckily, that didn't happen. By the time I put the net into the water, the big fish had rolled onto its side with a lazy-like motion, and I scooped it up and into the boat. The musky never made another flop or flip of its tail. It had actually knocked itself out by ramming the side of the boat. We finished that trip without anymore action and returned to the resort, where we measured the musky at forty-seven inches and weighed it in at twenty-nine and a half pounds. Now that I look back on that experience, it wasn't so much the size of the fish (oh, it was a nice fish,) but the way we ended up getting it. That fish took itself out of the game, so to speak, and we were the fortunate victors of the battle.

I am not sure why, but this particular summer seemed to be the year for oddities happening in my boat. On another occasion that summer I was guiding two of my regular customers from Chicago, brothers Bill and Frank Cunningham. We were musky fishing a nice weedbed along the east shore of Star Island, and it was another one of those bluebird days when everything seemed right with the world, except the musky fishing. I haven't been able to come to any conclusions as to why muskies, for the most part, seem to get more active as the weather gets nastier, but I do know it's true most of the time. Let me qualify that statement a little. I have caught muskies during times of nice bluebird type weather, but in looking back over the years, I have caught more of my larger fish when the weather conditions were not so good and maybe even a bit adverse, to say the least. Anyway, Bill and Frank were casting bucktails and spinners along a breaking weedline, and I was throwing a wooden surface bait called a "Mud Puppy." Apparently some other musky fisherman had beaten us to this spot, because there were numerous weeds floating on the surface along the break just above the under water vegetation. As I was casting and probably not paying particular attention, my bait pulled through a bunch of these floating weeds which trailed about eighteen to twenty inches behind my bait. I began a speedy retrieve to bring the bait to the boat and discard the weeds when out of nowhere a nice, stalky, forty inch musky came up and grabbed the weeds in its mouth in an attempt to hit my bait, I think. The fish wrestled with those weeds on the surface for what seemed to be fifteen seconds or more. My bait and hooks were a good ten to twelve inches ahead and away from the musky's closed jaws. The weeds were hanging out of the fish's mouth and being shaken from side to side. It was a humorous and yet helpless feeling to see the fish fighting those weeds and knowing there was nothing I could do about it. After awhile, the fish disappeared beneath the surface, and all was quiet again on top of the water, like nothing had happened. Frank, Bill and I just looked at each other with a look of disbelief. As I recalled later, that musky, shaking those weeds in its jaws, looked like a mad dog shaking an old sock from side to side and throwing bits and pieces of it here and there along the way. I have had similar instances occur since then, but none that lasted as long as that particular one did out there east of Star Island.

You might ask, "Is that all you did, was fish?" Actually not, as there were always kids and friends around. We swam and water skied during the mid-day hours between fishing trips. My cousin, Tom Horn, and I used to ski a lot, and on occasion we golfed or went hunting for arrowheads on the various shorelines around the lake. Janet Studley, who's father was a guide on the lake, lived just across the street from our resort, and she was always tagging along with us and enjoying all the swimming and skiing that was going on at the beach. She still is a good friend who, has done well for herself in city government in and around the twin city area of Minneapolis and St. Paul. It seemed like whenever the summers ended, Janet was still always around as a good friend to talk to and visit with because her dad, Frank Studley, was a teacher in the Little Falls school system. They wouldn't leave from the resort until just before school was ready to start.

Another enjoyment for me, besides fishing, was to fly over Cass Lake and surrounding waters in a small floatplane and take pictures of all the underwater sandbars and drop-offs for future reference, which helped me learn the lake structure a lot better. With visions of the contour of those structures in my mind, it was easier for me to negotiate the underwater terrain while floating on the surface in my boat. Don Gaard was a resort owner on Steamboat Lake, and he piloted a small, yellow, single engine, Piper Cub, two place airplane. Don also took aerial photos of other resorts from his seaplane and would sell them to those resorters as postcards which they could sell and use in their resort business. Don would land at our resort occasionally during the summer and take rides or pick me up so I could get some more pictures of structure in a different part of the lake. One time Don picked me up, and we took off in his Piper Cub, which had a stick control on the floor in the front seat. We usually flew with the side windows folded out and fastened down to leave the sides open so we could lean out and get a better view or picture of the lake. With the engine running and wind blowing in on the sides, it was very difficult to hear or to carry on a conversation with each other, so we didn't talk much. This particular time, Don seemed to want to talk more; since I was strapped (or belted) in, I had to lean forward to hear. He said, "You should have been with me over 'Big Winnie' yesterday." By "Big Winnie," he meant Lake Winnibigoshish. So, I asked, "What was so important that I should have been with you yesterday?" He answered, "I broke a crankshaft on this little baby while flying at about four thousand feet." I screamed, "WHAT !" He repeated himself, and I said to myself, "Why did you wait until we were in the air to tell me that good news ?" Then he said, "What?" and I answered, "Nothing." He told me about losing power, of course, and how he had to glide the plane down into the wind along a shoreline close to a resort and land it crudely without any power what-so-ever. He was able to negotiate all that and still keep his calm, while not panicking and nosing the airplane into the water. He was then able to get out of the plane, jump off the pontoon into knee-deep water and wade the plane to a nearby dock at the resort where he landed. He called someone he knew who was able to pick up a crankshaft and deliver it to him at the resort, and also help him install the new shaft. Don then taxied the plane around in the lake a bit to check things out and took off and went home for the evening. He did all this in the matter of one day's time. That in itself seemed amazing to me ! I still have the many slides and photos I took from up there in that little yellow Piper Cub while being piloted by Don. I take them out occasionally to review for my own satisfaction, and each time, I remember with deepest respect, Don Gaard, his pretty little yellow seaplane, and the many trips we took together and enjoyed the beauty of God's creation. A few years after that, Don and his son went up north somewhere to pick up another floatplane, as I remember, and on the way home, Don's plane lost power for some reason. Don tried to force land it on a small lake, but came up short of the water, due to lack of power and air speed. He died when he crashed into the trees. When the news reached us, we were very saddened. I remember going to my room, pulling out all those pictures, and remembering a great man whom I had been fortunate enough to know and fly with. I remember the rest of that summer, every time a plane would fly over, I would look up and hope that I'd been having a bad dream or something and maybe it was Don flying around taking pictures, but later reality hit and I realized I wouldn't see him for a long time.

The musky action continued that summer, and in mid-August we experienced another mini musky rampage. One evening, guide Cliff Riggles came in with four muskies, and there were four people in the boat ! Cliff reported that the fish were really moving and active. Unfortunately, they had to come in early as they had their limit. Ironically each person in the boat caught a musky, and the weights were impressive as they each weighed in at thirty-five, twenty-eight, twenty-five, and twenty-one pounds, and measured fifty, forty-eight, forty-six, and forty-two inches respectively. Cliff said, "They attacked the baits like mad dogs !" He also gave a complete rundown of each fish and how the person catching it acted and reacted. It was an interesting description as Cliff told it, and nobody could tell it better, because Cliff was one of those natural storytellers. The very next morning, because Cliff had everyone so pumped from the evening before, we all headed out musky fishing. The bite was still hot, and my boat managed four muskies and Cliff registered another three. The lengths of these seven fish were forty-eight, forty-six, forty-five, forty-four, two forties, a thirty-nine and a thirty-eight inch fish ! That evening after my dad had called a TV station in Duluth, Cliff, Dick Smith, Steve Stetz, Sr., Steve Stetz, Jr. and I took the five largest muskies to Duluth and showed them on the ten o'clock news. There was a problem, though; the Minnesota Twins were being televised and their game went into extra innings. I do not recall how many extra innings, but when the news came on, it was almost eleven o'clock and so the station manager decided we should wait and go on the sports segment, after the news and weather. The only problem was Cliff and I had six am guide trips scheduled the next morning, and it was a good two hour drive back from Duluth ! We sat back and waited patiently, watching all the workers behind the scenes looking at and stepping cautiously over and around the five muskies lying on the floor in the way of everyone and everything. It became quite comical to us as we knew we, along with the Twins, had really upset the proverbial TV schedule applecart this particular evening ! We made it back to Birch Villa at three o'clock in the morning, and Cliff and I did make our six am guide trips, although I'm sure we weren't functioning at 100% of our abilities. That one evening, one morning musky rampage really set the stage for a great ending to the summer, as it started a barrage of several successful musky trips the following two or three weeks for our guide service business. I remember Cliff saying a couple years later that he remembered that time as one of the most memorable times in his long guiding career.

Not long after that, it was time for me to put my boat away for the winter, pack my things for college and go back to Fort Hays for another year of classes. I said good-bye to my family, friends and the lake and was gone for another nine months.

Cliff Riggles and Larry Heitschmidt in their respective 18' Cass Lake guide boats.

The musky that rammed the side of the boat, knocking itself out.

The "three musketeers", Tim Monda, Steve Stetz and Merv clowning around.

Taking off in the Piper Cub.

Steve "Stephanie" Stetz dresses up as the Birch Villa Queen.

The Birch Villa "Paint Crew." Actually only Tim Monda, Larry Heitschmidt and Merv were the painters.

Don Gaard's Piper Cub we flew in to take pictures over Cass Lake.

Some views of the underwater drop-offs just off the SE tip of Cedar Island.

Underwater structure off the south side of Cedar Island. Notice the hole in the middle of a shallow sand bar.

A view of Star Island looking from south to north. Lake Widigo can be seen within Star Island.

A view of the Birch Villa Harbor from the air.

Cliff Riggles with Mr. and Mrs. Steve Stetz and Tim
Monda showing off the four muskies they caught one eve.

A view of east and west Potato Islands
with the mouth of Mississippi river coming into Cass Lake in the background.

Steve Stetz, Cliff Riggles (holding
musky), Steve Stetz, Jr. with a 34
pounder caught in Cass Lake.

1965

If this chapter had another title it would probably be, 'Beetle Spin,' because much of the summer was consumed with the introduction of this cute little lure to the Cass Lake area. We will get to that story in a few moments, but let us take first things first.

That year in school at Fort Hays, I was introduced to an exercise more commonly called, "the block." This was a time when teachers-to-be had a chance to do their "student teaching." For me it came during the spring semester, and I was assigned to a high school in southwestern Kansas in the town of Garden City, which is not too far from Dodge City, Kansas. I was advised to teach physical education, social studies and driver training, which were the areas I was focusing on for later teaching disciplines. My master teacher was a great gentleman named Kurt Shipley, who was then the boys' physical education and health teacher as well as the head varsity boys' basketball coach at Garden City High School. When I arrived at Garden City, Coach Shipley was packing equipment for state competition in the Class AAA state basketball tournament. He told me to get my things settled in the apartment I had rented with another fellow from Fort Hays, who also drew Garden City as his place of student teaching, and meet him (coach Shipley) back at the gym that very afternoon, as we were leaving for the tournaments! He told me he wanted me along because I had just finished four years of college basketball at Fort Hays, and he thought I could be of value to him and the team during the tourney. We left Garden City that afternoon for a week-long stay at the state tourney. Garden City won the tournament that year, and I received a lot of valuable experience that would help me later in my own coaching career. I mention this only because I was intending to graduate that spring, but I guess, God had other things in mind for me. My student teaching did not go as well as I had planned; in fact I felt like I was failing at the thing I wanted to do most in my life, teach. I would go home each evening from student teaching with a headache and a very tired feeling of non-accomplishment. After a couple of visits from my college advisor, we decided the reason for my feelings of anxiety and frustration were because I am an extremely organized person. While student teaching in physical education, I was not allowed that freedom. I was never sure what I'd be teaching from day to day because of the weather, and I guess that bothered me more than I realized. Because I was putting so much stress on myself, I even considered not going into teaching at all. The answer to this situation was rather simple, but at the time it hurt in many ways. We decided I should not graduate that particular spring, but go back to Fort Hays the next fall and take English courses all year in order to obtain a major in English. It meant another year of school, money out of my own pocket for tuition because now my scholarship was finished, and a change of attitude knowing I wouldn't graduate when I had planned. I finished college that year with a degree of skepticism and reservation; I wasn't sure whether I had made the right choice.

A great thing happened to me during those days of student teaching, however, and it changed me for the rest of my life. That's when I met Jan Smith, who later became my wife. She was in her first year of teaching in a nice town named Scott

City located just north of Garden City. We were introduced by my brother Larry and his wife, Juanita, at a women's town team basketball game, and it was love at first sight. Jan and I dated during the remainder of that spring and wrote to each other during the summer months while I was guiding in Minnesota and she was at her parents home in eastern Kansas.

I understand the Minnesota spring opening fishing season was a little slow for most of our guides that year, at least those were the reports I was getting from my parents. It was because of an early spring and unfavorable weather conditions, but that didn't affect me too much, as I was still in school and didn't arrive at Birch Villa until June second. My dad had a guide trip scheduled for me the morning of June third, so I didn't have a chance to allow any grass to grow underfoot. I recall that trip as if it were yesterday because there was a cold north breeze, and it was snowing! It snowed about two inches that morning, and our boat seats, tackle boxes, minnow buckets and nets were all covered with a nice thick layer of snow before noon. We did catch walleyes at an alarming rate though, and with full limits by mid-morning, we decided to give the northern pike a try. The northern fishing was unbelievable as we trolled over an area that would later produce a nice weedbed using flashy spoons to try to entice one of these long sleeky creatures to bite. There were few or no weeds yet, but the northern were there, and we had three limits of the pike on the stringer by noon when we went back to the resort with snow, fish, wet clothes and cold hands. It felt good to get next to the fire in the fireplace at the Birch Villa Lodge and to talk about the nice stringers of fish from the morning's catch. The twenty-four walleyes weighed an average two pounds each with two of the fish tipping the scale at five pounds. The nine northern, on the other hand, weighed an average of four pounds with one fish measuring nine pounds. The fish were not monsters by any stretch of the imagination, but it was a beautiful catch. I don't remember the names of the three men I was guiding that morning, but I do know that they were from a small town just south of Grand Forks, North Dakota. One man was an implement dealer, and the other two were farmers from that area. I remember all the complaining that morning, but after we got on the fish and the bite started there was no more grumbling from anyone. It was quite a nice way to begin another summer despite the weather. Now all of that seems like a blur in the past, but thanks to some record keeping and logging of a few guide trips it doesn't seem that long ago after all. The remainder of June went by like a flash with numerous walleye trips and many fish caught and cleaned. It seemed like no time before we found ourselves in the month of July. The walleye action had slowed considerably by then, so we shifted our attention to muskies a little more.

I recall an incident that took place during this time of transition from walleye action to musky hunting. My brother, Larry, was guiding a couple from Kansas, Harold and Dorothy Greenwood. They had gone out early to fish muskies that morning in early July, and since the muskies didn't seem to be active, decided to try some late morning walleye fishing before going back to the dock. They arrived at a location just north of Cedar Island where the rest of us guides had been fishing and were about to leave because our morning trips were ending. As the rest left, I stopped and visited with my brother to find out how the musky fishing went for them that morning. I also informed him we had our limit of walleyes and the bite was pretty good. As we pulled away, I noticed they all had their worm rigs hooked up, ready for action. Later we found out that action is exactly what they got. My brother told of trolling through this area a few times losing some tackle by getting it 'bit-off' as they fished. I thought to myself that was funny, because the lake had a very clean bottom in that area, so it must have been fish causing the problems. Sure enough, Harold had a heavy bite and after a few short seconds a huge musky surfaced with his worm harness hanging from its mouth! To make a long story short, Harold fought that musky around the boat for forty-five minutes with his six foot spinning rod spooled with old, weak six pound test monofilament. Fortunately, Larry had the big musky net in the boat because of the earlier stint of musky hunting that morning. As Harold played the big fish down, Larry got ready with the net and scooped the toothy critter into the boat. The fish measured forty-six inches and weighed in at twenty-eight pounds. As Larry's guide boat came across the lake, we all saw a musky flag waving in the breeze. Our thoughts at first were, "What's going on here ?" Then as the boat drew closer, we figured out that they had been blessed with a musky while fishing for walleye. Harold had the fish mounted, and, as far as I know, that was the only musky he caught during his entire life. Now that's a good example of irony for the simple fact that during the earlier morning hours, Larry, Harold and Dorothy had no musky action while actually fishing for them. So, they decide to try for a few walleyes and what happens ? They catch a musky on a worm!

It wasn't too many days after that when we were still fishing the same area north of Cedar Island and a storm moved in on us rather quickly, catching us off guard and making things a bit tense for us guides and our customers. As I recall, there were about three or four of us fishing walleye during the mid morning hours when the storm hit. We immediately headed for shore as the strong winds and then heavy rain began to force us off the lake. We usually watched the weather and we all had a healthy respect for the water and what these weather conditions can cause. This one was holding off and lingering out there on the horizon to the northwest all morning, but when it started to build and move in on us, it came fast! I was guiding with the launch, and when it started to rain everyone went down into the cabin to keep dry. That causes some problem as most of the weight is then shifted to the front or bow of the boat which causes the boat to more or less "plow" in the water. This causes more water to come over the front of the boat and slows the boat down considerably. It also causes the guide to take the brunt of the discomfort as he wants to keep the customer as dry and safe as possible. With this in mind we were heading west across the lake into a stiff northwest wind and driving rain so heavy I could not see twenty feet in front of the boat, but kept the twenty-four foot craft on an erratic course toward the resort. It took about twenty minutes to get across the lake from north of Cedar Island under normal conditions. My question was, "How long will it take me now?" I kept glancing at my watch trying to determine how long we'd been underway. I did not know where the other guides were with their faster boats, but we were all headed for the same place. In the driving rain, it was difficult to see anything, mainly because of the rain hitting me in the face and eyes. After what I thought was about twenty-five minutes, I put my hand on the throttle in order to be ready to cut the power just in case I came abruptly upon the west shore of the lake. In that instant I thought I saw a blur of something ahead of the boat, so I cut the power as fast as I could, and there before me loomed the Birch Villa dock with two other guide boats quickly unloading their passengers. I trolled the launch up to the dock where my cousin, Tom Horn, our dock boy, was waiting to catch us. He asked, "How's the weather out there ?" I responded, "It's good now that we're in here!" The amazing thing about this whole event that I've re-thought many times, is that we came through the harbor entrance (a twenty foot wide opening) at full speed before we knew where we actually were because we couldn't see anything. I firmly believe there was a guardian angel looking over and guiding us that day. It was a time when the guide needed a guide to help find the way home. The fourth boat that day ended up about a half mile down the shore at another resort, where they waited out the storm after calling and telling us where they were. I found out later the other two guides arrived at our dock before I did, but they both missed the entrance to the harbor by a hundred yards or more. It wasn't a fun experience as we guides were responsible for our passengers and that adds extra stress to the job, especially during this kind of storm condition.

There was one other time my brother and I had guide trips and we were fishing together just south of Star Island. It was a walleye trip and a fast moving storm swept in on us when we were caught in the middle of driving winds and rain. We both headed for the resort and about half way in, it began to hail! The hail stones were marble size and caused some considerable pain when they hit the body. My brother and I both used a seat cushion to hold up to protect our faces so it wouldn't hurt so bad, but the hail still pelted our hands. We both ended up with bruises from that ordeal. We managed to get back to the dock safely and waited out the storm again. It lasted most of the day, so we had to postpone those trips until a later day. We did get the trips in and, I must say, under much better conditions, as we caught some nice walleyes and jumbo perch.

As stated earlier this would be my Beetle Spin chapter. This summer made a great difference and an even greater impact on our guiding success for many years to come. It all started in July as the walleye fishing became tough; in fact it got downright impossible. All of us guides were having trouble figuring out the poor walleye bite. Cliff, Kutsey, Larry and I would try everything we knew and even some off the wall variations to try to get consistent walleye action, but to no avail. To add insult to injury, enter Grandma and Grandpa Weber from Illinois, who were having success at catching walleyes on a consistent basis. At first I noticed they were watching and fishing by the "solunar tables" in the newspaper each day. It seemed they were always on the water when there was some kind of active fishing action, however slight it might be. At least it was slight for us guides who were doing everything right to catch walleyes.....Right ? Right! The solunar tables are written and published in book form, but are also reprinted in various newspapers and magazines. These tables show times of different phases of the moon and usually tell when the major and minor active feeding times of wildlife occur. The Webers would quietly and discretely leave the dock at a different time each day. A time that was designated by the table in the newspaper, and they returned consistently with success and a nice catch of walleyes! Now when the customer begins to outfish the guides on a regular basis, it makes people wonder what's going on, especially the guides! It was getting both frustrating and discouraging. One day, after the Webers had shown the guides up for the sixth or seventh day in a row, Cliff said, "Merv, why don't you go over there and find out what they are using and how they're catching these fish ?" I said, "Sure, make me the grunt here!" I was curious, though, and approached the Weber boat with a sly finesse that would have made an FBI agent proud. I said, "How's fishing?" The Webers started to tell me how they were catching walleyes, what they were using, where they were fishing, and what times to show up! They told me more than I really needed to know, but I listened. One thing I learned as a guide is that you can learn a lot if you just stay tuned in and listen. I casually returned to Cliff and the boys with all the information the Webers had given, while they watched from their boat. Boy, I bet they thought I was dumb! Anyway the bottom line was, 'Beetle Spin'! Cliff said, "Beetle Spin! What the heck is a Beetle Spin anyway ?" I told him it was a little rubber bodied thing on a hook with a spinner attached to a safety pin-like wire thingy. Cliff looked at me and said again, "What the heck is a Beetle Spin ?" I knew it was useless to try to explain, and I'm not a very good artist, so I knew drawing a picture wouldn't do any good either. Finally I told Cliff that I had seen something that looked like a Beetle Spin at the bait shop in town. Cliff said, "Let's go; show me this thing." We went to town and sure enough there were some of these little baits, but these were called Mr. Twister spinners. Cliff bought a whole card of these Mr. Twisters, and I bought three for myself. I think they were sixty-nine cents each, plus tax, so that wasn't too bad. Now we were ready to go forth and be good guides again, but guess what ? The Webers continued to bring in nice strings of walleyes, while Cliff and I were still getting skunked. I think Larry and Kutsey were just waiting to see if this phenomenon was going to pan out and last. It was frustrating, so I approached the Webers again. They told me they had tried the Twisters, too, but they didn't work for them either. Oh well, you live and learn, so Cliff and I went back to the bait shop again. I don't know what the difference is, because the Twisters looked just like the Beetle Spins, the only thing different was the Twister had a wavy tail (which I liked better in the water) and the Beetle Spin had a split twin tail (which showed no action what-so-ever.) This time Cliff bought three cards of the Beetle Spins (white body with a red spot were the hot ones), and I purchased the last card for myself. That evening Cliff caught seven nice walleyes in his boat, and my boat ended up with nine walleyes and a nice northern pike. We stayed about a half hour longer than Cliff did that evening, so we ended up with a few more fish. It was easy fishing, as we found you could troll anywhere from four to twelve feet of water and catch walleyes consistently, and thus began the era of the "Beetle Spin!" As I write this during the fall and winter months of 2003-2004, we are still using Beetle Spins and still catching lots of walleyes, all because some guests at our resort showed us what, how, when and where! Thank you, Webers! My philosophy, you can always learn from other people, no matter how much you think you know about your trade; all you have to do is listen. The Beetle Spin era began for us about thirty-eight years ago, and that is a very long standing run of success for one specific artificial lure. I should add here that the Weber family used to come to Birch Villa Resort each year and Grandpa and Grandma's son still comes to Birch Villa. Their son, Carlisle, has carried on the tradition that he and his parents started some thirty-eight years ago. Carlisle uses Beetle Spins mostly, and even though some modifications have been added, like tipping it with a bit of night crawler, he's still catching his share of nice walleyes to this day.

Later that summer, near the end of July, I guided a man named Jess Kail and his son Jim on a musky trip. The Kails were from Maine and had fished for muskies once or twice back in their home state, but the result was only a small twenty-four inch fish that they released, back to its habitat, to grow bigger for a later fight. I really wanted to see them have some action and show them what Minnesota had to offer in the way of musky fishing. As we started out that day for a weed bed east of Cedar Island, I attached a red bucktail to Jim's line and gave Jess a black one to use. I tied on a yellow bucktail, and we began casting upon arriving at the designated spot. Now you have to understand here that when I guide, I use a method of "forward troll" which means that the person or persons in the front of my boat usually get first and second shot at the fish due to their position in the boat and the fact that we troll forward. It was that way with Jess and Jim as we trolled parallel along a weedbed casting out to the side and front of the boat. Within a few minutes I had a hit and set the hook only to find that my lure, which was third in line, was the one this musky chose to attack. I fought the fish quickly, and it turned out to be a stout forty-five incher which we netted and put on the stringer. I decided the yellow colored bucktail was the one for the day, so I gave it up to Jess and took his black bucktail hoping he would have the same result as I had with it. We continued on and within a few more casts I had another fish on about the same size as the first one. It turned out to be a forty-six incher this time, and so I gave Jim my black bucktail and took his red one hoping he would have the same luck I had and we continued on again. I even made a comment that it would really be weird if I were to catch a third fish, and everyone laughed. I thought to myself that at least they weren't mad at me yet. No sooner than I had spoken the words, I felt another hit and I was fighting yet another musky as my passengers watched. How could this be happening, I thought to myself as we netted the third fish and admired its forty-two inches of healthy body. What should I do ? I laid the red bucktail on the boat seat and said I was done, and they could catch the next fish. I thought to myself, this is a fine time to do that, after I've caught three muskies within about an hour and we weren't even half way to the end of the weed bed! Jess said that he still wanted me to fish because it was just as much fun to watch someone else in the boat catch a musky as it was to catch one himself. I reached into my tackle box and pulled out a white bucktail that I had never caught a fish on; in fact I never even had a follow from a musky with it. I felt like I was safe with this bait, and Jess and Jim would now get whatever action we might encounter, so we continued on. Yes, you guessed it! I saw another musky chasing my white bucktail, and I literally jerked and pulled it out from in front of this fish as it made a lunge with open mouth for my bait! Jess asked why I did that, and I told him I just couldn't let it happen again. That fourth fish was a smaller musky than the other three so I wasn't upset too much. We fished the remainder of that weed bed and two or three others, and both Jess and Jim had follow-ups and a few swirls or boils, but neither of them were able to connect with a fish. When we returned to the dock, Jess gave me a twenty dollar tip and told me he couldn't remember a fishing trip he had enjoyed more, so I guess he was happy with the result even though he didn't catch a fish. I told someone about that evening later and said, "It's one of those times where I couldn't win, but I also couldn't lose." Life gives us some rather unexpected twists sometimes.

This summer of sixty-five gave us some different experiences, but the older I get the more I realize that we continue to add to our list of experiences as time goes on. August gave me some great musky fishing that year, and we ended up the season with fifty-five big fish that we kept in my boat not to mention those smaller fish being let go or released to fight again another day. Again that fall I packed my things and headed off for my senior year of college. Since this would be my last year in college, I knew I would return next spring and not have to leave as early the next fall. Tom Horn had already gone back to Tulsa and probably was in school, so it was a little easier for me to leave since most friends were already gone too.

Jim Kail and Merv with two of the three muskies they caught while fishing in Cass Lake one evening with Jess Kail, (Jim's dad).

Merv holding two of the three muskies caught in Cass Lake while fishing with Jess Kail and his son, Jim.

Merv with a 26# musky.

Merv with some nice walleyes caught in Cass Lake on one of his guide trips.

Merv's Black Lab, Dutchess, accompanied him on many fishing trips.

1966

During the fall and spring semesters at Fort Hays I was able to take twenty-six hours of English classes, which enabled me to receive a double major in physical education and English, plus minors in social studies and driver training. At the June 1st commencement exercises for my graduation that year, my parents couldn't attend because of being twelve hundred miles away and operating Birch Villa Resort during a very busy time of the season. My brother and sister-in-law, Larry and Juanita Heitschmidt and their four children were able to attend, however, as well as a friend, Janice Smith, who a year later became my wife. I recall going through the graduation ceremonies and afterward Jan, my brother and his family and I went out to eat as a little celebration. Jan and I went to a movie that evening, and then I took her back to her sister's dorm on campus and we said our goodbyes for the summer, as I was leaving early the next morning to go back to Minnesota and guide again for the summer.

My cousin, Tom Horn, had come to Hays that morning to accompany me back to Minnesota to be our dock boy again for the summer. We had a good all-day trip and arrived at Birch Villa that evening of June 2nd to a welcoming group of guests and my parents. It was an easy start to the summer as I didn't have a guide trip for a couple days after arriving. I also had some exciting news to tell my parents, I had signed a teaching contract with the Scott City Jr. High School in Scott City, Kansas! I would be going back again in the fall, only this time I would be teaching English most of the time with a couple physical education classes three days a week.

The walleye season was mediocre during the month of June, but took a drastic change for the better as we rolled into the month of July. We turned from using minnows to a night crawler rig and even tipped an orange flatfish with a piece of crawler occasionally to entice the walleyes. It worked, and we caught even more and bigger walleyes during July which was usually a month when the walleye bite turned off completely or at the very least, slowed considerably. That year we kept catching walleyes all summer and our musky fishing suffered because of it. Everyone wanted to get a piece of that walleye action so most of our trips continued to find us on the walleye bars morning and evening. The guides didn't mind that too much because the fishing was fairly easy and business held up during a period of time that it usually slacked off. Those of us who wanted to fish muskies would schedule mini-trips or half-trips during the mid-daytime hours. We reduced the price and went out for two hours rather than four. This meant more time on the water for most of us, but at least we were able satisfy our "musky fever" somewhat.

The Beetle Spins were also working for us from late July through mid to late August that year, and as I look back, the walleyes never stopped biting. Oh, there would be a slow day or two and we would think it was all over, but then the walleyes had a way of proving we didn't know everything about their habits and started biting again. It was a great walleye summer and on one occasion I had a man and his two sons out for the morning "trying for some of those walleyes" as they put it. We were fishing a small corner or curve along a drop-off just north and east of Cedar Island getting bites using night crawler rigs in about fifteen feet of water. It seemed that when a bite occurred we would pull up only half a worm or less, that was left on the hooks. I could feel the walleyes biting the worm and just hanging on for a short time and then letting go and leaving us with a partial worm and no fish. I remembered a time in the past when this happened with minnows and we just left our rod and reel sit by itself leaning over the side of the boat until the fish was about to pull the rod in. We would then pick the rod up and jerk or set the hook and we had success at catching the fish. So, I told the father and his two sons to put their rods down on the bottom of the boat with the tip standing up and leaning out over the water. As they did this we would watch the rod tip and see when the walleye would take hold, only now, without our hand-held resistance the fish would continue to bite further up on the worm and we caught them. It took about an hour with this method and we had three limits of nice sized walleyes! I think we caught all but two of those eighteen fish with that no-hands method. I'm not sure why that worked, but after years of catching walleyes, I do know that they can be a frustrating fish because of their sometimes wary ability to sense when something is not right with their food and its availability. That man and his two sons continued to return to Birch Villa for many years to come and his wife told my mother that it was great to see her husband and his boys having such a good time together due to the fact that their dad was on the road a lot with his job. After hearing that, I was more pleased to know that this game called fishing is much more than just a game. It could be called, fishers of men for more reasons than we can ever comprehend. I truly believe the "Fishers of Men" named their organization because of a more supreme power and what it can do for us as human beings. Those kinds of experiences became more and more evident to me than just the pure enjoyment of catching.

Another experience that gave us a thrill that summer came one early August morning when I had a husband and wife out fishing walleyes directly in front of our resort. Now, everyone knows, you never fish on your side of the lake because there are no fish there, so usually we go clear across the lake. This man wanted to know why no one ever fished "out front?" I tried to be a little discrete in my answer by saying, we just feel there is better fishing out further in the lake. His wife spoke up and said she would just as soon fish close to the resort so that if she got bored or tired, we could bring her in and she wouldn't feel bad about disrupting our fishing time. I knew I was in trouble because I'd been through this kind of thing before, remember, (never try to out-fish women or children) so we fished in front of the resort. I guess from a guide's standpoint we wanted the customer to feel they were getting their money's worth, so we took them across the lake. We also wanted the guests to know that we did know another part of the lake! Getting back to the story, we were in front of the resort, fishing with Beetle Spins because there are a few under water weeds and the Beetle Spins don't snag on them as easily as some other baits. You can troll these baits fast enough to ride over the weeds, so there we were trolling along, and within about five minutes as fate would have it, this guys wife gets the first bite. She seemed to be having more fun than normal reeling this fish in and I thought she might be exaggerating a bit just to rub it in and show me there were fish to be caught here! As it turned out she caught a nice eight pound northern and then I told them that was another reason we didn't fish there very much because these weeds were full of northern pike. They wanted to know what was wrong with that, and I didn't actually have a good answer, but I did say that most of the northern weren't as nice as this one and we usually ended up saying something about these pesky little "snakes" or "hammer handles" as we called them, that was degrading to this species of fish. We continued to fish "out front" and they continued to catch fish abundantly! Not only did they catch northern pike, but the walleyes had moved in and we ended up with two limits of both northern and walleye. It was another one of those times when the guide eats humble pie and chalks it up to experience, plus being reminded of his old many times proven philosophy. At least I can look back on those experiences now and chuckle, knowing and realizing again that we humans don't know it all.

A rather sad thing happened late in August that year, there had been a man and his wife staying in our little number five cabin for the past three years. This cabin was also known as the "honeymoon cabin" because it was a small one bedroom unit that didn't have a lot of popularity due to its size, and the fact that most of our customers were more family oriented. These two were retired cattle ranchers from southwest Kansas and had been spending their summers with us at Birch Villa. Herb loved to fish and acquired a small fourteen foot fishing boat with a six horse power Johnson motor and kept it tied up at our dock and fished almost everyday. Lola, his wife, fished occasionally with him, but she was more content to stay at the resort and read or help my mother with meals or cabin cleaning whenever the need would arise. After having lived there for three summers, Herb and Lola were like family to us and we would enjoy watching them enjoy their retirement, doing what they loved to do most. Herb was a tall, big boned, solidly built man who had the disposition of a puppy. He had suffered one or two mild heart attacks, but was taking medication and exercising moderately each day. We would be working around the resort or dock and occasionally look out at the lake. There Herb would be trolling along in his boat enjoying all the comforts of his retirement. This was an everyday sight and we often teased Herb that he was keeping the fish population under control at least on our side of the lake, because he never got more than a half mile from the dock. If you wanted to know how fishing was, you could just ask Herb and he would usually answer, "They're really bitin' down by the wagon bridge!" He would also usually add, " I got into a whole school of muskies and they almost upset my boat!" Then he'd follow with that wide grin across his face and chuckle as he walked on his way. One day my dad, brother, a couple other guides and I were building new covered docks in our harbor. Herb was walking by to go to his boat for another day of fishing. He was across the harbor and we were putting the tin roof on the dock shed when my dad called out to him, "Hey, Herb, eyeball this for us, does it look straight?" Herb never looked up, he just kept walking, raised his hand and shouted, "Nail'er!" We laughed about that and to this day, our little inside joke has been used many times when someone asks for advice, "Nail'er!" One morning as I prepared my boat for a guide trip I looked out and saw Herb trolling by the harbor. He was sitting kind of slumped over, as he always did, with his fishing rod in his right hand and his left hand on the throttle of his outboard. I continued my duties as it was about seven thirty in the morning and we were due to go out at eight. My customers arrived at the dock about ten minutes early and we rigged their fishing rods and loaded them in the boat to head out on the lake. As we left the harbor I looked to my right down the shore and there up in the shallow along the shoreline under some overhanging trees was Herb's boat with Herb still sitting up clutching his fishing rod and still slumped over a bit. I knew this was not his routine as he never fished that close to shore. I headed the boat over toward him thinking he must have something wrong with his reel as he appeared to be looking down at it. As we approached I called out, "Do you need some help, Herb?" He didn't move or answer so I went even closer and had to turn off my motor and raise it out of the water because of the shallow depth. We coasted up to his boat as we floated along and I leaned out to touch him, but there was no response. Herb was not breathing and had apparently died of a heart attack. He looked as peaceful as ever and I knew at that moment he went out of this world doing exactly what he enjoyed most, fishing. I threw my coat over Herb, and we towed him and his boat back to the dock without any undue attention. After some delay of notifying Herb's wife, allowing her some time with him and letting the authorities know, I still took my customers out fishing. I know it sounds rather cruel, but there was nothing more I could do, and Lola had lots of friends around her to help ease the shock at the time. It wasn't a very good trip for me because I had my mind on Herb most of the morning and I truly don't even remember where we fished or how many walleyes we caught. All I could do was keep thinking all the thoughts of good things about Herb and about all the funny things he had done around the resort. When we got back to the dock that day I was scolded by the county water sheriff for moving the body and the boat from down the shore back to our dock. My dad stepped in and asked the sheriff if it would have been better to leave the body and allow some children, who might come along swimming, to find it. The sheriff cooled down a little and apologized, saying nothing wrong had been done as far as he was concerned. That was the last summer Lola spent with us as she later packed up their belongings and went back to Kansas for the winter.

I have to add here that this hit my cousin, Tom pretty hard because he liked Herb a lot. Years later, I think it was in 1994, cousin Tom and his wife Jodee returned to Cass Lake so Jodee could see first hand how beautiful this area really was. My brother Larry and his wife, Juanita took Tom and Jodee to Cass Lake in their motor home. They were camped at a place called Marclay Point Campground sitting around a campfire one evening watching the "aurora borealis" better known as the northern lights. Jodee was a bit startled by this beautiful phenomenon and it made her a bit uneasy to see these beams or rays of light moving and dancing up and down in the northern sky. It even made the evening seem a little eerie to her as she watched the moving rays. A loon began to cry out its uncommon high-pitched song, at least it was uncommon to Jodee. Being from Oklahoma and all, she had never heard a loon. Jodee said in a frightened voice, "What's that!" Of course, cousin Tom, being the practical joker, thought he would have a little fun with an old story, so he told Jodee about Herb's death in his boat many years before. As Jodee listened to the story all wide-eyed and intensely interested, Tom unraveled the details piece by piece, until he came to the end of the story. Jodee asked, "But what does this story have to do with that strange sound coming from the lake?" Tom quickly answered, "That's Herb's ghost!" Jodee scooted a little closer to Tom and he went on to explain that poor old Herb had died in exactly the same position he fished in, so no one knew he had died because he looked so natural sitting there. Tom went on to tell that no one knows how long Herb trolled and floated along maybe calling out for help, but not attracting anyone's curiosity or attention. It is assumed, Tom went on, that Herb's ghost comes back occasionally to call out in the night, just like that loon is calling to us now. With that, Jodee thought a bit and almost knocked Tom off his lawn chair when she realized he had been stringing her along.

Later that summer, Jan and a friend of hers came to Minnesota to enjoy a week in the Boundary Waters. On their way home they stopped at Birch Villa to spend a few days with us and to meet my parents, who Jan had not yet seen. During the few days they were staying with us they were given a cabin on the lake level and I took them fishing and we caught lots of fish. Jan later told me she didn't think she liked fishing until I took her out and she was able to have some success at the sport. She had only gone with her dad in Kansas and caught small bullheads which didn't taste as good as these fresh water walleyes and didn't bite as well as these Minnesota fish. The night before Jan and Linda were to leave to go back to Kansas, I had taken them to a movie. We had returned to the resort and Linda had gone to the cabin, but Jan and I went for a walk along the beach and on the dock. After a beautiful evening of stars and moonlight and northern lights, I walked her back to the cabin and on the steps of cabin number seven I proposed to her! She said, "Yes!" I don't have a very good recollection of the remainder of that summer, I can't imagine why. The neat thing was we were all going to be teaching in the same school district in Scott City, Kansas. By all, I mean my brother Larry, his wife Juanita, Jan's friend Linda, Jan and I, we were all now employed by the Scott City school system.

Since school started in late August, we packed up earlier than usual that year and headed back to Scott City where I would set up residence in brother Larry's basement until I could find an apartment of my own. A few more things that were exciting in my life happened that fall as school started, Jan and I were engaged in October. We had gone to Garden City after school on a Friday and picked out our rings and I purchased the engagement ring for Jan and placed it on her finger. She looked at me with a tear in her eye and said, "I'm so happy I could just cry!" I said, "I know, you already are crying!" Later that evening we attended the Scott City High School homecoming football game and Jan was the center of attention of course, showing off her ring and all. The rest of that year went by quickly and Jan and I got to see a lot of each other what with all the plans for our upcoming wedding in April of 1967.

Merv with man and sons – a stringer of small walleyes.

Warren, Craig and Jay Deeds of Scott City, KS with
walleyes caught leaving rod set in bottom of boat.

Brother, Larry, his wife, Juanita, and Jan Smith (my wife to
be) with a stringer of walleyes.

Merv with a 37# musky caught on a rainy day.

Merv's nephew, Lindsey, Matt Wilson, nephews, Doug and
Dave Eckert with some fish they caught in Cass Lake with
Merv as their guide on a one hour trip.

1967

As the spring of sixty-seven arrived, it found us still teaching in Scott City, Kansas, but with a few changes in our lives. Jan and I had been married on April 8th, and we were finishing a school year that had been filled with many activities and much excitement. We had not had a chance to take a honeymoon because we were married on a Saturday during the school year, took an overnight trip to Oakley, Kansas and returned Sunday to open our gifts and prepare to be teaching again on Monday!

When the end of the school year came, Jan and I took our honeymoon trip through Yellowstone National Park and the Black Hills of South Dakota on our way back to Minnesota for the summer. We arrived at Cass Lake on June tenth and moved into cabin number five for the summer. Yes, that is the cabin that Herb and Lola had occupied the three previous summers. It was a small unit with a combined kitchen and living room area, one bedroom and a full bathroom. It was perfect for a couple who, as of yet, had no children. It took a couple days to get unpacked and settled in, but the guiding service was being sought, and the summer finally and officially began as I took my boat to the waters of Cass Lake for the first time that year.

It was June twelfth and Elsie and Ed Jensen had returned to Birch Villa for the second time that spring. This was unusual because they had set a particular routine in the past, at least with their staying at Birch Villa. Usually they would visit the resort for the Memorial Day weekend, then again for their two week vacation in July and then again for the Labor Day weekend to finish off the summer season. I found out they had been at Birch Villa over the Memorial Day weekend that year, but the weather had been unfavorable to say the least, and they were not able to get

out on the lake to fish. Not to mention the fact that it rained so much, about all they did was go from the cabin to the lodge for their meals. Anyway, Elsie and Ed were back and the weather was great so I had the honor of taking them walleye fishing. I probably don't have to mention this, but after being away from the resort and off the water for about ten months, even a guide gets a little rusty and needs a certain amount of time to get back into the swing of things. It took almost half that first morning for me to even start feeling comfortable with my boat again. We did manage a few walleyes that morning, but it took awhile to locate a school of fish and then some strategies to get them to bite, due to the fact the walleyes were still shallow, the water was cold, and the day was bright and sunny. Now with cold water the fish seem to be a little sluggish and since they were in shallow water and it was a bright clear day we anchored the boat in about six to eight feet of water and cast our minnows out to the ten foot depth and retrieved them very slowly. We had tried a slight drift as there wasn't much of a breeze, but it didn't seem to work, so we tried slow trolling and even though we did have some bites, they wouldn't stay with the bait. I felt like we were moving to fast and that's when we tried anchoring. It worked, because on the first cast, Elsie hooked a nice two pound walleye and brought it to the net. Ed followed with another two pounder and the action continued like that for about an hour, first Elsie would get one and then Ed would come in with his share of the catch. They kept me busy netting fish and putting them on the stringer, but after an hour, the fish turned off and we never caught another walleye that morning. We did find a school of perch and caught some nice jumbos there, but time ran out on us and we had to be back at the resort so Elsie and Ed could be on time for their noon meal at the lodge. We did not want to keep the cooks waiting, and after all we did have eight nice walleyes and eight nice ten to twelve inch perch on the stringer. That wasn't too bad for the first time out in ten months! The next morning proved to be a little more fruitful for us and I took Elsie and Ed out again. It was partly cloudy that morning and there was a slight southeasterly breeze which set us up perfectly for drifting the south edge of Middle Bar, just out from Birch Villa. We left the dock at eight am sharp that morning and returned at ten am with three limits of walleyes. They were eighteen of the nicest two pound average walleyes you would ever want. On the first drift down Middle Bar we caught five fish and I didn't even throw out a marker because the walleyes seemed to be scattered all up and down the bar. Elsie had the most amazing touch and to this day I still claim that she probably was the best fisherperson I've ever had in my boat. Being blind didn't stop Elsie from enjoying the sport of fishing and not only that, she was aware of so many things going on around her. She heard the loons and all other birds as they called out, and she always made mention of that which made me realize that I was so used to those beautiful sounds that I didn't even hear them anymore. It was like Elsie had a way of bringing a person back to reality and helping one to re-focus on what we take so much for granted. Elsie would hear a loon out on the lake and raise her hand toward the direction it came from and say, "Look, there's a loon over there, can you see it ?" It was as if she could see it herself and wanted you to enjoy it with her. I recall a time when Elsie and Ed and I were fishing walleyes south of Cedar Island near the end of June, there were two loons in the water just ahead of our boat and as we approached I noticed there was a smaller baby loon swimming with them. I explained to Elsie that they were feeding their young one because it could not yet find food for itself. Elsie reeled up her line and asked me to turn off the trolling motor and see if she could hear the loons in the water. I thought the idea sounded a bit crazy, but I followed her wishes. I kept explaining to Elsie how each parent loon would take turns diving and coming up with tiny minnows, then they would each swim over to the baby loon and put the minnow in its beak to feed it. This routine went on for almost an hour as we sat there and watched the family of loons feeding and teaching their little one part of the process of life and survival. Our close presence didn't seem to bother the loons as they just went about the business of providing for their baby. Elsie would point toward the loons each time they dived or surfaced and would say, "Listen, you can hear the water ripple as they go down and come up!" It was exciting for Elsie to know she was that close to the loons and she even had Ed take pictures so they could enjoy them later. She explained to me that Ed would go through every picture with her explaining in detail what the scene was and how it looked.

The walleye action held up through most of June that year and unlike the preceding season, it did taper off in early July a bit, so we enjoyed some good early musky fishing too. That summer my boat tallied thirty-nine muskies kept and nineteen that were released, but not without some real dead times for action. It reminds me of a mid-July crisis we went through, I say we because I didn't realize until later that the other guides were suffering the same crisis. There was a two week stretch which lasted through the second and third weeks of July when I never had so much as a smell of a musky. I began to take it personally again and was only focused on my own fishing skills and abilities and thinking that I just wasn't cutting it as a guide because of the lack of muskies produced in my boat. I had tried everything I could imagine from throwing ninety-nine different lures at them to trolling (which I never did,) to live bait rigs (which have never worked for me,) to almost wanting to try hand grenades or dynamite. I decided the latter two were not a good idea even though I was getting pretty desperate. Once again Cliff, the senior guide, came to my rescue. He told me to take off the blinders and look around at what the other three guides had brought to the dock in the way of muskies over the past two weeks. I did begin to think back a bit and remembered that Kutsey and brother Larry had not been rocking the boat with any catches either. I think Kutsey had caught and released one small musky that didn't even measure thirty inches, but that was his total for two weeks. Cliff had only seen two muskies follow to the boat in that stretch of time, and he assured me those were very small fish. After talking with brother Larry, he told me he hadn't seen a fish either. It always takes someone, usually a well meaning friend, to pull us back to reality occasionally and Cliff had done just that again, as I recall this had been a minor detail along the way that had gotten to me before. So we kept on fishing for muskies as if everything was alright and it was. Once I realized it wasn't just me, it was happening to other guides, I knew it had to be more than likely the fish and the low profile they had been keeping for a couple weeks. As it turned out the muskies came out of hiding and began to get more active. My question was and still is, "Where do they go, and what do they do for that period of time?" I called it "Two Bad Weeks At Black Rock" and it was a frustrating time. We hit a frenzy time in my boat on two separate occasions after that terrible lull and I'm thankful for those good times as they help us to cover-up and forget about all the bad times we have on the water. On one occasion I had two men from Illinois who were staying at a resort on Wolf Lake, but wanted to have a guide take them out on Cass Lake for muskies. I was the chosen guide that day and I must say, I wasn't too excited about going after the long dry spell plus it was another one of those bluebird days. I took the trip and later was glad I did. We caught two muskies that morning with mirror like water and bright sun! The first three spots we hit produced nothing and I thought to myself we were still in a slump. The fourth spot which was an area I didn't fish very much seemed to be infested with muskies. I remember seeing eleven fish in about a one hundred yard stretch which blew my mind. It added new emphasis to the old saying, "when it rains it pours" because we were now experiencing the exact opposite of action over the past two weeks! What a change and what turned them on all of a sudden ? We did catch two of those fish on a second time through the area, and saw four fish besides. One fish weighed twenty-one pounds and the other was an eighteen pounder. I was back in the swing of things again, and remember saying a prayer of thanks to God for allowing this to happen. Excitement stirred around the dock as we came in, flying the traditional "musky flag." It seemed to pick up the spirits of everyone around and just like that it seemed like everyone was once again catching fish. In the next week, I believe the four guides, all totaled, had brought in fourteen muskies and we were on the way to having another successful season with the big fish of Cass Lake. There was one day in that great week when I took a man and his wife musky fishing and the lady caught her first musky, a twenty-four pounder that gave her as much fight as she wanted, but afterward she said it was one of the most rewarding and fun things she had accomplished. That fish jumped and dove and thrashed on top of the water like a wild animal trying to get free from its capture. This lady held on for a great fight and never relinquished or gave in to its efforts. Her husband was happy for her, having caught several nice muskies himself, he later told me it couldn't have worked out any better. That's what pleases the guide, the customer is happy!

We continued fishing walleye, northern and muskies into August that year with mixed result, it seems that if we caught big fish, we never caught very many, but if we got up in good numbers of fish, then they were small to medium sized. It worked that way for me on one particular trip to Pike Bay fishing for northern. I was guiding a father and two sons from Rockford, Illinois, and I don't know their name, all I can remember is that they were baseball nuts. The oldest of the two sons was supposedly being checked out by some pro scouts and he had high hopes of making in the major leagues someday. I actually think his father had higher hopes than his son, but then I guess that's pretty normal for most dads. This trio of fishermen made a baseball game out of their fishing time, remember, I said they were baseball nuts. They scored runs only if they caught a fish, they got hits for each fish that would strike their bait, and they collected errors for missing or losing a fish. Each one kept his own box score and each time we would turn the boat around or pull in our lines that marked the end of an inning. This game went on for four hours and it got to be interesting to see who was leading who at the end of our guided trip. I don't recall who won or lost, but they had fun doing it and that's what counts. I do remember the small northern were quite active that day and we managed to keep enough three to four pounders to fill their limits. The big surprise came as we made our last pass along a weed line before going back to the dock. I was trolling a small orange jointed bait called a Brooks Reefer and about fifty yards before the end of the weed bed I had this heavy hit on my lure. I set the hook and cut the motor as I began to play the fish at the end of my line. I knew almost immediately this was a good sized fish, but it had me fooled. Unlike all the quick hitting, fast running, small northern we'd been catching this fish was slow and powerful and deliberate in every move it made. I could feel the wide spread side to side motion of the fish's head as it tried to shake the hook, but with the line taut, was able to wrestle it to the boat for netting. As it came closer we could see it was a huge walleye and then I began to get nervous as one of the boys was going to land it for me. I kept telling him over and over as the big fish made run after run, "She's too green, not yet!" "She's not ready!" Then as quickly as it started, she was wallowing in the net. My netter had done his job and I told him I'd give him a homerun for that one! That didn't make me too popular with the other players, but they got over it as we measured the thirty-one inch walleye that tipped the scales at eleven and a quarter pounds. It was a fat, girthy fish and it eventually went on the wall as my first large walleye. I think it was the first walleye I had caught over nine pounds and I was as proud of it as my first musky. Needless to say, it aroused quite a commotion around the dock and resort that evening. When I started this little story, I said that we never caught a lot of big fish at one time during the last half of the summer and this trip was no exception. We did have three limits of northern, but none of them very big, however; the walleye was the bright spot in that trip as we came home triumphant.

That late summer was a good one for my wife, Jan, as she was able to go with me on several occasions. It went back to my old philosophy about "never try to out-fish . . ." and I think you remember how it goes from there. Jan would always outfit anyone else in the boat and it was usually me! One time I took her to a small area at the south side of Cass Lake called the "kettle" and we fished for northern pike with large sucker minnows and a bobber. We anchored the boat and I rigged Jan's line with a sucker and helped her half cast half throw the bait and bobber out to swim and float over the weed bed. Before I had my sucker rigged, she had a fish on and going with her bobber in tow, so I left my bait in the minnow bucket and waited for her resulting fight. With that type of rig you have to let the fish run, stop, run, stop and continue that sequence for about two or three minutes at least, then you have to decide if it's time to tighten the slack line, if there is any, and set the hook. She did everything right, with some good coaching I might add, and after setting the hook the fight was on! The fish was a good sized northern and after a few runs from and under the boat we were able to put the eleven pounder in the net and eventually on the stringer. It was Jan's first sizeable fish and she was elated about how much fun it can be. She later caught another eight pounder and I caught three small northern that I released. It was about time to go when Jan's bobber started acting perculiar and not at all like a regular northern bite. The bobber would lay over on its side shortly, turn upright and go just under the surface, stay there stationary for many seconds, then come back to the surface. It did that about three or four times and then finally just disappeared out of sight and under water. I told Jan it was probably a little bitty northern that couldn't even get the big sucker in its mouth, but after about two minutes I said, "Set the hook!"

She tightened the slack line and gave a heave on the fishing pole, again a sizeable fight pursued and this time as she fought the fish close to the boat we could see it was a nice walleye. I netted the fish for her and it was a healthy eight pound beauty! We went
home that day with three chunky northern and a big walleye that Jan had caught. The only thing I could tell her or anyone else was that she had a good guide!

A little later that summer my cousin Tom Horn had an opportunity to do something the dock boy doesn't get to do very often, go fishing. He was asked to accompany Cliff Riggles as he guided a man from Cairo, Illinois by the name of Homer Dick. They were going musky fishing and Cliff didn't want Homer to be his only companion, so he asked Tom to go along. Of course Tom jumped at the chance after clearing it with my dad as far as the dock boy's job was concerned. I told him to go and have a good time and I would watch the dock for him and my dad agreed, Tom needed a little break too. Homer had taken a liking to Tom and I think the feeling was mutual, so they got along just fine. They got along fine that is, until Cliff hooked into a rather large musky. After fighting the fish a short time, Cliff was in control of the situation and allowed the musky to swim by the boat a few times. Homer saw the big fish and said, "I don't want that thing in the boat with me, I've never seen a fish that big before!" With that, Cliff and Tom netted the muskie and began to lift it into the boat and Homer grabbed his jacket, put it over his head, and tried to crawl under a boat seat. Tom told this story afterwards and related that Homer got his head under the seat, but his back and butt were still sticking out and he was still yelling, "I don't want that fish in the boat with me!" It made for a funny story and we didn't let Homer forget about that time either. Homer was a great person, years before he had been a champion trap, skeet and trick shooter for Remington Arms Company before retiring. Homer was a regular at the resort and he always had a new gun or two that he loved to show off and share with others. One fall, Homer had come to Birch Villa for the deer season, rented a cabin and hired Cliff as his guide. It was an unseasonably cold fall during the deer season and Homer was having a problem staying in the stand Cliff would place him in before stalking around trying to jump a deer and run it toward Homer. Cliff became a bit frustrated after moving two or three deer past the point where Homer was to be, only to come by later and find out Homer had long since gone back to the truck and was enjoying a hot thermos of coffee, trying to warm up. After that Homer decided to wait a day or two and see if the weather changed before going back out again. Being a practical joker also, Homer was bored and decided to stir up a little excitement around Cass Lake. He drove out to one of the local farmer's places and bought an ugly old cow from the farmer for fifty bucks. Homer gutted the cow the same as you would a deer, had the farmer help load the cow on the fender of his car, tied it down, put his deer tag on the back leg, and drove back to town where he parked on the main street. He sat in the local café having coffee and watching out the window at all the different reactions people had as they stopped to gaze at and talk about this weird sight that had found itself right there in the middle of their town! Needless to say, I think Homer had a more memorable experience from that deer season than did most of the hunters around. Eventually, Homer took the cow to a near by rendering plant and donated her carcass to them for whatever she might be used.

Before the summer ended that year and before we were to go back to our teaching jobs in Kansas, I told my dad one day I was going to do a little scouting on Pike Bay as we wanted to keep tabs on when the walleye bite picked up on that body of water. Dad told me he had a small errand to run, but if the fish were biting to call him on the two-way radio we had equipped our boats with and he would meet me at the shore to fish with me for awhile. My dad loved to fish, but he didn't care to eat them very much. He also didn't have much time to do any serious fishing with all the work involved at the resort, so this would be a unique situation if he did, in fact, get to go. I was going alone this trip and usually when that happened I took my trusty black lab, Dutchess. This was no exception as she seemed to sense when I didn't have anyone else and she was in the boat before I could get there. Dutchess learned that when I got a fish on the line there was some degree of excitement involved and she let out little yips and quiet barks until the fish was in the boat. Then she would wait until the fish quit flopping and sniff it, then look at me as if to confirm her approval of the catch, go back to her seat and wait for the next victim. If there was a lull or quiet time without bites or fish, Dutchess would lie down on the floor of the boat and take a nap until something did occur. We had ventured across the bay, through the channel between Cass Lake and Pike Bay, and I had started trolling along a drop-off just outside a good weedline near the west side of the lake. The area being fished was over a mile long from end to end and the first pass along that drop-off produced five northern (one was an eleven pounder) and three walleyes each about two pounds. I called dad on the radio and told him the result of my first pass along the weedline and he responded by telling me he would meet me at the beach area on the northwest corner of the lake in about an hour. I agreed and told him I was going to troll back toward that spot and it would take about that long to get there. After trolling about half way to the beach and thirty minutes later, I could see dad's pickup sitting there, so decided to run up and pick him up. Another ten pound northern had been put in the boat along with one more nice three pound walleye. As I pulled into the beach area (which is very shallow) my dad was there to catch the boat, climb in and push us off, all in one easy move. He looked down at the fish on the stringer as he petted Dutchess and said, "That's a good looking catch already!" I agree and we motored back to the weedline I had been fishing for the last hour and a half. Dad connected first and I could see by the look in his eye he was enjoying the struggle with this northern. We netted that fish and it was another ten pound beauty. The northern seemed to have moved out at that time because we never caught another one, but whatever happened, it did allow the walleyes to move in and we sort of cleaned up on a nice stringer of those. Dad was proud as he had out fished me on the walleye side of the stringer, catching five and six pound fish back to back and blitzing me for the walleye part. We went back to the beach and dad took the pickup home while Dutchess and I journeyed back in the boat. It wasn't until I was back in Cass Lake that I realized as I looked down at the stringer of fish, I had more than my limit of fish, and I don't think the game warden would consider Dutchess a legal fisherperson! I crossed my fingers as I sped across Cass Lake, past the city boat dock, (where the game warden kept his boat) and on toward home. A boat came out of the city marina as I passed, but it was just an islander going back across the lake to Star Island where he lived for the summer. Most of the guests were gone for the summer, as it was mid to late August, so there wasn't too much excitement at the dock. Word had reached the resort by radio that there was a nice catch of twelve walleye and six northern coming to the dock, so there were a few late summer guests and resort staff there to greet us as we came into the harbor. I was happy because my dad really deserved that short time away from the hustle and bustle of the resort and we had been given an opportunity to have some quality time together before Jan and I had to go back to Scott City for the school year. It was a rather sad ending to that summer because not only were we leaving some great fishing conditions, we were saying good-bye to cousin Tom as he had just finished his fourth year as our number one dock boy and he would not be returning to Birch Villa the next summer because of other pursuits that lay before him in his life. He would go back to Tulsa, finish his senior year in high school, and then move on to hopefully bigger and better things. My brother Larry, his wife Juanita, and their four children, Lisa, Lori, Lesli and Lindsey began to pack their station wagon for the long twelve hundred mile trip back to Scott City, and I believe they had to leave a few days before Jan and I. Eventually we all made the trip safe and sound, not knowing the turn of events that lie before us and our futures in the upcoming year.

Merv holding a stringer of 18 walleyes he guided three men to in July.

Bill Dayton with some nice walleyes and rock bass he and Merv caught.

Homer Dick and Tom Horn with two northern pike they caught while fishing for muskies with Cliff Riggles.

1968

The school year in Scott City was a very good year, but the spring months brought many changes in our lives. In March, my brother Larry, his wife, Juanita, Jan and I made a quick trip to Minnesota so Larry could interview for a Speech Clinician job with Lakes and Pines, an organization which helped place speech therapists in cooperating schools around the Mille Lacs Lake area. Jan and I went along to help with the driving as it was to be a fast weekend trip. We left Scott City, Kansas on a Friday after school (since we were all teachers in that district,) and drove to Sioux Falls, South Dakota where we found a motel to get some sleep for the long hard day ahead. We were up early and on the road Saturday morning to meet with Al Baas, coordinator for Lakes and Pines, in Princeton, Minnesota at 9:00 am. After having breakfast, Al took us up Highway 169, visiting many schools on our way around Mille Lacs Lake and lunch in Isle, Minnesota. After lunch we journeyed east to some schools along Highway 65, and by mid-afternoon found ourselves enjoying pie and coffee at the Park Café in Braham, Minnesota, famous for its homemade pie. While having pie and coffee, Al introduced us to C. R. Lewis, the Superintendent of schools in the Braham district. Mr. Lewis discovered our reason for being in Braham and I told him after my brother got a job and taught in Minnesota for a year, my wife, Jan and I would consider looking for a teaching job in Minnesota also. Mr. Lewis gave us an invitation to come over to the Braham school and visit, as he was looking for two English teachers to fill positions that were being vacated that year because of one teacher's retirement and another one moving to Wisconsin. We went to the school and our visit with Mr. Lewis turned out to be an informal interview for me, for one of the English positions. After the Braham stop we traveled back to Princeton in the late afternoon and told Al Baas good-bye then began our return trip back to western Kansas. That evening we took a motel in Wilmar, Minnesota and Sunday morning were headed back to Scott City where we would resume our teaching duties on Monday morning. On Wednesday of that week a certified letter letter addressed to me, came to the Junior High school, where I taught. The principal, Don Hedges, came to my classroom with the letter, which had a self address from the Braham Schools, and he wanted to know what this was all about. Mr. Hedges knew we had gone to Minnesota the weekend before to see about my brother's interview as a Speech Therapist and the possibility of his getting a job in a Minnesota school. I opened the letter with Mr. Hedges present and was surprised to find a teaching contract for the position of English teacher in the Braham Schools. Mr. Hedges was interested to know what my intentions were and I told him what had transpired on our visit to Braham, but my wife and I would have to talk about it before making a decision. The following Monday we had made a decision to take the Braham job and I informed Mr. Hedges of our intentions, so he could begin his search for the position I would vacate. Yes, I signed a contract about two weeks before my brother, Larry! Since it was getting rather late in the school year we had a lot of plans to make and many new decisions to think about as we prepared to pack up and leave Scott City. Jan was pregnant with our first child and the doctor, Galen Fields, told her she would have to stop every hour on the twelve hundred mile trip to Cass

Lake, and stretch and walk around the car for the sake of not having any complications that might arise otherwise. My brother, Larry, had signed a contract to be the Speech Clinician for both Isle and Onamia school districts through the Lakes and Pines organization, so we decided to
move and travel together on our way back to Minnesota. It was quite a sight to see our little caravan traveling the highways, as I took the lead in a small, cab over, Ford pickup, with sideboards added and covered. Jan followed in our 1962 Ford Galaxie pulling a twelve foot U-Haul enclosed trailer, Juanita was third in the caravan driving their 1963 Ford station wagon pulling a twelve foot U-Haul enclosed trailer, and Larry followed, bringing up the rear in his 1961 Ford pickup with sideboards added and covered, pulling a fourteen foot U-Haul enclosed trailer. My little, cab over pickup would only go about fifty-five miles per hour top speed, so it was rather a long trip which took us two days to reach Onamia, Minnesota, where we stored everything in an abandoned creamery for the summer months. Larry Caldwell, traveled with us to be our dock boy at the resort for the summer. Larry's mother was secretary at the Scott City Junior High School, so she and her husband, Bill "Bob" Caldwell agreed to let Larry come to Cass Lake with us and be dock boy. After unloading everything in Onamia and getting all the trailers back to U-Haul, we continued the last, three hour leg of our trip to Cass Lake where we would work and guide for the summer. Before leaving Onamia, my little pickup had the transmission lock up, so I had to leave it with a mechanic to repair and come back to get it at a later date.

One of the earliest memorable experiences I had that summer occurred early in June as I was guiding a group of men from the Twin Cities who were fishing with their company known as Hart Motor Express. I've heard it said that "history repeats itself" and there was no exception to that theory as we were fishing in the launch because of the size of the group. It had been a rather poor, slow morning and the walleyes were not being cooperative at all, but in a last ditch effort to salvage something from the almost
disastrous day we were having, I steered the launch along the North Cedar bar. I recalled a few years prior to that when we were having the same slow unfortunate luck and within an hour there on North Cedar our boat limited out with walleyes. I mentioned that bit of trivia with the men aboard and they hastened me to try circling up on the bar as we had done in that prior experience, so I obeyed their wishes, knowing it would probably not do any good and on the first time around we boated three average sized walleyes. I thought to myself, "Wow!" "This can't be happening." It was happening and after a few more passes around the shallow center part of the sandbar we had twenty-six of the nicest looking walleyes a guide could want after three hours of nothing. The walleyes were all average in size, about a pound and a half each, none were big and yet it made a consistently, well balanced stringer to view. The men in this party of five all agreed that it was in fact, "history repeating itself!" Upon arriving back at the dock I found the other guides had done equally as well only they had a few larger fish. It was usually my practice not to fish near or too close to the guides in the open fishing boats when guiding from the inboard launch mainly because it was louder and a little more difficult to maneuver and when fishing in shallower waters, seemed to spook the fish

more. That morning was no different so we stayed away from the others most of the time as a common courtesy to them and the tough fishing conditions. The ironic result of that trip was the fact that the other guides had been having a difficult time being able to get on the fish the same as we had. It seems that the others had their success at about the same time, but in a different area of the lake. We started becoming more and more aware of the windows of time the fish were actively feeding and more times than not, we found consistent feeding periods across the lake. At certain times of the year we could sometimes pattern the different bars to produce walleyes earlier or later in the day than others, and we would adjust our fishing patterns to match those periods.

The muskies were active that year earlier than normal, or so it seemed, and my boat took several in the twenty-five to thirty pound class. One of the trips in early July produced a twenty-eight pound "boxcar" as I called it. The fish was only forty-two and a half inches long, but was very girthy and built squarely like a boxcar. I'm not sure what the girth measured as we hadn't started measuring muskies around the middle during that period of time. I was guiding three men from Kansas, actually two of them were my wife's cousins, and the third was her uncle, Clyde Moore. They all seemed like uncles to me as the cousins were older than I was. Frank "Babe" McQueen and his brother, Leonard McQueen and their wives had made the trip to Cass Lake along with Uncle Clyde and his wife Mildred to fish Minnesota waters. We had fished muskies during the early morning hours for about three days and these men were quite impressed with the size of fish that had been following our baits to the boat so we could get a good look at them as they came up, swirled around and retreated as quickly as they had appeared. During the afternoons these three men would either go out by themselves or take their wives out for a try at the walleyes, but come evening I would be guiding them again, in search of that elusive musky. These three and their wives were great people and I don't think I've ever laughed as hard as I did when they were all together. They knew how to have good clean fun and still enjoy themselves on a vacation such as this. The fourth morning I took the men musky fishing again with Uncle Clyde toward the back of the boat next to me, Cousin "Babe" was in the middle and Cousin Leonard up front. There was this small weed patch near East Potato Island in Allen's Bay of Cass Lake and we had seen a couple nice fish in that area the day before, as they had followed to the boat. So, we decided to try it again and as I eased the boat forward along the break or weed- line, Babe had a musky follow and jump over his lure, lying on the water right by the boat. We trolled on past the spot and I mentioned to the fellows that we would come back to that fish after giving it a chance to regain its composure, in about twenty or thirty minutes. After fishing the remainder of that area, we returned to the small weed patch to give the musky another shot at a lure. This time we had all changed baits and were casting something different than the first time through. I had also reversed the movement of the boat, so instead of going forward, we were back trolling along the weedline. Both Clyde and Babe had cast straight off the side of the boat over the weed bed when I pointed toward the area just off the back corner of the boat and said, "The fish was right back here, you'll hit it within the next two casts!" About that time, Leonard, in the front of the boat, cast over the other two lines right at the exact spot I had pointed to when making my statement. He couldn't have pinpointed the spot any better with a thousand casts of practice and the water erupted with a huge boil and splash as the fish hit his lure the instant it struck the surface. The fight was on, and needless to say, so was the unorganized commotion of the four men in the boat trying to get their lines in under Leonard's line with the musky going furious on the other end. After all lines were clear and Leonard was finishing the fight with this big fish, I tended the net and when the time was right, scooped the fish up and into the boat. It was the "boxcar" musky I had mentioned earlier in this segment of the story and had a very large girth. I remember watching Leonard fight the fish and it seemed as if the musky was stiff and couldn't turn short and quickly like most of them do, so once it was in the boat, the girth spoke to that thought and told us the fish was just built short and stout. I had only seen one fish with those kind of features before that time, and it was the musky Cliff Riggles had caught back in September of 1957. That musky was only forty-eight inches long and weighed forty-two pounds. The girth on that fish must have been twenty-eight or twenty-nine inches, but whatever it was, I was impressed with its strong looks. Anyway, Leonard went home a happy man, and the other two didn't seem to mind the fact that he had accidentally, on purpose, cast out over their lines to get first dibs on that musky. Leonard never did hear the end of that little incident and everyone had a good time joking and kidding with him about it every chance they got. It was just one of many nice muskies caught during those early weeks in July.

The middle of July that summer there was to be a plane load of men flying in from Oklahoma to fish walleyes. The "dog days of summer" had come and the walleye fishing had gone from worse to 'worser,' as one of our veteran guides exclaimed. We actually were not looking forward to those guide trips because it seemed rather useless to go out when nothing was biting. The big, two-engine plane (I think a DC-3) landed in Bemidji, Minnesota at the airport and the men were picked up by bus and transported to Cass Lake for a three day weekend of fishing. There were eighteen men in all, including the pilot and co-pilot, and they were taken to their respective cabins to unpack, relax, get ready for dinner and enjoy the great Minnesota evening before hitting the water the following morning. This group was from the Haliburton Oil Company in Tulsa, Oklahoma and they were all employed by Haliburton who gave them the fishing trip due to a good year for the company. They were going to fish all day Saturday and Sunday, but only until noon Monday, then pack up to fly home that afternoon and be back at work on Tuesday. That first morning on Saturday was a disaster as everyone tried minnows, jigs, artificial lures and about everything they had in their tackle boxes. If I recall correctly, we caught three walleyes and four perch total for the eighteen men plus five guides. Twenty-three fishermen fished for four hours and that was all we could muster up. After lunch I told the group I was going to town to get night crawlers, and asked if anyone else wanted any. Of course the other guides instructed me to get night crawlers for them too. After the trip to town we prepared our boats for the afternoon/evening trip and we were all off again for another adventurous experience. Cliff Riggles was guiding three men in his boat, my brother, Larry had three men, Ally Clark, another local guide had three men and I also had three. Kutsey Nornberg drove the launch on this occasion and his crew of six men had never caught a walleye. The first hour was warm and calm with the fish seeming to be affected by the same fate as those of us fishing. At 5:00 pm we saw Cliff stand to net a fish, the first of the afternoon, as far as we knew. At 5:05 pm Larry netted a nice walleye right in front of my boat and right where I was going to be in another few seconds. Action picked up gradually and night crawlers seemed to be the answer to our problems all of a sudden. At eight o'clock, just three hours after the action started in Cliff's boat, we were all back at the dock with limits of walleyes, all caught on night crawlers. It was like the difference between night and day from fishing that morning with no result, and now with huge success. The walleyes were all caught in twelve feet of water just on the edge of a break or drop-off way out north of Cedar Island in an area called the "duck-bill" which from an airplane, looks much like a duck's bill. It is also a very difficult area to fish with more than one boat trolling, because of the small size and sharp drop on the break of the bar. So, with five boats, how did we finally pull it off? We anchored up on top of the break and cast the night crawlers toward the deeper water with a three foot worm harness and spinner. Just ahead of the harness leader we used a quarter ounce trolling sinker and pulled the rig slowly up the drop until we felt a tug, and then it was, "set the hook" and "reel em' in!" It was honestly that easy! You've never seen a happier bunch of guys, even the guides were excited about this mid- summer jump out of the fishing slumps. The fish averaged two pounds with about eight or nine four to five pounders thrown in for a nice bonus. All totaled, that afternoon we had caught one hundred eight walleyes among the five boats. Many of the fish were quickly cleaned and we all had walleye for dinner that evening, man, could those guys eat! I think they were all used to eating those Oklahoma catfish back then and when they got a taste of the fresh Minnesota walleye, it was a real treat! On Sunday we were back on the water with these same men again, but the action wasn't as heavy as the afternoon before. There was a good amount of fish caught that day and if memory serves me correctly, the group only needed nine fish Monday morning to fill their limits to take home. Sunday had been another calm day and made for more difficult shallow water fishing success, but there had been fish caught and we were all looking forward to a big T-bone steak dinner in the lodge. The steaks were brought from Oklahoma and tasted as good as the name sounds, especially if you are hungry like we were. During the dinner Sunday evening I asked the pilot, who happened to be sitting next to me, if they could do a fly-by the next day after they left the airport in Bemidji. He said they had planned to do that, so I asked him how low they could come with that big DC-3. He paused, looked out the window, and said, "How high are the trees around here?" "Wow!" I said. Everyone around laughed and then we couldn't wait to see them off the next day about one o'clock pm. We did manage to catch enough walleyes the next morning to fill all their limits to take back to Oklahoma, but only three of our guide boats went out as some of the men chose to sleep in and relax before the trip to Tulsa. We bid them good-bye at one o'clock pm and about an hour later they flew by the resort about one hundred feet off the ground! We were all standing on the dock watching as the big plane flew eastward straight over the lake and away from the resort making a long banking turn toward the north over Star Island. As they turned back west and then south we could hear the big engines slow and the plane came even lower right down over the trees along the west shoreline. When they flew by, we were all waving and you could see the faces of the men as they looked out the little windows which lined the side of the plane, and they were waving back. The pilot rocked the huge plane back and forth as if to be waving the wings at us in an effort to say good-bye. I have seen pilots do that in small planes, but I had never been witness to that happening with such a large aircraft at this low altitude. As they roared over, and I do mean roared, (because the pilot was giving it all the thrust the big plane probably had,) they ascended over the town of Cass Lake more than likely rattling every window in town. It is one of those occasions one doesn't easily forget, even over a lifetime of memories.

The day after the Haliburton gang had gone home there were no guide trips on the docket for any of us guides, so what did we do ? Kutsey had some work to do at home and Ally Clark had his job to attend to back in town at the L & M Oil Company. Cliff Riggles, my brother Larry and I did what any fishing guide would probably do, we went fishing by ourselves. Since Cliff didn't like fishing with night crawlers, because they are packed in messy worm bedding and it gets the boat dirty, he wanted to go back to minnows and try some different spots. Larry and I agreed, but I went to town and bought some golden shiners, because I knew they would be the perfect answer to the slow attitude the walleyes had been taking toward minnows. After fishing a couple spots without much luck we found ourselves off the north eastern tip of O'Neil's Point (we called it Anderson's Point) on Star Island. Cliff was guiding, and of course, was giving me all kinds of teasing about "my" golden shiners and the fact they hadn't produced a walleye yet. In my stubborn German way I made up my mind to keep using the golden shiners. It was a 'do or die' situation and I had decided to show these guys I meant business. After four hours and having finally found walleyes in about twenty feet of water along the drop off near O'Neils Point, we had eighteen nice walleyes on the stringer. My golden shiners had produced one of those walleyes, but Cliff and Larry had caught the other seventeen with just a plain old river shiner. I guess I showed them who was right! I didn't think it was too funny at the time, but we did have many laughs over that story later.

That summer came to a close much too soon, but not before we had caught thirty- seven muskies in my boat which was good considering the fact we had taken more walleye trips than usual, and not as many musky trips.

Another reason which added to the seemingly short summer was my wife, Jan and I had made several trips to Braham, Minnesota, where we were moving to after leaving western Kansas earlier that summer. We did find a house and manage to get everything moved into it by the time we were ready to go back for the school year. Those trips to Braham took away from our guiding time a lot, because it meant being gone at least a whole day if not more. It was an easy transition for us moving from Kansas to Minnesota as everyone in the Braham area was helpful and willing to lend us a hand with whatever we needed.

September seventh through ninth was the first annual International Muskies Inc. tournament and of course having guided Gil Hamm that summer several times, I was in! Gil was basically the founder of Muskies Inc. and promoter of the big tournament. He had come to Cass Lake during the summer months and fished with almost all of us guides out of Birch Villa. Gil was a fireball of a man to say the least, and his enthusiasm was contagious as he introduced the art of musky fishing to what would become literally thousands of fishermen and women. During the tournament I guided two men, Johnny Moore from Ankeny, Iowa and Jay Kuanbeck from the Minneapolis area. The first day we had several follows from muskies, but none took the bait. The second day we were fishing an area east of Cedar Island late in the morning when Jay had a hit. He was using a six foot, rather limber rod, casting a sucker colored Suick jerk bait when the big fish hit and the excitement was in full swing. The musky never jumped as it swam near the boat three or four times in what seemed to be a cruising mode. We could see about an inch of the big lure sticking out on each side of the big fish's jaws and I kept yelling for Jay to, "Set the hook, set the hook!" Jay would reef back on the rod tip, but I could see that it probably wasn't hooked and the tip of the rod would easily give way to the weight of the fish. I honestly think the musky didn't even know there were hooks in or close to its mouth. On the fourth pass by the boat, the musky opened its mouth and the lure simply slipped out as we watched the monster lazily swim away. I knew Jay had just lost what would have probably been the largest fish in the tournament! We were all stunned by the sight of the fish which would have been a fifty inch plus contender! It was rather quiet in our boat as we continued to fish and kept seeing visions of that big musky in our minds. There were a few more the remainder of that day, but no more takers. The third day, Sunday, we were to fish until noon and then attend the awards banquet. It was a rather slow morning as we only turned one fish and it was a small musky just curiously looking at the strange bait as it swam near the boat. Later, at the awards banquet, it finally hit us that the fish Jay lost on Saturday would have been the big winner because the first place fish was a forty-eight incher. The first place fish was a nice one, but we, and especially Jay went home knowing he had lost the bigger musky that weekend. Maybe next year was the thought I am sure we were all thinking on our way home.

Late summer turned to fall and then to winter, and I remember shoveling more snow by December twentieth than I had ever shoveled all together in Kansas! Early on the morning of December twenty-fourth, I rushed my wife to the Braham hospital, after she had gone into labor and she gave birth to our daughter Cristi Jo, our first child. The snow had been building up and the neighbors were all worried that we might be snowed in, or our car wouldn't start, or some other catastrophy might occur which would delay getting Jan to the hospital. They had all kinds of helpful hints and ideas about what we could do in the event of an emergency of some kind. One neighbor even offered to come with his snowmobile and take her to the hospital if we had problems and couldn't get there. We were grateful for all the attention and concern, but as it turned out there was no historical blizzard and the car started, so we made it to the hospital in time for Cristi to be born under normal conditions. She was the greatest of Christmas presents and claimed most of our time during the remainder of that winter.

The Heitschmidt caravan as Larry and Merv's families
moved from Kansas to Minnesota.

Merv with a nice 16# northern pike he caught.

As the spring of 1969 arrived it was somewhat different for us as we only had to prepare for a three hour trip to Cass Lake from our home in Braham and not the usual twelve hundred miles we were used to making each spring from our old home in Scott City, Kansas. In fact, it allowed us the freedom to be at Birch Villa Resort many weekends before the school year ended to help my parents prepare the resort for opening fishing season and the upcoming summer.

That spring the walleye fishing was next to spectacular as the season was warm and brought with it some very normal weather patterns. The walleyes had spawned early that year and during the opening weekend we were able to locate and catch large numbers of hungry fish. It seemed like every spot we fished produced fish and that made the guide's job pretty easy. There were many fish being caught that spring and I remember spending lots of late hours in the fish cleaning house at all the local resorts where we cleaned fish. There were many nights we cleaned fish until two or three o'clock in the morning which didn't allow time for very much sleep as we would have to be up by six am in the mornings to tend to the early risers and help them on their way to another day of fishing, as well as getting our own guide boats ready for our eight o'clock departures. During one stretch of about two weeks I recall cleaning fish every evening past midnight and guiding two, four hour trips each day plus trying to help my parents operate the resort. The full stringers of walleyes that came in each day were awesome, as we would see the guides usually having eighteen to twenty-four each time they took a party fishing. As I look back on those days now, it seems the fishing pressure has taken that kind of consistent walleye fishing away, both in numbers and size. Now days you don't usually see stringers of eighteen to twenty-four two pound average walleyes consistently being caught. There are large numbers of walleye still being caught, but the average size has diminished somewhat and sometimes even the large numbers are hard to come by. I remember one of the trips during that time frame when I guided three men on a morning excursion. We went out on a location we called "middle bar" which was straight out from the resort about one half mile. There was a mild southeast breeze which set up some very good drifting conditions and we were using a half ounce trolling sinker with a three foot leader and a plain, long shanked, number four Aberdeen hook. The shiner minnows we used were about three inches long and we threaded the hook in through the minnow's mouth, out the gill and then through the body near the back or under the dorsal fin. We would bounce the bottom with the weight and keep movement on the minnow as we drifted slowly along the drop-off in about twelve feet of water. When a walleye picked up the minnow you could feel a slight resistance on the pole or line as the walleye nibbled up on the bait. We usually tried to relax the pole a bit by letting the tip of the rod go back toward the fish and after a few tugs from the fish, set the hook when we felt the fish had the minnow far enough in its mouth to be hooked. Sometimes we had to wait longer or give the walleye more line before setting the hook, but it was an effective method and usually proved successful. On this particular outing the walleyes were hungry and aggressive, so within a few drifts and about an hour and a half of easy fishing, we had our limits of walleye which totaled twenty-four! Yes, even the guide caught his limit that morning. The men in the boat were happy, to say the least, but they also wanted to know what we were going to do for the rest of the four hour trip. I could understand that they wanted to "get their money's worth" from the trip and most would have been happy with just the limits of walleye, but these fellows felt that there should be something more. We tried trolling for northern pike, but they weren't as aggressive as the walleyes that day and we were only able to catch two small wiry northern within the next hour and a half. Now we had an hour left in the trip, so I suggested trying another weedy area for a last attempt at a sizeable northern, and we tried casting crank baits over the weeds. In that last hour we caught and released five more walleyes and never had a northern even take a look at the lures. Two of the men even tried spoons and one of them caught one of the five walleyes on his spoon. We did make a full trip out of the morning and the fellows I had out must have thought it was a good day as they tipped me quite well. I went back to that weed bed a few more times, but only to find the small northern had moved in and apparently moved the walleyes out, because we didn't catch another walleye in that spot.

The walleye fishing held up very well until just after the fourth of July that summer and that was good, because the muskies were beginning to turn on at that time and our guide trips turned more to the attention of the musky fishermen. On July tenth I took a father/son combination out on a musky trip in the evening. It happened to be Harmon Braaten and his son Rich, and after getting to the first spot we called the "rock pile" due to the fact there were lots of rocks located there, I looked down and realized I had forgotten the musky net. It seems I had put the net aside at the dock earlier that day when giving the boat a thorough cleaning and had forgotten to put it back. Rich was in the front of my boat and his dad, Harmon, was in the middle between us as we began our casting. I believe the Braatens were from Albert Lea, Minnesota and had been coming to Birch Villa for some time, spending a week of their vacation time fishing. They had tried for muskies on two or three occasions, but had not been too successful, so they hired me as their guide to show them a few spots and how to fish for these elusive, toothy creatures. I mentioned that I had forgotten the net, but we would fish anyway, hoping that if we did hook into one of these big fish, we could somehow manage to get it into the boat before it got off the hooks. No more than having told them of the missing net, Rich set the hooks on a furious jerk and the water exploded as the musky "blew up" on his white, in-line spinner, bucktail. The fight was on as Rich struggled against the weight of the strong, beefy musky. It jumped three times clearing the water each time, twisting and turning in an effort to free itself from the hooks it had closed its jaws on, but Rich held on and brought the fish to the side of the boat as it played itself down and became more and more tired from the tough struggle. Now it was up to the guide to try to manage a safe and successful attempt at landing the musky. Actually the fish gave up without much of a problem and I was able to slide my hand under its gill plate just above the gills and hoist it into the boat where it gave a few futile flops and then came to rest allowing us to remove the one treble hook stuck in the side of its jaw. Rich was congratulated by his two companions and the weighing and measuring took place. The musky weighed in at twenty-four pounds and measured forty-five inches in length. It was a pleasant trip from there on as we saw another four fish follow lures to the boat and one of those even took a swipe at Harmon's jointed pikie right at the boat, but missed its target and swam away unscathed. Rich got to fly the musky flag on the way back to the dock which caused quite a stir as this was the first of many decent fish to come into the Birch Villa dock that summer and Rich said later that he even got tired of lifting the fish for pictures while others were snapping their cameras in order to take home another memory from their summer vacation at Cass Lake.

Not long after that I took my wife and a man named Glen Rogers out musky fishing to that same rock pile area. At the time, Glen owned and operated the bait shop that is located on Mille Lacs Lake at the junction of highways 169 and 27 just north of Onamia, Minnesota. He was my only customer and since it was such a nice evening we took my wife, Jan along since she had never caught a musky yet either. Jan and Glen were both casting red, musky sized, spinner baits and Glen was in the front with Jan between us in the middle of the boat. We had made a late evening start and didn't have a lot of time to fish before dark, so I took them to the "hot spot" as Glen called it. After about a dozen casts Jan set the hook on a hit which we couldn't see as her bait was running fairly deep. The fish surfaced and jumped once so we could see it was, indeed a musky. It seemed to be a rather scrappy fish as she fought it for what seemed like an eternity. The musky would sound toward the deep water much like a larger fish would do, but after about three of those deep runs it played out rather fast. This time we had a net and the fish was brought into the boat without much of a struggle. It weighed a sound twenty-two pounds and measured forty-two inches. Jan got to fly the musky flag this time and much to the enjoyment of the ladies who were present at the dock to witness the nice musky, which was her first. Glen and I caught a little teasing, but again after suggesting she had a good guide, things quieted down and we were able to salvage a little respect from the crowd since we were acting as a team and not just individuals. Actually this was not the first time Jan had outfished me and I couldn't have been happier as it was her first musky! We tallied thirty-nine keeper muskies in my boat that summer which was pretty good considering the few number of times we ventured out after the elusive fish.

Our cousins from northwest Missouri and northeast Kansas, Clyde Moore, Leonard and "Babe" McQueen and their wives came back for an August fishing trip. One morning I was to take the men walleye fishing, but the wind was blowing about thirty miles per hour out of the west and about the only likeable spot to fish from our location on the lake was right in front of Birch Villa which is located on the west shore. We were fishing with night crawlers and a crawler harness and the perch were tormenting us something terrible that morning. I decided to move further down the shoreline to an area where the sand bar, loaded with underwater vegetation, made a distinct curve back out into the lake almost in the opposite direction. We drifted very fast with the wind, out along that curve and drop-off, just at the edge of the weed line. We had to add more weight to the worm rigs just to keep them closer to the bottom in an effort to find a hungry walleye or two along that area. As luck would have it the walleyes were concentrated there and we caught some very nice fish in a short time. It was difficult fighting the wind, netting their fish, keeping the boat on the right depth, and trying to make the most of what started out to be a bad windy situation. Leonard asked me what we called this bar, since all the others we'd fished had names, I told him we just called this one "out front." Later, after we had gone in with twenty-four nice walleyes, Leonard was telling Cliff, the senior guide, about our luck that morning and asked Cliff what he called that bar. Cliff told Leonard that bar was named, "Merv's Curve" because that was where Merv always fished to get away from a hard blowing west wind. He was mostly right about that, but not long after that everyone around the resort and some locals from town started calling that spot, "Merv's Curve!" It isn't every day a person has a fishing spot named after him and even though it's unofficial, I like to think that since Cliff named it that, I felt pretty privileged. I haven't seen it marked on any contour maps of Cass Lake, but we still chuckle about how the name caught on with many of the locals at the time. We did fish that area for a week or so and that concentration of walleyes lasted throughout those days, but not as good as it was that morning when it became known as, "Merv's Curve." I've fished that curve many times since and will always remember the good times with Uncle Clyde, Leonard, Babe and their wives as we fished and laughed over many experiences we had together.

Late that fall we were back to catching walleyes as well as muskies and one morning we awoke to a very heavy fog covering the entire lake. All the guides were to have fishing trips that morning and being the macho guides we thought we were, had decided to "go for it" and get out on the water with our parties and show them we knew this lake even in the fog when we couldn't see beyond our boat. Cliff was the first to leave and I followed about five minutes after he left the dock. I used my depth finder and headed my boat straight east watching as the first drop-off went deeper and deeper. I knew we would soon come upon "middle bar" and so by watching the depth stay steady at thirty to forty feet before it rose with the bottom, I felt I had a pretty good handle on where I was. As the depth came up to ten feet I was confident that this was middle bar and so we started trolling parallel to the drop-off. We did catch two small walleyes and for the most part that was keeping our interest alive, at least until the fog burned off and we could get to other parts of the lake. After about forty-five minutes of fishing in that heavy fog, we heard another boat approaching from a distance and it was headed directly toward us, at least from the sound. I grew a bit nervous, hoping the boat would either stop or see us before it collided with our craft. It did slow down and stop. I could hear the voices as plain as if they were in the boat with us and I could make out Cliff's voice as he spoke above the noise of his small trolling motor. They came closer and closer when all of a sudden, there they were, right next to us. Cliff shut off his little motor and I did likewise. He asked, "Where in the heck are we?" I thought this was a little strange as Cliff grew up on this lake and I was always asking him different things about the lake. If anyone could negotiate the fog it would be Cliff, and here he was asking me where we were. Now, I don't have to tell you, but I became a little concerned because for the first time the thought hit me that maybe I wasn't where I thought I was. Cautiously I answered, "I think we're on middle bar." Cliff said, "Holy cow, I thought I was on North Cedar Bar!" Now, North Cedar was about four miles away and I knew I had not ventured that far away from the resort. We both fished in this spot for awhile and as the fog began to burn off, sure enough, we were in fact on "middle bar." Cliff figured that he had made a big circle and had come back to about where he started. He said he had the compass out on his wooden boat seat, but it went crazy somewhere out in the middle of the lake. We laughed about that one for a long time too. I'm not sure where Larry and Kutsey ended up that morning and I don't think they knew for a while either, but we did all make it back to the dock safely and we all had walleyes on the stringers too. It wasn't until sometime after that, I had a similar experience. It was a foggy morning and I was fishing two men from Fargo, North Dakota. We left the dock in a very dense fog, headed for the north side of Cedar Island, stopping occasionally to listen for any other boats that might be wandering around in the fog like we were doing. About halfway across the lake my compass lying on the cushion in front of me started to go around in circles. Actually the needle went around in circles, not the compass. I would pick it up and try to make it stop, but it would start circling again like before. After some time with this situation I gave up on the compass and just went with my own instincts. We found what I thought was an area north of Cedar Island and started to fish. After about an hour the fog began to get patchy as the sun started to burn it off and little by little we could begin to see an outline of trees in the distance. When the fog lifted enough for us to see where we were, I had guided them to Pagoda Bar just east of Star Island. We were only about a half mile and one bar away from where I had intended to be, and the fishing in either of those two spots left something to be desired. We did manage a few walleyes, but all in all it was a slow morning. I later found out that Cass Lake has a lot of heavy mineral contents in the soil at the bottom of the lake and that was probably the cause for the runaway compass. Either that or my compass was a cheep one that wouldn't hold to a good solid heading.

That fall, Bill Paulson, from my hometown of Braham and Johnny Moore from Ankeny, Iowa joined me in fishing the Second Annual International Muskies Inc. Tournament. We fished all day Friday and Saturday, September sixth and seventh, and Sunday, September eighth until noon. We boated two sub-legal muskies which didn't count and saw many others that followed to the boat. At one location I stopped in the middle of a large weedbed and before I could get the five and a half horse kicker motor started, both Bill and Johnny made simultaneous casts off each side of the boat. As luck would have it they both set the hook on large muskies simultaneously, and as fate would rule, both fish were lost in a matter of seconds. I know without a doubt, both of those fish were fifty inch plus fish! That was as close as we would get to the trophy that year.

The school year started in late August with workshops and then early September with students in school and our fishing on Cass Lake turned to weekend excursions only. The late walleye bite held up good that fall right into the middle of October. We were catching nice walleyes in forty-five to sixty feet of water as they went deeper with the "turn-over" as the locals called it. There were a few weekend trips then to help our parents close the resort for another season, and finally winter eventually set in and covered the lake with ice seeming to give the fish a break from the ever constant pressures of fishing.

Jan's first musky.

During the winter months I was teaching English and coaching basketball which took a lot of quality time away from my family and the fact that my wife Jan was pregnant with our second child didn't make it any easier. March twenty-eighth came with a bang as our son Chad was born during the Easter break. We were excited parents as Chad was our second child and now Cristi, our daughter of a little more than one year, had a new little brother. It made for some interesting and trying times for Jan, as she was a full time mother of two children only fifteen months apart, not to mention the role of full time housewife as well.

The spring of 1970 came and again there were many weekend trips from Braham to Cass Lake in order to help my parents get the resort ready for the opening fishing season in early May. There were cabins to be cleaned, water to be turned on, wooden resort rowboats to be scraped, painted and put in the lake to soak so they wouldn't leak, the launch to be scraped, painted and put into the water and many other odd jobs that come with getting everything tidy and ready for business. It was always an exciting time as we prepared for meeting new people and greeting the old repeat customers back who made Birch Villa a part of their summer plans.

The walleye fishing proved to be good again as it lasted through all of May and June. The guides were busy throughout those two months bringing in many nice stringers of walleye. The thing I remember most about the early fishing that year was the amount of larger walleyes being caught. One day in early June, Cliff came in with a party of two and their limits of walleye which included two seven pounders and two Six pounders followed by a four pounder and a three pounder. That same day, Kutsey had guided two men to their limits of walleye that included an eight pounder, two six pounders and a four pounder. Larry guided three people to limits of walleye and their stringer had a three, four and five pound walleyes respectively. My boat with three lady school teachers from North Dakota came back to the dock with limits of walleye and our catch included two five pounders, three four pounders and a three pound lengthy fish that should have weighed seven pounds, but was a skinny twenty-seven incher. There were several trips with that sort of catch, but I believe that one day was the most impressive of all. On another occasion I was guiding two older widow ladies from Racine, Wisconsin. We were fishing a sandbar called "West Cedar" bar catching an occasional walleye, but action was rather slow. One of the ladies happened to get her line in the motor while I was netting a fish for the other lady. As I attempted to turn off the motor and raise the prop out of the water to free the line, we drifted into shallow water on top of the bar. While I was loosening the caught line I glanced down into the water and there were walleyes swimming all around us near the bottom. After freeing the line I let my minnow down among the walleyes and immediately had a nice two pound fish grab the minnow aggressively and get caught. I mentioned to the ladies the fish were there and they put their lines down and each had a nice walleye on before I knew what was happening. In the course of the next few minutes I quit fishing and just tried to keep up with netting fish for these two women. They were having the time of their lives and were looking over the side of the boat trying to be selective with each fish that tried to bite. They would pull the minnow away from the smaller walleyes to allow a larger fish to grab the it. I was reminded of catching perch in the bull rushes when I was a kid, choosing which perch I wanted to catch because of its size. This went on for about thirty minutes and I had walleyes flopping around in the bottom of the boat before I could get a chance to put them on the stringer. We went in that morning with our limits of walleye, all about two pounds each. Those two ladies were so excited that one of them told me later she had to go to the bathroom before all the excitement started, but she forgot all about it when the action took place. They returned to Birch Villa many times, but I doubt they ever caught walleyes that easily or in that short amount of time again. It was a once in a lifetime experience as I don't recall ever having caught walleyes like that before or after the experience we had.

Musky fishing was good again that year as Bill Paulson came from Braham several times in pursuit of this ever elusive fish. Bill was a fortunate and blessed musky fisherman as he seemed to have luck every time I took him muskie fishing. I truly believe he caught a musky every time he came to Cass Lake and sometimes he would connect on three or four fish in a given weekend. He had owned and operated a bait shop and sporting goods store in Burley, Idaho, and had fished salmon in most of the rivers and streams around Burley. Bill came to Braham, Minnesota to manage the Dahlman Rubber Division, a part of the Dahlman Company where potato diggers and machinery were manufactured. He later started his own business called Preimier Products, a small business that produced small parts for ATV's and rubber bungy straps with its injection mold machines. The business is still being run by his son-in-law, John Peterson, in Braham. Bill called me one time in July on a Thursday and asked if I could guide him and a friend, Stan Harper, for muskies that upcoming weekend. I checked my schedule and confirmed that I would indeed be able to guide them and would be ready for them Friday evening if they arrived in time. Bill said he would definitely be there in time to fish Friday evening, and he was. We made our trip that first evening and had some action, but didn't catch a fish. Stan Harper, his companion, also worked for the Dahlman Company and seemed to get into the swing of this musky fishing without any trouble. In fact, Saturday morning came and it was very windy, blowing a strong gale out of the west. We tried to fish some of the weed lines in the outer part of the lake, but were blown off almost every weed bed we fished. In the afternoon, with the wind still blowing, we left the dock not sure of where we would fish, so we decided to troll the weed line just in front of the resort, It was not my first choice and I had never caught a musky there, but there were nice cabbage weeds along the drop and it was out of the wind somewhat. As we made our first pass along the drop-off right in front of Birch Villa, Bill had a hit on his shallow running Cisco Kid lure. As I looked back, there was a nice sized fish thrashing on top of the water. It was a musky! "Wow!" I thought out loud as I shut off the motor. Bill played the eighteen pound forty inch fish to the boat for netting and that was the first musky anyone in my boat had caught at this location. There were a couple nice northern caught by Stan during that trip out and we ended the day with more than I thought we would get considering the windy conditions. Sunday morning brought a more pleasant day and Bill conncected again on a twenty-two pound fish, this time clear across on the opposite side of the lake. Bill and Stan went home that afternoon with visions of another trip in the near future.

Just two weeks later, Bill came back for another weekend of fishing, this time bringing another friend, Russ Sutton, who owned and operated a small business in Braham called Isanti Tool and Die. Again we were confronted with a strong west wind on Saturday morning so Bill suggested we fish in front of Birch Villa to start the day. I wonder why ? We started to troll exactly as we had two weeks earlier. We passed by Birch Villa's harbor without a strike, but about fifty yards further, Russ had a tremendous strike! The fish hit so hard the reel literally popped off his rod and Russ was holding the reel in one hand and his rod in the other! As we looked back, we could see the fish on the surface trying to throw the jointed pikie Russ was using. In an effort to help keep the line taut while we gained our composure I gunned the motor slightly and tightened the slack line. Bill came to Russ' rescue and put the reel back on the rod while Russ kept cranking. There was a problem with the reel seat as it would not tighten down on the reel. So Bill used his hands as a clamp and held the reel tight on the rod while Russ continued to crank the fish toward the boat. After turning the motor off, we managed to net the musky, but not before it gave Russ and Bill all the fight they wanted under those circumstances! It was the first musky for Russ and weighed in at an even twenty pounds with a length of forty inches. There is never a dull moment with a musky on the end of the line and this incident proved that theory to be even greater under the existing conditions.

In August that year, my cousin, Bob Moore, from northeast Kansas (Clyde's son) brought his family to Birch Villa to enjoy some fishing. The first time out I took Bob to Buck Lake on a musky trip. Buck Lake is a small body of water connected to Cass by a small shallow inlet located along the north side of Cass Lake and is navigable by boat for access into the lake. The first spot we hit was a small weed bed just to the north of the inlet to the lake and as we prepared to fish Bob asked, "What do I do ?" I told him to just cast out over the weeds and retrieve the jointed pikie back to the boat at a pretty fast rate of speed. He did just as I told him and on his very first cast a huge musky followed his lure right to the boat. Bob was sitting down and didn't even see the fish! I saw it and estimated it to be in the twenty-eight to thirty pound class, a very healthy looking forty-eight inch fish. We didn't catch a musky that trip, but Bob got a taste of what it was like and still returns to Cass Lake each year in an effort to catch that wall hanger. During Bob's stay at Birch Villa, we took his wife, Karen, and their two boys, Scott and Brian out fishing a few times and they had some success at both walleyes and northern pike. While Bob was there, Bill Paulson came back for another weekend of musky fishing and Bob went along each trip to see this lucky man in action. Bill didn't disappoint us as the first trip out on a bar we called Anderson Point, he caught a twenty-three pound musky and countered it with a nice twenty-eight pound, forty seven inch fish to best his previous record of twenty-six pounds. Bob got to witness firsthand what it was like to boat a musky and experience the excitement that goes with it.

Bill came back to Birch Villa another time in August and it was raining when he arrived later than usual that Friday evening, so we decided to wait for Saturday morning. It was still raining the next morning so after sitting it out in the lodge visiting and about three pots of coffee later I said, "What do you want to do, Bill?" Bill replied, " I came to fish and I have rain gear, so let's either go musky fishing or I'm going to pack up and go home." We went musky fishing and after about three hours of nothing, with rain water dripping off our noses, we began to wonder if what we decided was the right thing to do. About that time I had a hit on my red, in-line bucktail, and the surge of the fish set me back in unsuspecting surprise. As I fought the rain away from my eyes and the thrashing, jumping musky on the end of my line, I forgot all about the conditions and excitement quickly began to rise within me. I could tell by the feel of the fish's power and steady ability to go where it wanted and do what it wanted that it was a big musky. The fish played down and Bill netted it for me. As we gazed down at the fish, I think we both realized it was bigger than we thought. Upon weighing and measuring it we found our thoughts were verified, as it tipped the scale at thirty-seven and a half pounds with a fifty-three inch length! We fished a little longer, I caught another twenty-four pounder and then went back for a late lunch. We had seen two other muskies follow that morning and they were also nice sized fish, plus Bill had caught a twelve pound northern pike as a bonus for the morning. My dad saw us flying the musky flag as we approached the dock and he was our only welcoming party despite the rain which was still coming down. Dad took pictures for us and later I entered the larger musky in the local big fish contest at LeRoy's Bait Shop in Cass Lake which won a nice plaque and first place for the week. That fish was the third largest to be registered at LeRoy's that summer. We talked my dad into going with us that afternoon as we needed a third license in the boat to technically be legal, but the rain continued and by mid-afternoon without seeing a musky, our hopes became dashed as it seemed to rain even harder the longer we stayed out. I remember my dad standing there reeling his bait in, with rain dripping off his nose, not enjoying it at all and Bill saying to him, "Are we having fun yet, Al ?" My dad replied with a "Humph!" laid his rod down and said, "Are we going in ?" We laughed and Bill and I put our lures and rods away and we headed in. It was or had been a good day regardless of the weather, but we couldn't convince my dad of that. Sunday turned out partly cloudy, but best of all the rain had stopped. Bill and I went forth again and this time we headed across the lake in another direction to a spot we called Beringson Bar. It was our first stop that morning and as I pulled up to where we would start the casting, Bill cast out over the weed bed saying, "First in, first on!" He always said that, but nothing ever happened. That is not until this time, I didn't even have the big motor turned off let alone have the small trolling motor in the water when Bill yelled, "I got one!" I looked up and sure as his luck would have it, he did indeed have a musky on his line! As I scrambled to shut down the motor and get the net, Bill had the seventeen pound musky at boatside. I don't think he let the fish fight, he just cranked it in. It was a quick moment of excitement, but the best part of the moment was when Bill said, "I'm going to release it." "What!" I shouted. Bill had never released a musky other than a couple he'd caught earlier in the twenty-some inch class. This was to be an historic time in the life of Bill Paulson and I was there to witness his first decent release! I not only congratulated him on the catch, but commended him on the release. Bill had heard us talk about "catch and release" in recent months, but he said he would never do it because he worked hard for these fish and he wasn't about to let one go. Bill was a life member of Muskies Inc. and had been signed up by Gil Hamm as I had been, but he had a hard time letting go of the idea to release his fish. In reference to the release patches many other Muskies Inc. members were beginning to display on their jackets, Bill jokingly told me one time he was going to design a patch that said, "I ate mine!" I laughed at his humor, but I believe, at the time, he was halfway serious about it. Bill did release that musky and did so with many others as time went by.

A week or two after Bill had fished with me and made his first release, all the guides were sitting around the dock house on a cool rainy day visiting among themselves and with a few guests who happened to pop in to see what was going on. There were a few kids on the dock trying to catch some of the small panfish that congregate there for protection from the larger fish that prey on them. Every once in a while we would hear a voice proclaiming to the others to come see this big fish. One of the guests became curious and went out to investigate this disturbance that was causing so much attention. The guest eventually came running back to the dock house to tell us there actually was a big fish swimming in the harbor from side to side in an effort to find the entrance for its escape. We all went out to further investigate the situation and sure enough, there was a huge musky that probably swam into the harbor accidentally and couldn't find its way out. My brother Larry and I ran to my boat and I backed the boat out of its stall while Larry grabbed the musky net. As we moved back the musky swam directly toward us and Larry put the big net in front of it and the fish swam in and turned as if to say, "Here I am, pick me up." Larry lifted it out and after many pictures we took it out of the harbor and released it. It was an old looking musky that measured fifty-three inches and we estimated it to be thirty-five pounds. It was a long rather thin fish and seemed to be missing most of its teeth. We don't know if it was sick or not, but it wasn't too aggressive, nor did it put up much of a fight, and it swam away slowly and lazily.

It was getting late in the summer again and our thoughts began to turn to our teaching career, but we still made those weekend trips to Cass Lake to get in all the guide trips we could. Bill Paulson and Johnny Moore fished with me in the third annual International Muskies Inc. tourney that year. We didn't come as close to the first prize as we had the two previous years, but Bill did manage a forty inch musky which gained him a few small prizes and gave us a small amount of consolation for our efforts. The main thing was the tournament was growing and we were hearing more about "catch and release" musky fishing, which made us feel good about preserving our fishery.

The tourist season came to an end early that year and we spent weekends at Birch Villa again, helping with the winterizing process and putting our boats in storage for the winter months. Jan and I made a few trips to Birch Villa during the month of October to do some grouse hunting and in November we came back for the deer season. That was a great bonus for me as I topped off my year with a nice two hundred pound, ten point buck.

Russ Sutton and Bill Paulson with
Russ's 1st musky.

Merv holding a 37½# musky caught on
a rainy day.

Bill Paulson with Merv's 28# musky
caught in the rain.

Reuben Bjorklund, Merv and Don
Wieczorek with walleyes and northern
from Cass Lake. The big one weighed
15#.

Bill Paulson with his "first in - first on"
musky.

1971

Early in the year our family experienced another big event in our lives, as we purchased a newer home across town from the house we had been living in. The newer home was a three bedroom rambler style with beautiful butternut paneling in the living room area. It was difficult moving during the early spring months and know we would be gone for the summer, not being able to enjoy our new home until we returned from Cass Lake for the fall. Once we set our minds to this fact, I think it was easier to leave for the summer and we did make a few trips back home to take care of yard work.

First, I'll say 1971 was the year to behold as far as fishing goes, but the musky fishing was next to spectacular, to say the least. Our weekend trips began early as we journeyed from Braham to Cass Lake again getting the resort in order for the upcoming season. Our first trip actually started on President's Day weekend in February when Jan, myself and the two little ones, Cristi and Chad, made the trek to Gram and Gramp's house as they called it. Cristi was two years old and Chad was almost one, so they did not accompany Jan and I on snowmobile across Cass Lake to Star Island where we took trails from south Star Island to Lake Windigo in order to fish for crappies through the ice. Grandma was happy about that as she could have a few precious hours to spoil the grandkids. The parents didn't mind either as it gave them a little time by themselves to relax and enjoy some time together. It was a beautiful ride by snowmobile, especially after reaching the island, and we were able to take in the beauty of Star Island's huge green towering pine trees. It was one of those moments when you wished time could stand still for awhile to prolong the enjoyment and beauty of it all. As we made our way along the trails over fresh fallen snow the branches and bows of the huge pines were laden with the new snow and offered up a majestic scene that remains unforgettable in our minds. It was on to the lake within the landlocked perimeters of the island and see if the crappies would be cooperative. Behind the snowmobile we towed a sled-like cart on skis with runners under it to carry all of our equipment. It was actually called a "cutter" and made for a very useful piece of equipment as the kids loved to ride in it as well as providing a means with which to transport goods and equipment where we wanted to take it. After pulling onto Lake Windigo we went to an area of the lake where we found about fifteen feet of water and I started drilling eight inch holes in the ice with a manual hand ice auger. After the first hole was drilled and ice was cleared out with the ice scoop, Jan began to fish with the crappie minnows we had brought along. I remember very distinctly that I wasn't able to get the second hole drilled before Jan had a nice three quarter pound crappie on the ice. Hurriedly I worked a little faster to finish cleaning out the second hole and put my line down baited with a minnow. During the finishing up of hole number two and before I was was able to catch my first crappie, Jan had a total of three fish on the ice. Those crappies were hitting fast and furious and we knew without a doubt we had stopped at the right spot, not to mention the fact I never had to drill anymore holes. The two I originally drilled produced our limits of fifteen crappies each, so there was no need for any more. We had come prepared to use two lines each, but our second lines never got taken out of the sled.

The Windigo crappies are a rich black color and the first one Jan caught was the smallest of the bunch. The largest weighed one and a half pounds, but most were about a pound each and they made for a tasty meal at Gram and Gramps house that evening. Jan and I went back to Windigo the next day and caught our limits to take home and enjoy at a later date. We have found that after bringing fish home we put them in the waxed type milk cartons with water and freeze them. When they are taken from the freezer and thawed for cooking there are no freezer burns and taste almost as fresh as when they come out of the lake.

In March we were able to start making many weekend trips to Cass Lake so we could help my parents begin getting the resort ready for another year. It was a nice spring and the weather allowed us to do some early painting that normally we couldn't do so early in the year. Years before my dad had set up a plan that each year we would paint four buildings on the resort property and rotate the process in order to have a fresh coat on all the buildings every four years. Usually we were painting during the tourist season in June and July, but this year provided enough nice weather for us to finish before the fishing opener in May. It made for a much easier summer and we didn't have to feel pressured during the time our guests were present.

This particular spring and early summer was much like the last as far as the walleye fishing went. There were plenty fish caught and the average size was hold-ing steady with an occasional seven or eight pounder coming in as added bonus fish. We had even done a little early musky fishing in June that year which was a bit unusual. I recall one day in late June when another man from the Braham area, Reuben Bjorklund brought a friend, Ernie England to Birch Villa for some walleye fishing. Actually Reuben was from a small town north of Braham called Grasston, and Ernie lived near there on the Snake River. Reuben was a school bus driver and hauled both our children to school when they became old enough to attend the Braham Area Schools. He was also the bus driver for our boys basketball team which I coached during the winter months, so I got to know Reuben quite well. Reuben was also a rural mail man and carried mail near his hometown area. I knew Reuben and Ernie were to arrive at Birch Villa about noon on a Saturday so I took a guide trip that morning with some guests from the resort. After a great morning of walleye fishing we pulled up to the dock with three limits of walleye where Reuben and Ernie were waiting. Reuben's eyes widened as he saw the catch being lifted onto the dock on the stringer. I had left a marker buoy out on the lake marking the spot where the walleye were Caught that morning so we could return and hopefully catch another limit for them. After a quick lunch, cleaning and gassing up the boat, we headed back to the marker buoy to get in on some more of this good walleye action. It wasn't to be, as we tried everything we could think of to entice those fish to bite, it was like they had turned off completely. After about two hours in that spot we had one small fifteen inch walleye on the stringer, so we decided to try a few other areas that had recently been producing walleye. It was getting late in the afternoon and since Reuben and Ernie had planned to return home that evening we were feeling the pressure of not being to get them any fish. We had tried a number of good walleye areas, but nothing was biting and I asked them if they had ever fished for muskies. Neither of them had ever held a musky rod before so I talked them into giving it a try. I had three musky rods in the boat and gave them each an outfit rigged with a floating type crank bait. Just in case they had a problem with backlash or tangled line these lures would float when at rest in the water. We started casting an area where we had seen muskies in the past, but mainly in order to give them a chance to learn the proper casting technique. They had some problems to begin with, but before long, had each mastered the art of getting the lure out and bringing it in without experiencing a backlash or bird's nest as we sometimes called it. As guides, we referred to this occurrence as a "professional over-run" on the reel as the line would outrun itself and gather up in a huge mess or backlash. The term "professional over-run" made it sound more like a technical problem than one of our own doing. With them having mastered their casting abilities we went to an area east of Cedar Island where I had seen a couple muskies a few days before when they followed our lures to the boat without hitting. I remember it like it were yesterday, there was a slight southerly breeze and as we drifted along the weedline just next to the drop-off we could see our lures as they hit the water and trailed in toward the boat. Conditions were almost perfect and I had a feeling inside that is difficult to explain, but it gave me a sense of excited anticipation that puts a person "on alert' so to speak. The feeling sort of makes you tingle all over inside and gives you a greater sense of readiness for what is to come. As we slowly drifted up to a curve in the weed line I mentioned to Reuben and Ernie that this was a good spot to see a musky. Ernie was in the front of the boat casting over about ten to twelve feet of water just outside the weeds. Reuben was in the center casting directly over the weeds and I being on the shallow end, casted up on top of the bar into shallower water. I felt that we were covering the area very well as we drifted nearer the curve in the drop-off. I could see what looked like a sunken log or deadhead, and placed a cast up near it along the bull rushes and started the retrieve. I was using a yellow in-line bucktail spinner bait, and as the spinner caught hold and began to flutter around and around, the log began to turn and change direction, following my bait toward the boat. I cranked a bit faster and the log that suddenly became a fish swam quickly with the same speed as the bait staying about six feet behind it. I slowed my retrieve and the big fish slowed accordingly, but still continued to follow the bait as if to be chasing the lure away. This routine lasted all the way to the boat and at the last second, as my lure was rising away from the fish, the big musky made a sudden lunge for the bait. What took place in those next miniscule seconds was phenomenal to say the least. The huge fish opened its mouth and spread its gills wide to resemble a fifty-five gallon barrel coming at my lure and I seriously think my heart actually stopped beating for an instant. The musky was intent on one thing and that was to devour my bait. With a sudden rush the musky missed its mark and came flying out of the water toward the boat and over the top of my lure! As the fish left the water we could Hear it inhaling with a loud sucking noise as if it were going to literally inhale the entire bait. It made an eerie sound that actually sent shivers up my spine at the time. When it hit the water with a splash and swam back toward the direction it came from, I looked at Reuben with water dripping off my face and clothing wet, and he was standing there in awe with water soaking most of the front of his body as well. All he could say was, "Wow, I've never seen a fish that big alive in the water!" We made quite a few casts in the direction of the big fish's escape route, but to no avail. All this time Ernie was quiet and seeming to exhibit a feeling that he wasn't sure if he wanted that fish in the same boat as he. As is my practice, we kept drifting along for about a half hour in order to allow time for the fish to regain its composure and hopefully forget what had happened in that brief moment of time. We then went back to that same curve and started as we had before, drifting and casting our way up to it. As we reached the curve I looked for that familiar log that had been lying there so peacefully before, but it was not to be seen. As Reuben and Ernie cast over their respective areas I tossed my lure up near the bull rushes again, close to where the big fish had been pretending to be a log. As I began my retrieve this shadowy figure came charging out of the bull rushes again in pursuit of my lure. Again I hurried the speed of my lure and slowed it down, only to have the big musky do likewise in another series of attempts to follow the lure and seemingly chase it away. It was like an instant reply of the same action we had seen just a half hour before. It was weird and uncanny the way that fish used the same action as before. Again, right at the boat, the huge musky made its surge and charged my lure with all the gusto it could muster. It made that same inhaling, sucking noise as it left the water, and again it missed my lure and literally flew completely over it and also clearing Reuben's lure in the process. We were both drenched again like as before and as we stood there in awe, I watched the fish hit the water and swim toward Ernie's end of the boat and over his line. Ernie reacted quickly to an uncommon feel on the end of his line and as we watched, he was hanging on to his rod for dear life, he had a fish on! I couldn't believe it was the same fish because the one that had dampened us and our spirits went cruising on over his line too. No matter what had happened, the situation that now presented itself was the plain and simple fact, Ernie was fighting a musky. The fish fought hard and long and Ernie couldn't seem to get it turned or headed toward the boat. It was about a twenty minute struggle and the fish was gradually playing down, but still Ernie could not seem to get the fish headed in our direction. I noticed as Ernie pulled back on the rod the fish would keep swimming away, but as it grew more tired and became weaker it would lose ground and Ernie would pull it in backwards. We could not see any part of the jointed pikie lure on the end of Ernie's line, so we figured the fish must have swallowed it entirely. As the big musky finally tired and Ernie pulled it to the boat backwards, I was able to get it in the net and into the boat. The fish gave one flop on the bottom of the boat and bled about a quart of blood onto the floor. This was the first time I had seen a musky do that. They usually lose a little blood, but very little from the mouth and usually from the tail or maybe the gill area more often than any place else. The fish was dead after that last flop and I think even before it bled out. I grabbed the line and began to work my way toward the lure. The line was not coming from out of the mouth, but rather from under the gills. The lure was entirely imbedded in the throat of the fish and had cut or tore into the main artery or juggler vein. After thinking the whole plot through, this was the same musky that had followed my lure twice before, but on the second attempt had come down into the water, on top of Ernie's lure, and had literally sucked the lure in through the gills and not the mouth. It was an experience I shall never forget, and as I stated before, one of those once in a lifetime happenings that will not likely repeat itself. The musky weighed thirty-seven and a half pounds and was fifty-two inches long. Ernie won first place in the local contest that week and received a nice plaque for his catch, plus the fact that his fish was the longest musky registered all summer and took second place for the season. He had the fish mounted and displayed it at his home on the Snake River by Grasston, Minnesota. I'm sure Reuben and Ernie forgot about the poor walleye fishing that afternoon and on their way home, which was a late night trip, they probably were wide awake replaying the event of catching that big musky. It is probably the fish story I enjoy telling the most, as I relive that moment every time I tell it.

Bill Paulson came back to Birch Villa many times that summer and continued his lucky streak in fine fashion. I believe Bill caught and released fourteen legal sized muskies that summer before the big musky tournament on Cass Lake in early September. On one of those trips Bill and I were fishing muskies and casting along a weedy drop-off which ran close to the shore on the south side of Cass Lake. We were approaching a cottage or summer home with a floating swimming raft anchored near the drop-off just in front of the cabin. Since it was August, there were four teenage children diving and swimming off and around the raft. As was our practice, we trolled out around the raft and away from the swimmers so as not to disturb their fun. Just as we were far enough past the raft, Bill made a cast back up toward the break line of the drop-off and the instant his musky sized Mepps spinner bucktail hit the water, a musky exploded on it. It was not a huge fish, but it did jump about three times between us and the kids at the raft. Bill fought it to the boat, I netted it, we took a couple quick pictures with Bill holding it up, and he released it back to the water. We hadn't noticed, but the kids had all seen this battle, the jumping fish, the weighing and picture taking, when one of the boys yelled, "How big was it ?" Bill replied, "It was forty inches long and weighed eighteen pounds." With that, one of the girls said, "I'm not swimming around here anymore!" Then she dove into the water, swam toward shore, picked up her towel and walked to the cottage. The others followed her and we chuckled to ourselves as we fished our way on down the shore and along the weed bed. I don't know if those kids ever went swimming there again, but the next summer, that raft was anchored in shallower water in front of the same cottage.

A nice young couple came to the resort that summer looking for a muskie guide, and I was readily on hand to accommodate them. I say they were young, actually they were about four or five years older than I was, but they still seemed young. Their names were Bev and Myron Barrie, from Waseca, Minnesota where Myron was employed by the original Herter's Inc., a full line sporting goods outlet that was probably ahead of its time as far as the business end of things is concerned. That is only my observation of the business and not intended to cause hard feelings to anyone. It was a great outlet and mail order sporting goods business that I was sorry to see closed. Myron and Bev hired me as their musky guide and even though we didn't catch a musky that day, we did have some action with follows and surface swirls as the fish made passes at our bait. We did build a relationship which has lasted through some thirty-two years of being friends, taking family vacations together, and doing a lot of hunting and fishing together. Before the musky trip was over that day, Myron and Bev had invited Jan and I down to Waseca to do some fall pheasant hunting. We accepted the invite and we've been good friends since.

We had another fog experience late that summer, Cliff and I each had two customers who wanted to fish for walleyes. I was going to head across the lake to a place known as the "Girls Camp," because there was actually a girl's camp near there. It is located north and east of Cedar Island and is approximately six miles from the resort. Cliff was headed for an area known as "Strawberry" which is a sand bar extending out from a point on the south shore near Strawberry Lake. We both left Birch Villa dock at the same time and headed into the dense fog, stopping occasionally to listen for other boats, and trying to keep on the safe side to avoid any unnecessary accidents. After traveling through the fog and keeping my boat on as straight a line as I could for what I thought was giving myself ample time to arrive at the Girl's Camp bar, I slowed down and began to watch the depth finder until we came up on the shallows where we began trolling for walleye. As we trolled along the break line I was confident we had landed on the correct location. Within about ten minutes time I could faintly see the outline of an approaching boat. It was Cliff! As we got got closer I asked if he had decided to come to the Girls Camp instead of Strawberry. Cliff said, "We're on Strawberry." I told him I thought we were on the Girl's Camp bar and he replied, "We're far from it." Since Cliff had grown up on this lake and knew it like the back of his hand, I followed his lead and assumed I had gotten off course somehow and ended up at Strawberry. Within about an hour the fog began to lift and both Cliff and I were amazed to find we were fishing just east of Cedar Island. I was about a mile and a half short of my destination and Cliff had over shot Strawberry by about a mile. That sort of thing had happened before with similar outcomes and one time Cliff ended up where I was going to be and I found myself where he was to be fishing. The fog plays funny tricks on a person's mind and it isn't always a pleasant feeling.

September came and with it the musky tournament and found Bill Paulson, Johnny Moore and I fishing together again. The first day, Friday, brought cooler than normal temperatures, but other than that, fairly good musky conditions. We raised a few muskies, but none were takers so we finished the first day empty handed. We didn't feel too bad about it because at the bean feed that evening we found out no one caught too much to speak of. There had been a few smaller fish registered so there was still hope for us to compete. Saturday dawned a beautiful morning and at about ten o'clock am we found ourselves fishing the rock pile behind about twenty other boats. It was like take a number, get in line and wait your turn. We waited until the last boat got far enough ahead before we began to follow them along the path all the others had taken. About one hundred yards along the bar, Bill said, "Scoot the boat ahead." I said, "What, it's forty feet deep out there!" Bill replied, "I don't care, I saw a muskie surface about twenty yards ahead of the boat." I tried to tell him it was useless And that fish was probably just cruising around checking out all the commotion. Again he requested, "Just pull ahead and let me cast once or twice over there." Knowing Bill's luck with muskies and his many gut feelings that proved successful, I scooted the boat ahead and let him cast. He was using his favorite lure, the Mepps Giant Killer with a blaze orange blade and yellow bucktail. It was a little heavier lure and he let it sink a bit deeper before retrieving. On his second cast he set the hook and shouted, "I've got one on!" At first I thought he was joking, as he sometimes did, and tried to make me think he had a fish. This time he did have a fish on, and it was a nice musky! I glanced at the depth finder and it read forty-five feet. After a short battle and one nice jump, Bill brought the fish past the boat a couple times and on the third pass it was close enough for me to net. We unofficially weighed the fish at twenty-nine pounds on my trusty D-liar scale and we were off to find the flagship to get an official weight and register the fish. The tournament officials weighed it in at twenty-nine pounds, two ounces. In those days there was no release yet and all fish were kept and registered according to weight. The release thing came a few years later in the tournament rules. We fished the rest of that day with only a few follows and one fish that took a swipe at Johnny's lure by the boat. We did hear that Bill's fish was leading the tourney after two days of fishing. We had another half day to hope it held up and try to get a bigger one. Sunday morning was another good day and we went into Buck Lake, a place we had not fished yet in this tournament. As we entered the lake we began fishing just inside the entrance Following the weed-line and drop-off toward the south where it cuts in toward the shore. We were all three casting off the left or port side of the boat perpendicular to the drop-off. I cast my Pflueger Muskil with red bucktail way up into shallow water and from out of nowhere a musky hit it with such a force, it almost pulled the rod out of my hands. This fish did not jump, but did make several nice runs in, out and around the boat until it tired and Bill put it in the net. I figured it didn't jump because one of the treble hooks was in the lower jaw and one in the upper causing its jaw to be locked shut. Since it couldn't open its mouth the fish probably didn't sense it could throw the hooks. We weighed it at twenty-nine pounds and headed off to look for the flagship where I could get it officially weighed and registered. The official weight was recorded at twenty-eight pounds, fourteen ounces, just four ounces less than Bill's musky the previous day. It was about eleven o'clock and we had to quit at noon, so we finished out the tournament fishing near the Potato Islands. Johnny had another small musky take a look at his lure, but it wasn't interested enough to take the bait. Noon came and we arrived back at the dock with our second fish hoping it would qualify for a place in the top four, as that is as far down as the tro-phies were awarded. We attended the awards banquet later to find that Bill had caught the first place fish and mine was in second. Bill won a sixteen foot boat, trailer, twenty-five horse Johnson outboard and a nice twenty-four inch trophy for his first place fish. I won a depth finder, boat anchor, four boat cushions, a musky rod and reel, many lures and a nice eighteen inch trophy. Bill and I had come to the tournament together so on the way home he offered to buy all my prizes from me to equip his new boat. Since I already had a fully equipped boat, I agreed and after collecting for my guide services from he and Johnny for the three days, I was feeling pretty flush as far as my wallet was concerned. My wife didn't mind either because she got to go on a little shopping spree, as I shared some of my earnings with her. The trophy still stands in my rodcrafting workshop where there have been many stories told and memories remembered related to that three-day tournament.

There were a few more trips to Cass Lake that fall for some late season guiding and fishing. We ended the summer with fifty-nine legal muskies in my boat and it proved to be a very successful one without a doubt.

To top it all off, in November that year I went deer hunting with a good friend of mine from Braham, Loren Christenson. We traveled to northern Minnesota to a deer shack Loren, his brother, an uncle and others shared specifically for deer hunting. It is located near Effie, Minnesota and they have different areas named for each hunter in the heavily forested land they hunt on. I recall "herd clearing," "doe ridge," and "buck draggin'road" just to name a few. I was hunting on the spot they called "herd clearing" all day Saturday of the opening season. It was cold and there was a fresh blanket of new fallen snow. I remember sitting in the tree stand and shivering most of the morning until Loren's uncle came by about noon when we sat on a nearby log and had lunch together. It was still cold when he left and I got back up in the tree stand and shivered some more. At three o'clock I looked at my watch and when I glanced up, there stood a big buck that looked like a horse with antlers. It was about a hundred yards across a small swamp standing broadside to me, so I raised my trusty old Winchester Model 94 lever action, pulled the hammer back and aimed directly at the heart region through the open sights and pulled the trigger. The buck jumped as if startled and bounded straight ahead disappearing into the woods. With gun in hand I jumped to the ground from the ten foot platform, I didn't take time to crawl down. I had to run around the edge of the swamp to get to where the deer had been standing when I took the shot. There on the snow was some deer hair, so I knew I had at least hit the animal. Upon following the tracks I could see they went from side to side showing the buck had run and jumped erratically in an effort to escape. About fifty yards away I found the big ten point buck lying in a heap, a hole right through its heart. The deer was gutted and as I started to drag it out I found that was going to be useless as I needed help, it was much too heavy for me to drag alone. Thinking and knowing there might be timber wolves in the area, and knowing I couldn't hang the big deer without help, I found a low hanging spruce brow and drug the deer under it to conceal it for the time being until I could return with help. It was about a mile back to where Loren was sitting on his stand and by now it was getting late in the afternoon. I hiked the trail back as fast as I could and found Loren in his tree stand. He asked, "Did you get one ?" I answered, "Yep." He laughed and asked, "Where is it then ?" I replied, "It's out by my stand, can you help me drag it in ?" He laughed again and said, "You didn't get a deer, cause I didn't hear a shot." I said, "Yes, I did," and showed him the empty cartridge. He said, "You could have had that empty cartridge in your pocket all the time." I took off my jacket, pulled up my sleeves and showed him the dried blood on my hands and arms. He exclaimed, "You did get one!" I answered, "Yes, now are you going to help me ?" Loren came down out of his stand and asked, "How big is it?" I thought to myself, \lquote two can play this game.'Then I answered saying, "Oh, it's just a small spike buck." So we walked back to "herd clearing" and when we arrive Loren asked, "Where is it?" I said, "Right over there under that spruce tree." As he pulled the limb of the tree back revealing the ten point rack, he said, "Spike buck my foot!" He added, "Boy, that's a nice buck." The two of us each grabbed one side of the antlers and started to drag the deer back to the trail. After much grunting and groaning we decided the buck was still too much for the two of us to pull all the way back, so we walked the mile and a half back to the deer shack to get my snowmobile. We rode double which was difficult on the rugged terrain under the thin layer of snow. We had our guns cased and riding on the running boards on either side of the snowmobile, but when we reached the deer, Loren's gun had fallen off so now we would have to look for it on the way back with the deer, in the dark. With the buck tied to a rope hooked on the rear of the snow machine we began our trek back to camp. Something was wrong, the snowmobile would not pull the two of us and the deer too. We decided that I would pull the deer back with the snowmobile and then come back to get Loren as he literally felt his way back along the trail in search of his cased gun. I took off with the deer in tow, but when I reached a low swampy spot in the trail, the snowmobile would not pull the deer through. This buck was proving to be more trouble than he was worth. I unhooked the rope and went back to get Loren. He had not yet found his gun and I hadn't seen it along the way in the headlight. We rode the snowmobile back to the deer and pulled the buck across this span of swamp that the snowmobile couldn't accomplish. Going through the swamp was rough as we couldn't see where the clumps were and our feet would sink down into the muck as we pulled the heavy animal across. About halfway across we found Loren's gun stuck partly in the mud. It was a good thing he had it in the case as it didn't get wet or dirty from the swamp muck. It took us some time to get everything together and finally tied the deer back on the snowmobile, so I drug the buck back to camp while Loren walked most of the way in the dark. After untying the rope from the snowmobile I did go back to meet Loren and we finally made it to camp. Upon getting the buck hung in the tree at a safe height we went into the shack to change clothes, warm up and have a bowl of stew that the Uncle had prepared and kept warm for us. It was ten o'clock pm and we were not only tired, but hungry as starved wolves. It was a trophy buck for me that weighed two hundred twenty pounds field dressed, and made a beautiful shoulder mount to hang in the den. I often think of that span of time from when I shot the buck at three o'clock in the afternoon until we had it hanging at camp by ten o'clock that night and often ask myself if I would do it again. At my age and this stage of my life, I probably wouldn't be able to do it again, but I'd sure give it a healthy try.

Yes, 1971 was a good year and left many wonderful memories with lots of good friends that I shall cherish the rest of my life.

Jan Heitschmidt with crappies on the ice in Lake Windigo.

Reuben Bjorklund, Ernie Englan and Merv with the 37½# musky that inhaled Ernie's lure into its gills from behind.

Nephew Lindset Heitschmidt, Chad, Cristi and Merv holding a 48", 37# musky.

Merv and Bill Paulson with 30# and 18# muskies caught in July.

Guide, Larry Heitschmidt with a 23# musky he caught in Cass Lake.

Merv with a 39# musky in Leroy's Bait Shop.

Bill Paulson and Merv with a 14# northern pike and 20# musky caught in the rain.

Bill Paulson and Merv with 17# musky.

Merv and Bill Paulson with 29# 2 oz. and 28# 14 oz. muskies. First and second place fish in the annual September musky tourney.

Bill Paulson and Merv with 1st and 2nd place trophies in the annual September musky touney. The boat and trailer Bill won is in the background.

Sholder mount of 10 point buck Merv shot in November.

For the most part, this year started off like any other, weekend trips to Cass Lake, preparing the resort for the upcoming season, getting boats ready for summer use and doing whatever needed to be done before the opening fishing season. These weekend trips were taking place while we were finishing another school year, and making our move to the resort for the summer and another season of guiding. Something I have failed to mention before was a fishing trip that several friends and I had been taking in Canada over the past few years. I haven't mentioned it because the trip really didn't have anything to do with Cass Lake or any guiding experiences, which this book is basically focused on, but I felt this excerpt important enough to be shared. The fishing trip being referred to is one that some teacher friends and I took to a place called Reed Lake located in northern Manitoba, Canada. Reed Lake is only a mere five hundred miles north of Winnipeg, Manitoba and Winnipeg is the halfway point from our homes in east central Minnesota. When we first started going to Reed Lake about two hundred miles of the highway north of Winnipeg was gravel. The trip took about twenty-one hours and we usually drove it straight through. There were six of us and the plan was to take two vehicles pulling our own boats and rotate drivers every two hours. While the driver put in his two hours the next driver would ride shotgun to help keep the driver awake and talk to him along the way. The person who had just finished his two hour drive would then sleep in the back seat and this routine seemed to work quite well as we always made the trip safely and somewhat rested without too much jet lag from the long trip. Our group had been making this trip for a few years now so the routine was well organized and the team effort, on the part of everyone, made this annual expedition very enjoyable. My friends and companions were Ron Lykins, a fellow teacher in Braham for over thirty years, Al Hanson, Irv Erickson, Bob Gilbert and Dave Franko, all teachers in the neighboring town of Mora, Minnesota. Our routine upon arriving at Reed Lake was to unload all equipment and food onto the government dock where we would then launch the boats. After parking the vehicles and trailers we loaded the boats with half the equipment, most of which was mainly the tents and more bulky items that would go to the campsite on the first of two trips. With two men in each boat loaded with half the gear, we made our way across the lake to the campsite while the last two men would remain on the dock to watch and care for the other half of the equipment and food. The trip across the lake was usually about five or six miles so it took some time for the boats to return empty and pick up the remaining supplies and last two men who stayed ashore. This routine was practiced each year due to the safety aspect of it all to help insure a positive and successful week long experience. While the two empty boats with only the drivers came back for the second trip, the other two men who first went across with the gear would begin clearing the campsite and setting up the tents. When we returned to the campsite with the second load and all six fishermen were finally together again, we began the arduous tasks of setting up camp for the week. There were two tents for sleeping, one tent for food and equipment storage, and a tarp-like covered shelter to cook and eat under in case of rain. The equipment was carried into the storage tent along with the food, the cooking facilities were arranged under the lean-to cover, everyone put his bedroll and bag of clothing in its respective tent and we even had a place back in the woods where we assembled a makeshift bathroom out of a six gallon plastic pail with no bottom and an old toilet seat someone had brought along. After everything had been set up and organized it was usually time to go fishing. As I mentioned, we had been making this our routine for a few years, but something happened this year which altered our plans and interrupted the routine drastically. We had left Mora, Minnesota about nine am on a Friday morning in early June, the week after school had ended. After driving all night we arrived at Reed Lake about twenty-two hours later on Saturday morning at seven am. While unloading and getting the boats launched at the government dock we noticed three men and a teenage boy doing about the same thing next to us. This was common practice then as most fishermen camped out on one of the many islands in Reed Lake. The strange thing about their set-up was they had two canoes situated about three feet apart, but tied together near the front and back with two two-by-fours each about six feet long. They loaded their gear into the canoes which consisted of sleeping bags in plastic bags, food for a week for all four, tackle and tackle boxes, camp cooking equipment, extra gas, lanterns, and a six horse power Mercury outboard fastened onto the two by four at the rear and between the two canoes. Then all four of these guys boarded the canoes, two in each, and they pushed off heading out across the big open part of the lake. There was a pretty steady southerly wind that day as they headed out at an angle to the direction of wind and waves. We commented on how overloaded they seemed to be as the canoes rode low in the water and they disappeared from view behind a nearby island. Our thoughts went back to loading the sixteen and eighteen foot Lund boats equipped with thirty-five horsepower Johnson outboard motors each with a Johnson six horsepower kicker motor used for trolling purposes. Our first trip across was a safe one, but we noticed the wind coming up a bit and we were anxious to get across to our campsite to unload the first half and then return to the dock for the last two men and remaining gear before conditions grew worse. On the return trip I was in the lead, driving my eighteen foot boat and more or less breaking the waves for Irv who was following with his sixteen footer. The wind was increasing in velocity and the waves were probably two feet high by this time so we were taking it slow and easy with empty boats in the somewhat rough water. As we approached the halfway point going back to the dock, I caught sight of something black floating in the water ahead. As I slowed the boat and grabbed the object it turned out to be a large black plastic garbage bag full of what I presumed to be garbage. There were usually lots of boats going to and from the only government dock on the lake, so I figured this garbage blew out of someone's boat undetected and I would do the proper thing and take it in for disposal. When we finally reached the dock I handed the bag to Dave Franko and told him to put it in the garbage can near the dock. He asked what it was and I suggested it was probably someone's garbage. He said it didn't feel like garbage so he opened the bag and it contained a brand new down filled sleeping bag still in its original package. Dave took the sleeping bag over to the lodge by the government dock and asked the owner if he could keep it until the bag's owner came back to claim it. The man at the lodge didn't want anything to do with it since the owner probably wasn't one of his customers, so Dave told him to let the claimer know we found the bag and it would be safe in our vehicle until we came back during mid-week to buy gas, so he could pick it up then. Dave put the bag in one of our cars and came back to the dock to help with the finishing touches of loading the boats for the return trip across the lake to our campsite. About halfway out, I was in the lead again and for some reason glanced around over the lake and caught a glimpse of something like a flash to our starboard side, but probably a quarter mile out. I slowed the boat and Irv came along side asking what was wrong. I told him I thought I had seen something in the water to our right, so I stood up and there about a quarter mile out was someone in the water waving a canoe paddle in an effort to catch the attention of a passerby, which was us. As we turned toward the individual we spotted more items floating in the water, another black plastic bag, gas cans, tackle boxes, food items and other various things connected with camping. We picked up most of the items as we headed toward the submerged canoes and campers. It was the group of four whom we had seen earlier, overloaded and heading across the lake in their two canoes strapped together. The two men in the back of each canoe had gotten out and were holding onto each canoe, waving their canoe paddles. They were very large men and seemed to be somewhat in a state of panic. The other two, a father and his teenage son were still seated in the front of each canoe with the son appearing to be in a state of dazed shock. All four were cold and shivering with faces and lips blue from the almost icy forty degree water. We estimated their canoe had taken on water and semi-submerged about forty-five minutes earlier and they urgently needed to be helped somehow. Not wanting to approach too closely due to the fact the two larger men were in a state of panic, and our boats being loaded, wouldn't have taken too much more to cause us to take on water and possibly submerge us too, we cautiously tied my anchor rope to the front of one of the canoes. Everything was under water except for about six inches of the top front of their canoes, so we slowly began to pull them toward an island approximately another quarter mile away. It was slow going as the opposite canoe veered off to the side acting like a rudder and pulling us the wrong direction. We were fighting the waves, telling them to hang on and we'd pull them to safety, and all this time Irv was out gathering up the other floating items he and his boat could salvage. We felt it important to keep talking to them getting them to respond and yet making them feel like they were going to be alright. While the opposite canoe was pulling the wrong way, I decided to go with the flow and take the same course, but also bring the boat around in large sweeping turns back toward the island, and it worked! I'm not sure how long it took, but I know these four men were in the cold frigid water for over an hour before we finally landed on the rocky shore, out of the wind, on the lee side of the island. As the feet of the two larger men, probably two hundred seventy or eighty pounds each, touched the rocky bottom, they began to scream and literally cry out in pain. They told us later it felt like pins and needles on the bottoms of their feet, like when your foot goes to sleep, only exaggerated by about a hundred times. I can't imagine the pain they must have endured, not to mention those cold, icy temperatures and length of time in the water. We managed to help those two up onto shore and pull the canoes up as far as we could while Irv and Bob built a fire out of some dry wood they found on the island. I thought the first two men were going to jump right into the fire as they were shivering intensely trying to warm themselves. Dave and I set to work on helping the father and son out of their canoes, but the teenager was in such a state of shock he wouldn't talk to us nor would he take his fixed, staring trance off the world ahead of him. He just sat there with both fists clenched around the gunnel of the canoe, looking stiff as a board. As we tried to help him slide backward in the bottom of the canoe, since his legs were under the support strut or crossbar of the canoe, we had to lift and scoot him back first to get his legs clear and lift him out. Every time we would move or touch him he would cry out in pain and it became agonizing for us because we wanted to help, not hurt him. Finally we just picked him up, slid him back, raised his stiff body up over the canoe and carried him up by the fire, all the time he was crying and screaming in bitter pain. It was hard on us all, but it had to be done and his dad thanked us for it later. His father, although tested by the same pain, helped us remove himself from the canoe and then we carried him to the fire to begin a warming process. Now, we still had our boats and gear to contend with and the wind was steadily increasing, so we told the four men we would take our equipment back to the campsite and return to help them get back to the landing and their vehicle. They begged and pleaded with us not to go and leave them on this island, but we had to let the other two men in our party know why we were not back so it presented quite a problem. After lots of persuading and much deliberation, we suggested that we leave one of our gas cans and a tackle box with them as a sign of trust that we would return to help them. They agreed and we were off toward our camp leaving them to warm by the fire that was now beginning to take the chill off the edges and help them to get some feeling back into their bodies. Upon arriving at camp, Ron and Al were there to meet us wondering where we had been and what had happened. As we unpacked the gear and stowed it away the story was unfolded to them with every detail revealing the fact we had to return to help these four back to their pickup at the dock. It was decided that four of us would return to them with empty boats to help them back to shore. Since Irv and I had our boats, we were destined to go, then Ron and Bob volunteered

to go with us to continue and finish what had actually become a rescue of great magnitude. As we made our way back across the lake the wind had not eased at all and the waves were still two to three feet high. We found the four men still sitting by the fire, I don't think they moved while we were gone. It was decided to put the men in our boats and pull the canoes back to the landing, but as we prepared to gather their gear and get the canoes ready, it started to rain! The wind was still blowing so we decided to put the men and gear in our boats and carry the canoes upside down across the gunnels of our boats. After everything was loaded and the men were in we pulled away from the island. I took the lead and knew the wind was going to cause some trouble, especially with the canoes across the gunnels, so I had two people hold the canoes secure and prepared for the worse. With the rain coming down we could not see the shore or the dock a little over two miles away, and there were two rock piles somewhere directly between us and shore. The rock piles were about forty yards apart and rose above the surface about three or four feet. As we came out from behind the island the waves slapped at us and the wind pushed at the canoes across the boat, but I aimed the boat in the direction I thought we should head. Saying a prayer, "God be with us and guide us through this to safety," I gunned the motor and Irv followed close behind as we made our way toward shore. What seemed like an eternity probably happened in only a few minutes, but about halfway back to the dock the rain stopped and we could see the dock, but where were the two island rock piles ? I slowed the boat and Irv came along side asking if I saw the rock piles. I told him I hadn't and as we looked back at the rains moving off across the lake the rock piles appeared and we had gone midway between them. Think what you want, but I know there was somebody looking out for us that day, and I don't think I have to tell you who it was. The angels were with us through that situation. We continued on and got the men safely back to their pickup, helped them load their gear, put the canoes on the carrying rack and saw that they got the new sleeping bag back that we had first found floating in the lake several hours before to start this whole nightmarish affair. They had decided this was enough and were going to return home to Rugby, North Dakota. The boy was still in a state of shock and not speaking and we were concerned not only for him, but the other three as well, because they had endured a lot of extreme losses of body temperature. I'm convinced these four would have become fatalities that day if we wouldn't have been there. I don't say that to give credit to our group or myself, but it is a fact that we never saw another boat on the lake that day probably due to the existing conditions, and those men would have experienced hypothermia in a very short time. We learned later the ice had just gone off the lake just a few days before and the water had not warmed a whole lot so I think forty degrees was estimated a bit toward the warm side. I gave two of the men one of my business cards for guiding which included my phone number and address and asked them to contact me later and let me know how they came through the ordeal. I never heard from either of them, but during the summer, back at Birch Villa Resort I did talk to a man from the Rugby, North Dakota area who gave me a very sketchy report of their outcome. His side of the story revealed that one of the men lost circulation in one of his legs and it had to be amputated below the knee, the teenager had some psychological problems and the dad had a nervous breakdown shortly after returning home. This information was never verified officially, but those were the facts given to me secondhand. Needless to say, the remainder of that week on Reed Lake was not as pleasant as in years past because all six of us were concerned and mentioned several times the condition of the men and wondered how they were doing. It certainly brought home a point to us, it is much safer to make the trip twice with half the gear than taking a chance on risking everything for the sake of saving a little time and gas. Our week on Reed Lake ended and we were on our way back to Minnesota, but the memory of that rescue kept playing in our minds all the way home. Since school was out and my family and I had already moved to Birch Villa for the summer, the men dropped me off at Cass Lake and were on their way back to Mora, Minnesota, to their families and summer jobs.

Walleye fishing was sluggish, but steady during the month of June as it seemed like a hit or miss situation each time we went out with a guide trip. If I remember correctly, the weather was kind of up and down too, as one frontal system seemed to move through on the heels of the last. There was never a weather pattern that seemed to be consistent for more than a day during the entire month. There was one situation that surfaced during that period of time which has remained in my memory and was rather an unexpected gift. I was guiding two men from New Ulm, Minnesota whose names were Leo and Gilbert, that's all I know because I don't believe I ever heard their last names. They were older men, probably in their late sixties or early seventies, but they loved fishing for walleyes. The two men enjoyed just being out on the lake and seemed to notice many things about nature that most people don't recognize or just take for granted. The fishing was slow that late June morning and we had tried several locations without a trace of a walleye. It was a difficult transition time for us because we were using minnows for bait, but would take night crawlers along in order to keep check on these fish as perhaps they might become more enticed by the worm rather than the minnow. On this particular day neither had worked, so at noon, when we were supposed to be going in, I suggested trying night crawlers again and we would move to one last spot called "kettle bar" which was located just southwest of Cedar Island about a half mile. Leo, trying to be positive after four hours of getting skunked, piped up saying, "We'll get 'em now!" I didn't really know if he was being positive or sarcastic, so I took it as a positive comment for the time being. We motored up to the drop-off, threw our crawler rigs out and began a slow troll in about twenty feet of water along the bar. I don't think we had gone fifty feet when Gilbert yelled, "I've got a snag!" There were a few deadheads or logs along this stretch of bar, so I began to back the boat toward the snag, while Gilbert reeled his line in. As we kept backing I noticed Gilbert's line seemed to keep the same angle and the boat was not getting back far enough to consider freeing the line. I watched his rod tip and didn't detect any more than the steady bend it had from Gilbert's reeling it in, but still the line was maintaining a consistent angle down into the water and behind the boat. I said, "We should have gotten back over your snag before now, what's wrong here ?" With that I took Gilbert's rod, lifted the tip and felt the steady pull of a fish, a big fish! Now I quickly handed the rod back to Gilbert, turned off the trolling motor and said, "You've got a fish!" "A big fish!" I exclaimed. Then he began to get excited and fight the fish, but I told him to take it easy and just keep a steady pull while reeling and lifting his rod tip to keep the line tight. Apparently after the walleye had eaten the night crawler it just kept swimming and all we were doing was following it back down the bar thinking it was a snag. It was a hot, sunny, still day and we could easily see down into the water probably twelve feet or more, so when the walleye first came into view, it looked huge! Gilbert handled the situation quite well and finally brought the fish beside the boat where I netted it and brought it into the boat. It was a plump beauty weighing seven and a half pounds and turned out to be the biggest fish Gilbert had ever caught. That caused much excitement in the boat as Leo said, "See, I told you we'd get 'em, didn't I ?" I replied, "Leo, it's a nice fish, but it's only one fish." Leo chirped back, "Ye of little faith." He had me there and we continued fishing up the bar. Again, not thirty feet along, I had a fish on, and it was another hefty feeling walleye! It came to the boat with some resistance, but eventually gave in and was netted and turned out to be a four and a half pounder. Now there were two good looking walleyes on the stringer and Leo's comment was coming true. It seemed like the fish were keeping track who was catching that day as Leo set the hook on the third walleye which turned out to be a five pound golden colored beauty. Things began to get interesting now and we started to show more of the enthusiasm we had lost about three hours before. It had been hot and humid with no wind and a bright sun, but all of a sudden we forgot about the heat and were enveloped in a fish feeding frenzy. To make a long story short, we fished that area for another forty-five minutes before the walleyes turned off and quit biting. It was one of those times when we were at the right place at the right time, and that's how a lot of successful fishing plays out. We ended that trip with six walleyes, two weighed four and a half pounds, one was a five pounder, two more were six pounds each and the seven and a half pounder that Gilbert first caught was the largest. We returned to the dock an hour and a half later than expected, the other guides had come in on time, but had been skunked, so a little overtime paid off. Those kinds of trips, with that many big fish didn't happen too often on Cass Lake, at least not for me, but I believe it is due mainly to the deeper average lake depth. You don't see too many ten pound plus walleyes taken, but when you do, it's a bonus. It's a known fact that fish further north in deeper water lakes don't grow as fast compared to the warmer water and longer seasons of lakes in the south, because of the greater length of time for growth. The fish do get larger over time and obtain different habits in the northern lakes, but it takes more time for that growth to happen.

That summer I began guiding a family from De Kalb, Illinois, who had been coming to Cass Lake for a few years and stayed at a neighboring resort called Sah-Kah- Tay Beach Resort. Sah-Kah-Tay was located just across the street from Birch Villa and We knew many of its guests as well as our own. Ken and Doris Hintzsche and their Family were into the farm scene and had originated and maintained a very successful chemical fertilizer company with Ken's brother, Rich. Ken's family rented a nice cottage at Sah-Kah-Tay during the month of July each year and his brother Rich would rent the same cabin during the month of August. We had been using the ever trustworthy Beetle Spins during mid-summer months and Ken's first time out produced limits of average sized walleyes for his party of three. He was hooked, so we tried to schedule one or two guide trips each week for he or some part of his family. It was fun guiding them because regardless of the outcome, they always enjoyed the time on the water and made something of a positive mood for whatever the luck had been. It got to be a friendly contest as one time I would guide the men and the next time out the women would try their hand at it. They would tease each other

when one side out fished the other. There were many good times in the boat as we fished, visited and got to know each other during those hours on the water. I wouldn't want to take sides, but I truly believe the women did out fish the men on most occasions. There was one trip that summer when Ken brought two friends that were visiting for a few days, we were fishing the "west Cedar bar" as we called it and the walleyes were cooperating seeming to like the Beetle Spins. We had been at it for almost three and a half hours with twenty-three fish on the stringer and only one to go for our limits. Ken said, "One more and we can go in,"

Sometimes that last walleye can be the toughest to get and this was no exception. We fished for another hour, it was well past the time to go in, but not one more fish took the bait. We arrived back at the dock, took pictures, and began to fillet the walleyes while they were still fresh. As I removed the fish from the stringer we counted twenty-four! Someone had miss counted and we had our limits all along! I won't suggest who counted the fish, but I think the guide took credit for it.

During August that year I had another fog experience. It was another dense fog as usually happened that time of year when temperatures began to cool. I was guiding two men staying at Birch Villa and no other guides had a trip that morning, so I was on my own, so to speak. We headed across the lake for an area known as Norway Beach, because that's where we had been having luck, still fishing with the Beetle Spins. The slight breeze was in the northeast so I quartered the waves and headed for our hopeful destination, stopping on occasion to listen for other boats in order to keep it safe to travel through this denseness. As it turned out, we came upon a drop-off and began to fish parallel to it, trolling the Beetle Spins in about ten to twelve feet of water. In a short time the breeze picked up and blew the fog away and revealed a beautiful stretch of Norway Beach, right where we wanted to be! The walleyes were semi-cooperative that morning as we boated ten and couldn't muster any more, even after trying several other spots. The men were happy with that as they had been fishing for nearly a week on their own and had only caught two walleyes and a perch.

In September, Bill Paulson and Stan Harper came north to fish the fifth annual International Muskies, Inc. tournament with me, only this year we decided to fish the big waters of Leech Lake which lies a few miles to the south of Cass Lake. It was a new experience for us as I had only been on these waters a few times before. As it turned out, we saw many nice muskies follow to the boat, but they all seemed to be lazy and listless and we came away empty handed. Bill had returned to Cass Lake several times during July and August and continued his fortunate success, landing a musky almost every time he came. There were no really large fish that year for Bill, but he did acquire a new theory about the sport. It seems that every time he caught a musky there were these little dark gray colored birds called terns flying about nearby. Bill nicknamed them "musky birds" and every time he saw some he would say, "We're in luck, I see the musky birds again." It was probably just a coincidence, but whenever we had musky action, there these little birds would be also. When ever we came in without having had much luck and someone would ask, "How'd you do today?" Bill would explain that we saw nothing and usually end the conversation by saying, "That's it in a nutshell." He always had these little sayings that captured the attention of whomever he was fishing with. One of his pet sayings in the boat, whenever we reached a new fishing spot was, as he stood up and cast out first, "First in, first on." Then he would give a little chuckle because he knew he was the first to cast his bait. That year we ended up with thirty-six legal muskies in my boat which was down a little from some of the more recent and previous years.

A very big decision had to be made that summer as my parents decided to either turn Birch Villa over to my brother and I or sell. My dad was sixty and mom was fifty- nine at the time, and they decided after about seventeen years in the business, there were other things they wanted to do before getting too old. They wanted to travel a little and just settle down to a little slower pace of life. My brother and I along with our wives talked it over and decided one of us would have to give up our career in teaching and take on the full time job of operating the resort. Neither of us felt we were in a position to sacrifice our careers at the time due to seniority at our respective schools, and after having spent many years with our parents at the resort, also wanted a little break away from the tasks the resort requires. I didn't want to give up the guiding part of my already established summer life and my wife and children were enjoying the lake more each year, so we decided to work out a way to come back for the summers in order for me to guide. My parents did sell the resort in October that fall to a couple named Marv and Shirley Topper (pronounced Tow-per) and their son Jack. The Toppers were from the Chicago, Illinois area and with the resort, Marv agreed to buy my guide boat and motors.

During the winter and early spring months that year and the next, I purchased another new eighteen foot Lund fishing boat equipped with a thirty-five horse power Johnson outboard motor and a six horse Johnson as a trolling motor to be used as a guide boat. My wife and I also purchased a fifty-five foot used mobile home with two bedrooms which we moved onto a site at Sah-Kah-Tay Resort on the hill above the cabins. We had made a deal with the owner, Rich Becker, to have the mobile home there and guide for him at the resort, in turn for free site space. Rich's parents, Stan and Lil Becker actually operated the resort for Rich, so he wasn't around very much. It allowed a place for my family to live during the summer months while I continued to guide on Cass Lake. So as you can see, there were some big decisions to be made during the fall of 1972 and the spring of 1973.

Merv and Ron Lykins with nice walleyes caught on
Reed Lake, Manitoba, after the amazing rescue.

Merv with back-to-back lake trout caught in Reed Lake Manitoba. One weighed 30# and the other was 28#. Ron Lykins is seated in the foreground.

Ken Hintzsche and Kenny Jr. holding a stringer of walleyes caught on Cass Lake while being guided by Merv.

1973

My parents had retired to a nice wooded lot near Midge Lake west of Cass Lake approximately five or six miles located just off U.S. Hwy number two. Dad had continued working a part time job as mechanic for the Deep Rock Oil Company in Cass Lake, and my mother was content to be housewife again after seventeen years in the resort business. My brother, Larry, retired from guiding and he and his family continued to reside near Mille Lacs Lake in a small town called Wahkon, Minnesota. My wife, Jan, our children and I, made our summer home at Cass Lake where I continued to guide summer fishermen and their families. It was a new and different life for us as we had moved a mobile home onto a lot at Sah-Kah-Tay Resort, and while I guided, Jan was full time mom as she and the children would enjoy the beach as much as possible. Jan also helped with the usual weekend chores of cabin cleaning for both Birch Villa Resort and Sah-Kah-Tay.

I had a new and larger eighteen foot oversized Cass Lake made fishing boat, equipped with two new motors, a thirty-three horsepower Evinrude and a smaller six horsepower Evinrude used as a "kicker" or trolling motor. We had made a few early season trips to Cass Lake that spring to prepare the trailer for living and to do some early season guiding. Cliff Riggles was still guiding as was Kutsey Nornberg, but due to age and other interests of income, they were both slowing down and guiding less than in years past. I don't remember anything out of the ordinary as far as fishing went that spring, but the walleyes were aggressive and hungry, and we took every advantage of that as we could. Marv Topper, the new owner of Birch Villa would accompany me on occasion in order to learn the lake and get an idea as to how and where we did most of our fishing as the seasons and habits of the fish changed. On one such occasion, we were slow trolling with shiner minnows in about twelve feet of water, along a sharp drop-off, when Marv yelled, as he set the hook, "I've got a good one here!" We had picked up a few average sized walleyes and this just might be one of those bonus fish as we referred to the larger ones. As Marv continued to reel and pump the fish toward the boat it surfaced and jumped. It was a small musky! Marv had only fished a few times for walleyes that summer, but never for muskies, he didn't even own a musky rod! He played the fish to the boat and I netted it with the walleye net, but his eyes were wide and the look on his face was that of total surprise. He was shaking and looking down at the musky as I told him we had to release it quickly because it probably wasn't legal. He protested as he wanted to keep it to show his son, Jack, and his wife, Shirley. He said questioningly, "That's the biggest fish I've ever caught, and you want me to put it back ?" I felt bad, but the law is the law and the musky measured only twenty-nine inches, just one inch short of the minimum size required to be a keeper. He didn't want to risk a fine, so the beautifully marked musky went back into the water healthy and eager to find its place of habitat. There was one other man with us who had not seen a fish as large as this one either, so it was quite a treat for him as well. After finishing out the guide trip, we made our way back to the resort with half a dozen walleyes and three nice northern pike. Marv was telling everyone about his first musky and how he had to release it duc to its sub-minimum size. I believe Marv became hooked on musky fishing that day as he went to town and bought himself an outfit and lures with which he would start his musky fishing career.

Our musky fishing this particular summer left something to be desired, to say the least, as we only boated twenty-one of the big silvery creatures. One of those came from Wisconsin as our family took a few days off in mid-June to travel to the Hayward Lakes area where we fished the Chippewa Flowage and Lake Winter Reservoir. Myron and Bev Barrie and their family accompanied us and Myron, his son, Mark, and I fished for a Wisconsin musky. We were not accustomed to fishing "stained water" as the locals called it, and that took us some time to get used to it. I was told the reason for the "stained water" was due to the abundance of various roots of trees growing along the water ways, mainly the tamarack trees, which caused the water to become a darker, brownish color as it soaked the roots and gave up this dark hue. We had been more used to fishing the clear water lakes of Minnesota and Canada which was somewhat different. Fish in clear water hit or strike by using their sense of sight, but fish in darker or stained water have a tendency to strike more at a moving shadow or noise created by the lure. After fishing the "Big Chip" as they referred to the Chippewa Flowage without any action, we ventured on to the Winter Flowage, a reservoir with water backed up into a forested area with many stumps standing. It was tricky because of the many stumps and trees in the water, and as we drifted among them casting, we were thinking and wondering how we would manage to battle a musky under these conditions. Our fears were answered as I got a strike next to an upright tree. Fortunately it was a small musky and I was able to bring the fish to the net as Myron brought it into the boat. It was a thirty-nine inch, fifteen pound Wisconsin musky! That was my first musky caught in Wisconsin waters, and I had managed to keep it from getting tangled around a stump, which we felt was a feat in itself. That was the only musky we would catch on this particular trip, but we vowed to return again at a later date to give it another try. A couple things happened during our stay in Wisconsin that make memories last to tell another time. One of those incidents involved my three year old son, Chad. We were camped in a campground on the Chippewa Flowage near a resort called Herman's Landing. My family was in a pop-up type, tent camper with snap down canvas sides and one night Chad rolled over in his bunk and against the side only to have the snaps come loose. He slowly slipped about three feet down to the ground outside the camper, still in his sleeping bag! As he awoke, he realized he was alone outside, and at that time I awoke to hear him whimpering. After opening the door on the rear of the camper, I saw him standing there in his sleeping bag, unable to walk and still half asleep. We managed to get him back into bed and he fell asleep almost immediately as if nothing had happened. We did make a few adjustments as I took his position near the side and allowed him the inside position. Our daughter Cristi, who was four years old, took up my original position next to mom on the other side of the camper. The next morning Myron's family all asked what had happened during the night, as they had heard Chad outside the camper. The very next night the second memory occurred, a skunk had wandered into our campsite between the two campers and was scrounging for whatever leftovers we had overlooked or hadn't cleaned up. Myron had heard it and hollered across to our camper, warning us of the unwanted visitor. Between the two of us yelling at the skunk from our respective campers, it finally realized it wasn't wanted and wandered off, probably on its way to some other campsite looking for a morsel of some kind. I must say there were some tense moments as we didn't want to startle the varmit too much, causing it to spray our campsite, but we lucked out and the skunk had headed on its way.

After returning to Cass Lake it became a summer of full of guiding as I was actually the only fulltime guide remaining at the resort. There were many customers wishing to be guided for walleyes and the "Beetle Spins" had come into full swing after the minnow era faded for the summer.

July rolled around and the Ken Hintzsche family returned to Sah-Kah-Tay requesting at least four or five trips per week through all of that month. We made most of the trips as the weather cooperated and the Beetle Spins continued to be the main bait for walleyes. The Hintzsche women vs. the men continued and I still believe they outfished the men most of the time. There were never a lot of big walleyes caught, but the numbers of "good eaters," those fifteen to eighteen inchers, were abundant. We did occasionally catch one in the twenty to twenty-six inch category and those became the bonus fish. Ken Hintzsche and his son, Kenny, Jr. made many trips with me and very seldom did we not catch a bunch of walleyes. They would often remark that it was amazing how we could keep catching large numbers of walleyes consistently without much of a variation. It was always a joy to fish with their family as they made a fishing trip more than just fishing. They had fun teasing and joking with one another and still were able to relax and enjoy all nature had to provide, which is the way fishing should be.

Bill Paulson made several trips to Cass Lake during the months of July and August, and usually always brought his blessed luck with him. One morning we were musky fishing off the east side of Cedar Island approaching another boat with six people, planning to stop and move around them, so as not to interfere with their fishing. One cast before we were to move, Bill had a musky hit his Mepps lure near the surface. The fish jumped four times and thrashed violently on top of the water between the two boats, giving us quite a show. As we netted the musky, a cheer went up from the other boat and they applauded Bill's catch. It was a nice forty-nine inch twenty-eight pound beauty with fantastic spotted markings on its sides. We drew near to the other boat as they requested a closer look and they were snapping pictures of Bill and his musky. There was one more small musky that morning which measured only thirty inches and was quickly released. Sometimes Bill came alone if he couldn't find anyone else to accompany him, but many times he brought a friend to enjoy the companionship, and this particular time I believe it was Stan Harper, from Braham, who never caught a keeper musky. The three of us fished Portage Bay of Leech Lake that summer as we had planned to fish Leech again during the International Muskies Inc. tournament in September. It was more or less a time of getting used to Leech and its musky areas in an effort to be ready for the upcoming tourney. When September came we found ourselves staying at a small resort near Federal Dam, in a cabin which was close to where we would launch Bill's boat and fish the two and half day affair. It was a good lesson in humility as we had many follows by the ever sought after muskies, but we came away empty handed and all we had to show for our time on the water was a fourteen pound northern pike, which Bill had caught the first day. It was a good time though and we did have good food at the banquets which were served.

It seemed fall came much too early that year and I found myself draining the trailer water and winterizing it for the freezing winter temperatures. This all happened by the first part of October and I stored my boat as well, at the Sailstar Marina located on the southwest shore of Cass Lake and managed by none other than the Larson brothers, Connie and Corky Larson. So it was back to Braham for the winter and my teaching and coaching duties in the school system there.

By now my guiding business was well established and there were many repeat customers returning each year. It was during this spring season, after the fishing opener, I brought eight fellow teachers from Braham to Birch Villa for a weekend of fishing. It was a fun weekend as we had a chance to "get away" and enjoy the out-of-doors along with our usual kidding and teasing. My dad and mom always enjoyed meeting the friends I taught with, and dad would jump in and tease right with the rest of us. He would string you along with some wild, but believable tale, only to drop an embarrassing punch line on you and leave you baffled by his unique ability to "pull the wool over your eyes." If I remember correctly, he did that to Gary Livingston, Art Kaunonen and Loren Christenson the first evening we arrived at the dinner table. Of course everyone else was there to enjoy the tease and serve as a reminder to those three for years to come. Others in the group were: the late Ted Melcher, Darrell Glidden, the late Don Keith, Paul Gurholt, Butch Erickson, plus my brother Larry and I who served as guides for the party. We caught several walleyes and many jumbo perch during the weekend and enjoyed a wonderful fish dinner prepared by my mom, who loved to cook for large groups. It was even rumored that some of those guys "mooned" the other boat as they passed each other on the lake. It was never made too clear as to which ones were the "mooners" and which ones were the "moonees," but it did cause quite a stir among the teaching staff back in Braham later. I know it was all in fun and it happened almost thirty years ago, so it's just water under the bridge at this point.

We were enjoying a comfortable summer of fishing and enjoying the lake with many people who had established themselves as regular customers and friends. The Hintzsche family was there during the month of July and we enjoyed catching many walleyes on the ever famous Beetle Spins. Bill Paulson came several times to fish the elusive musky and was usually blessed with luck whenever he came. I remember one day when Bill and I were out musky fishing in a particularly weedy area and I mentioned to him that if we hooked a decent sized musky we would have to fight it through the heavy weed cover. I also mentioned it would be especially difficult for him as he was using an eight foot medium heavy salmon rod. I guess Bill became a bit edgy and "on guard" more than normal, because as fate would have it, he got a strike. He set the hook with such a force it pulled the fish's head up and above the surface of the water. Without so much as a slight pause he began cranking furiously, keeping the musky's head out of the water all the way to the boat. I never even had time to reel my line in when Bill was yelling, "Net it, net it!" The fish was beside the boat thrashing and splashing on the water as Bill kept a tight line not allowing the musky any freedom. I scrambled to get the net under the fish and bring it into the boat before Bill got too over excited about losing it to the heavy weed cover. Fortunately it was a small musky measuring only thirty-five inches and it was released. The entire catch lasted only a matter of a few seconds and after the release I said, "That has to be the shortest lived musky catch I've ever seen!" Bill remarked, "I thought you would never get the net ready." I know the fish was back swimming in less than a minute and probably didn't even realize it had been caught. We laughed about that one for a long time to follow. I also learned to be a bit more cautious after that whenever I warned Bill of any circumstances which might cause him to be overly sensitivity. He literally took me at my word as he decided in his own mind not to let a fish get the best of him.

One day in July I had come in from a guide trip shortly after noon only to find my lunch waiting, but my wife and children were already on the beach, as was their usual custom. After eating I put on my swimsuit and went to join them for a nice cool dip in the lake on this warm afternoon. A strange thing happened to me on the way to the beach as I walked past several of the new guests. I was approaching my family when an attractive lady who was sunbathing, raised up and in a rather loud voice said, "Merv, will you please bring me a drink ?" I was surprised to see she was looking at me as she said it! I looked to my wife as she was looking at me to see what I might have to say. Needless to say, I was speechless for a moment. I looked back to the lady and replied, "Pardon me, what did you say?" As she looked up at me she said, "Oh, I was just asking my husband to bring me some refreshment." Still stunned by her first remark, I said, "Oh, I see, well my name is Merv." She laughed as she processed the thought of what she had just said earlier. She apologized saying, "I'm sorry, I didn't know." I said, "That's OK, I'm just not used to hearing my name like that, especially from a stranger." We all had a good laugh over it and we still tell that story today, to anyone new to our friendship. Her husband came to the beach bringing her a beverage and we were introduced, "Merv, this is Merv!" As it turned out their names were Merv and Sonja Michalyshen, from Winnipeg, Manitoba. They were vacationing at Cass Lake for the week and they had two sons, Mark and Jason, who were about the same age as our children. The kids became good friends as did we, the parents, and our friendship has continued over the past thirty years. We have visited them at their home in Winnipeg and get to see them almost every summer at the lake. They have also become good friends of the Hintzsche family from DeKalb, Illinois, who have been regular customers of Sah-Kah-Tay resort for almost forty years.

In August Jan and I took a week long trip to Rainy Lake in Ontario, Canada with our friends, Myron and Bev Barrie. We camped out on an island and fished mostly for muskies, but also for walleyes and small mouth bass. Jan caught her third musky that week, a fifteen pound, thirty-four inch beauty that she released back to the Canadian waters. Myron and I also caught small muskies which we released, I believe they were about the same size as Jan's fish. Then it was back to Cass Lake for the remainder of the summer and more guiding.

Back at Cass Lake the musky action was in full swing and as my record shows, we were able to boat twenty of the nice fish, the largest weighing in at thirty-five pounds, nine ounces. All these came in just three short weeks of fishing in August.

September rolled around and school started as we found ourselves back in the swing of teaching and coaching. Bill Paulson brought a friend from New Mexico along with us to the Seventh Annual International Muskies, Inc. tournament that fall. His friend's name was Charlie Stevens and Charlie had never been musky fishing before this tournament. I just knew Charlie was going to "hit it big," or at least catch a musky in the tourney, but it was not to be. He did have one hit and a few follows, but none of us did very well that year either. We had come back to Cass Lake after trying our luck on Leech Lake a few years and getting blanked. It wasn't much better, but we did manage one thirty-eight inch release and a chance at some prizes. I had caught the musky, but after entering my name in the hat for prize drawings, I came up empty handed.

The total musky count added up to forty-six keepable fish that summer, plus several small muskies we released which did not make the thirty inch minimum size limit.

Late fall walleye fishing was very good that year on Cass Lake as I had several weekend guide trips in October. It presented a uniquely different approach as compared to the normal routine of walleye presentation. By late October we were fishing in forty to sixty feet of water and catching two pound average walleyes. It required the use of a two or three ounce trolling sinker in order to get the bait to the bottom. We used minnows for bait and hooked them in the tail and would slow troll or drift over the area, allowing the walleyes to bite and chew up on the minnow for quite some time before setting the hook. It was a method that seemed to work well at the time and it proved successful for us during most of that month.

I did manage one musky trip in November and even though we had several large fish follow our bait, we could find no takers. Our line would freeze with the water on it as we reeled the baits in time after time. After a few casts we would have to peel and chip the ice off the tip of our rods as well as from the line. It was a cold process and did not help in the long run as we returned home without a musky.

By Thanksgiving the lake was mostly frozen over and the boat was in storage. It was time to switch gears and enjoy the winter months to wait and anticipate the next up coming fishing season.

1975 - 1978

These years were much the same as many of the past, making our annual move from Braham, Minnesota each June, after having made many weekend trips expressly for guiding early fishing parties. During most of these spring months the walleye fishing was good for the most part. After having made the moves each June we would settle in for a wonderful summer of fishing and netting opportunities.

In early July of 1975 I had the privilege of guiding a man named Kip Sillers. I am not sure of his hometown, but he was from Illinois, staying at Sah-Kah-Tay Resort. We were fishing muskies on the east side of Cedar Island having many follows, but no direct hits. In the four hour trip we had fourteen different fish follow our baits to the boat only to turn and swim away with little or no interest. Kip and I had lunch together after returning to the dock. Kip asked if I would be upset with him, if he were to return to east Cedar Island on his own, and try for one of those muskies. I assured him there would be no hard feelings and that is what this game was all about. Later that afternoon Kip returned to the "hot spot" as he called it, and landed a nice forty-two inch musky. I was guiding another couple for walleyes on the north Cedar bar when Kip came to find us. He was excited and informed us he had caught the fish and just wanted to thank me for showing him a good spot and how to fish for the musky. It was gratifying to know that he had been successful, but more importantly, the lasting friendship we had made just because of the enjoyment of the sport.

About one week later, a similar incident happened in much the same way. I had guided a man named Lonn Tauer on two unsuccessful musky trips after witnessing many follows by these big fish. Lonn took one of the resort boats out by himself accompanied by his wife, Patricia, and caught a forty-seven inch musky which he had mounted. On that occasion I was guiding three men from Grand Forks, North Dakota on another walleye trip. We were fishing on the north side of Star Island and Lonn had caught his fish on the south side of Cedar Island in an area we call Strawberry Bar. He came looking for me after his catch and had traveled a good ten miles by water trying to locate where we were fishing. As he pulled up with a wide grin on his face, I knew exactly what had happened and shouted to him, "How big is it ?" His response was, "How did you know I caught one ?" After informing him of the telltale sign of the look on his face he said, "I guess that would give it away." It definitely did and he went through the entire sequence of events which led up to his fine catch. We all listened intently as he rambled on and it cost me an extra half hour of time making up for the loss of time we encountered listening to his story unravel. As it turned out, we were thankful for his interruption, because the walleyes went on the bite late in our trip and we managed to finish with fourteen of the golden colored beauties. Had Lonn not detained us, we would have probably moved on and missed the late walleye bite.

I fished with the Hintzsches again that summer and the Beetle Spins worked wonders for us as usual. Ken Hintzsche caught a nice seven and a quarter pound walleye on one of those trips and it made for topping off a great summer of fishing for him.

Myron and Bev Barrie returned to Cass Lake in 1975 and during one four day stretch we fished muskies along with my nephew, Lindsey and Myron's son, Mark. It was a warm stretch of consistently warm weather and the muskies seemed rather lazy
and listless. On the fourth day we were about ready to call it quits when Myron had a hit on his black bucktail spinner. We had been drifting along a weed line break and the musky surfaced behind Myron's bait. We thought it had missed the lure when all of a sudden it turned back and inhaled the bait with a quick thrust. Myron played the big fish around the boat several times and as it grew tired and played out we managed to get it in the net. It was a mountable sized fish measuring forty-eight inches with a huge girth to make it look even larger than it was. Since Myron is a taxidermist, he kept the trophy and took it home to mount it and display it in his recreation room. I think it was one of the first big muskies Lindsey or Mark had been able to witness being caught. That made it a special trip for all of us, just seeing the look on those two boy's faces was something I shall always remember.

Bill Paulson made several trips to Cass Lake again that summer, landing eight muskies and finally getting a fifty inch beauty to mount for his den wall. Bill and his friend, Russ Sutton, and I fished the Eighth Annual Muskies Inc. tourney again that fall, catching three sub-legal sized fish, but having a good time in all the excitement.

As the 1975 season came to a close, we had boated another thirty-six legal sized muskies and released numerous others.

In 1976 there were many early walleye trips which proved successful for the most part, but the summer musky action which followed made a definite impact on my boat's total production. We boated fifty-six legal muskies that summer with several measuring fifty inches or more. We were having more follows that year as well as catching more and larger fish, a fact, I think was due mainly to the recent introduction of "catch and release." Bill Paulson returned with a young man named Mark Packard, and for four days we produced seven muskies all caught and released. The largest of those measured fifty-two inches. At one point six muskies had followed our baits to the boat on eight successive casts. One of those fish, which we estimated at about forty-eight inches followed Mark's jointed Pikie Minnow bait to the boat and grabbed it straight on. Mark didn't have a chance with that one as it just crunched and jawed and thrashed on the water beside the boat, all in the time of about five seconds. Mark was holding on and pulling back, but the big fish never allowed the lure to position itself for a good hook set. It just kept biting and crunching the wooden bait in its teeth and then let the lure go as it turned and made its escape. Mark was wet from head to toe and we had a good laugh over it, but he was feeling bad about not getting to fight it a bit longer. He did finally catch a musky, but he didn't think the forty inch fish he caught was nearly as big as the one that got away.

That fall I had the honor of fishing in the Burger Brothers Musky Tournament held on Lake Andrusia and Cass Lake. Lake Andrusia is located just upriver on the Mississippi chain above Cass Lake and we headquartered out of Fin and Feather Resort. I was excited because along with the Burger Brothers there were the

Lindner brothers, Al and Ron, also Ron Shara, Larry Bolig, Ted Capra, Tom Fudally and many others who were all good musky fishermen. I was paired up with a man named Roger Swanson the first day of the two day tourney and we saw several muskies follow to the boat, but we had no takers. The second day I was paired with Tom Fudally, who was designing proto-types of the famous Fudally Reef Hawg musky lure, at the time. We had gone back into Cass Lake and I was guiding Tom along a drop-off as we both cast models of his proto-types up onto the shallows and retrieved them in short

jerking movements back to the boat. The muskies were active that day and Tom caught two nice forty inch plus fish which we would learn later gave him a second place finish. I don't even recall what his prize was, but I do remember several of the others, including the Lindner brothers, trying to get his proto-type lures out of the boat to give them a good look. Fortunately, Tom had the lures locked in the rod locker and they could not get at them. I say fortunately, for Tom, as he went on to design several musky lures which are still being widely used today by musky fishermen all over the United States. This tourney took place in late August and was enjoyed by all.

About two weeks later, Bill Paulson and I, along with Russ Sutton, fished the Ninth Annual Muskies Inc. tourney on Cass Lake, only to catch two sub-legal muskies. We always had a great time fishing and meeting other musky fishermen at the various banquets and just getting to know many of the others and the different methods used in pursuing the ever elusive musky.

I managed another dozen or so musky trips that fall in what I call the post tourney season, but on Cass Lake the musky fishing seemed to slow down considerably at that time of year. We did boat five muskies during the post tourney season, but they were all smaller sized fish generally in the forty inch class. We did see many larger fish follow lures to the boat, but they seemed to be only curiously looking at our baits before swimming off.

The spring of 1977 started with a terrific walleye season as I was able to guide several parties to many sizeable fish. A group of men from the Little Falls, Minnesota area came to Birch Villa for a short Saturday and Sunday morning walleye adventure. They actually arrived on a Friday evening in early June, but fished only two half-day trips on Saturday and another on Sunday morning. Saturday turned out to be fairly uneventful as we caught many fish of average one and a half to two pound size. I believe we finished that first day with a total thirty-one walleyes for the group of six men. It was a good day as Cliff Riggles, the other guide, and myself were both pleased with the way these men caught on to the walleye tactics we were so used to using. The walleyes were not biting aggressively and these men were learning the easy, patient way of letting the fish have line for a bit and then setting the hook. It was great to see them having fun and I don't think they were at all disappointed with the size. They were more interested in the numbers and that is what they were getting. On Sunday morning we headed out to a place we called "middle bar" about a mile from the dock. I was following Cliff's boat, a good distance behind, and we were catching an occasional walleye, just enough to keep it interesting. As we came near a corner of the drop-off I allowed my boat to slide slightly into deeper water from a depth of twelve feet to about twenty feet of water.

On the turn, my three clients set their hooks on fish simultaneously! Little did we know or realize at the time these were all large walleyes. When I saw the first fish come near the surface I said, "Wow, a seven pounder!" Then as I glanced to the other side of the boat I exclaimed, "Two more!" Fortunately the first fish was netted quickly and came out of the net with ease. It allowed me to rush to the opposite side and with one swoop, net the other two! I believe I was more excited than the three fishermen who caught the fish. We caused quite a stir for the boats around us as we weighed each fish individually. The largest of the three was an eight pound four ounce beauty and the other two came in a close second, each weighing seven and a half pounds. It made for a beautiful stringer as we finished out that trip with three limits of walleyes for the customers. Cliff's boat wasn't as fortunate with size, but they did manage their three limits also. These men had eaten some of the previous day's catch the evening before and now they were able to fill their limits to take home. Cliff and I each got our share of fish to eat from that catch, something which was a rare occurrence for us most of the time. The men went home happy and did return a couple weeks later only to find the walleye bite had lessened considerably compared to their first time out. The second trip allowed them only partial limits as we really had to work hard for a few fish.

July came and with it the musky rush made a swing into full motion. I recorded thirty-one musky trips during that month alone. During that span of time we boated forty-two muskies and released all but one. It was a fifty-two inch fish that weighed thirty-seven pounds. Warren Hedlun was the lucky fisherman in that instance and since it was his first musky, he had the trophy fish mounted. Warren was from Peoria, Illinois and had never fished for muskies before, but he became a believer in the sport and returned many times to try for other muskies. He was hooked and told me a few years later that he had given up his bass fishing to concentrate more on muskies. He said he still fished for bass on occasion, but muskies had taken over his priorities.

Bill Paulson returned to Cass Lake again and my record shows he boated another eight muskies in 1977. I do believe Bill was the most blessed musky fisherman I have ever fished with as he always seemed to catch the big ones every time he came to the lake. We fished the Tenth Annual International Muskies Inc. tourney together again that fall and Russ Sutton joined us. Bill did manage a forty-two inch legal musky in that tourney, but did not make the prize list. I only made three post-tourney season musky trips that fall as the Junior High football and Cross Country coaching seemed to take up much of my time at the school. There were football games to scout for the varsity coaches on Friday nights and then the Saturday Cross Country meets to attend which didn't allow too many weekends on the water. No muskies were caught during the post-tourney season and the boat was put into storage for the winter before I wanted it to be.

The spring of 1978 brought the same early trips and move to Cass Lake as in previous years. Spring walleye fishing was a little tougher this year for some reason, we couldn't find a logical theory to explain the up and down, hot or cold habits of the walleye. One day a person might have a good catch and the next would prove to be almost fishless. Some mornings were better than the afternoons, but then some afternoons would produce better walleye fishing than the mornings. Just when a person thought he had found a consistent pattern, it would change and you would have to go searching again in hopes of finding the right combination. It was a rather frustrating early summer as we worked through the good walleye season with limited results, finding no consistency in the habits of the fish. It wasn't until mid-summer when we finally began to catch walleyes with regularity. Of course we went through the minnow and night crawler stage with very little success, but when the transition time from live bait to artificial occurred, the trusty old Beetle Spin came through. I don't know what it is about the Beetle Spin that makes it so productive, but I do have a couple theories in mind which might be a logical explanation if nothing else. I feel that the rubber split- tailed body of the lure resembles a mayfly larvae, and since they hatch in the water, it provides plenty of easily accessible food for the fish. The other idea is the fact that the spinner blade acts as an attracter and simply entices strikes by feeding walleyes. The flash of the spinner probably looks like a shiny side of a minnow to the fish, and of course, the minnow being the main diet of many fish makes it more realistic to them. Many times during and after a large mayfly hatch I have observed how fat and full the stomachs of walleyes were. It seems as though they were as tight as a drum and almost ready to burst, but after being caught, they usually regurgitate a yellowish, slimy substance from their stomachs. It is my opinion that the fish feed on these insect larvae at such a gluttonous rate, they stuff themselves beyond normality and when brought into the boat, throw up the excess which cannot be readily digested. Again, this is strictly my opinion, but I truly believe the Beetle Spin does resemble a nice, big, fat, juicy mayfly larvae just waiting to be devoured. We had stumbled on a simple but great bait and weren't going to argue with the success it brought us.

My cousin, Tom Horn, and his wife, from Tulsa, Oklahoma, came to Cass Lake that summer again and during their stay we caught many walleyes on the ever popular Beetle Spin. Once again we found ourselves on "middle bar" during a mid-afternoon walleye excursion. The sky was clear with bright sun and the wind was blowing from the south at about fifteen miles per hour. We trolled over the top of the sand bar at a depth of four to ten feet catching average sized walleyes that seemed to be on a feeding frenzy. In two hours we had boated thirty fish and returned to the dock with our limits. My cousin and his wife were impressed with the catch and couldn't understand why the walleyes were so aggressive toward the small, but productive Beetle Spin. Again, it was one of those memories that will linger in our minds forever.

Cousin Bob Moore, his wife, Karen, their two boys, Scott and Brian came to Cass Lake again for a week of rest and relaxation. Bob, his boys and I fished for walleyes mostly, but on a few occasions, went musky fishing. Bob caught a nice five pound walleye one evening on a Beetle Spin. Pictures were taken, the story of its catch was told many times, the fish was cleaned, put in the freezer and when it came time to leave the fish was gone. We believe someone took the fish, not by mistake, but on purpose, because it had been marked with Bob's name, address, and fishing license number on the white freezer paper it was wrapped in. We did suspect a young gentleman who was staying at the resort, but he had left a day earlier and we had no way of proving our suspicions. Bob remarked, "If he needs the fish that bad, let him have it." There wasn't anything we could do about it and after all, it was just one fish, so Bob went home with one walleye shy of his limit. During that week Bob became known as "the most rested fisherman," because he liked to lie down in the boat while we were fishing. He would put his line out and hang on to his fishing rod while lying either on the boat seat or on the floor of the boat. When the musky fishing was slow, he had been known to even tie a pop can or an old shoe to the end of his line. He didn't have a kitchen sink, so I guess these items were his next choice. On one occasion, while dragging an empty pop can along side the boat, a musky swam up to take a look at this weird bait. Everyone in the boat saw the fish and Bob got pretty excited, wondering if he should maybe put some treble hooks on the can, just in case a musky decided to take a bite on it! During the week Bob and his family were at the resort, two teacher friends of mine from Braham arrived with their families. Terry Bodeen was a science teacher and coach, and his wife, Mary Kay, taught in the elementary school in Braham. Ron Grundyson, a physical education teacher, and his wife had come for a little rest and relaxation. The two men would fish while the women were content to enjoy the beautiful beach with my wife and children. Cousin Bob joined Terry and Ron as we made a few fishing trips together, mainly for walleye. One day, while fishing a place called the "Pagoda Bar," we happened to get into a nice school of walleyes and caught fourteen before the bite was over. The size of the fish weren't large, but we had managed to catch a good number of fish at a time when walleye fishing was tough. There was one outstanding fish that Ron had caught, it was a three inch walleye that could hardly get its mouth over the small hook on the worm harness rig he was using. We took his picture with it before he had a chance to release it and we didn't let him hear the end of that story for a long time.

The musky action was in full swing by mid-July and I was fishing with a friend from Braham, Minnesota. His name was Gene Okerlund, and he was a loan officer in the local bank in Braham. We were fishing muskies in an area called the "kettle," and Gene caught two walleyes, a four and a seven pounder on a large Cisco Kid musky lure. It was an eventful trip only because we were fishing for muskies and didn't even see one of the big fish follow a lure to the boat.

A week later I was guiding a party from Waseca, Minnesota, they were the Katz family. Chuck and Rea Katz were the parents of young Bill Katz and we fished the area on Cass Lake known as Allen's Bay. Bill caught a small musky that day on a bass lure called a Heddon Vamp. The musky took the bait on the surface as it hit the water after a well placed cast. Bill played the fish like a pro and I netted the forty inch, twenty pound musky on its first pass by the boat. It was Bill's first musky and the first time he had been fishing for them. He was excited and I think his parents were even more pleased with his ability to play the fish as if he had done it many times before. Later that year I was told that Bill had been in a terrible auto accident near his home town and almost lost his life. It was a rather sad time, but I was encouraged to know he had survived and I was even more relieved when he returned to Cass Lake the next year to fish muskies with me again.

I was again fortunate to fish with the Hintzsche family again that summer as the Beetle Spins continued to produce many walleyes. Myron and Bev Barrie returned for their annual trip to Cass Lake as did many others including Bill Paulson, on his musky trips, mainly during frequent weekend visits. Bill and I fished the Eleventh

Annual Muskies Inc. tourney again that fall, along with Myron and Mark Barrie from Waseca. I was fortunate enough to land two, forty-two inch muskies in the tournament that year and had earned a fourth place finish, worth three hundred fifty dollars in prizes. It had become a total release tournament and witnesses from another boat were required to see the live release of each musky as it was put back into the water, before signing a contestant release form. Bill Paulson and Myron Barrie had each caught sub-legal sized muskies during the two and a half day ordeal, but their fish were short of the minimum size required to register a fish. The state's minimum size limit was thirty inches for muskies, and the Muskies Inc. organization had made it their minimum size limit for the tourney as well. We all felt it was a good sportsmen like rule and I feel it definitely helped the musky fishery for the future.

We finished the season with another twelve, post-tourney musky trips, catching eight more legal sized muskies before the boat had to be stored again for the winter. As it turned out, we boated a total forty-seven legal sized muskies that summer and several others which fell short of the minimum size limit by state law. I considered it a very successful year and found the result of catch and release to be more and more gratifying with the release of every musky, as time went on. It doesn't seem to matter what size the released musky might be, it just makes one feel great to watch those fish swim away, under their own power, to live to fight another day.

As I write about these different adventures of fishing, I am reminded, too, of the fact that each year brings us back together with the many friends who return to the resort. John and Judy Seville, Don and Jody Inman and family, Les Tideman and family, the Steve Stetz family, Bruce and Karen Melin and their four boys, Bill and Jane Donahue and family, and many more who have become very good friends over the years. They all return each year to make it feel like a big family reunion. Those memories have been and are embedded in our hearts for life, and we cherish every little bit of time we can spend with them. Looking back over the past forty some years, those are lasting relationships we will never lose track of, as long as we live.

Ron Lykins and Merv with their limits of opening day walleyes.

Ron Grundyson holding his 3" walleye. Terry Bodeen is in the background.

Gene Okerlund with a 7# walleye caught on a musky lure.

1979 - 1982

I would call this chapter, 'the Hayward years' as will be explained and described. It became a time of great transition in the lives of our family, as we made a choice to move from the teaching position in Braham, Minnesota and the summer fishing guide service that took us to Cass Lake every year. During the winter months of 1978-79 we had decided to purchase a bait and tackle store in the town of Hayward, Wisconsin, made an offer through the help of a real estate broker, which was accepted, and had become the proud new owners of our of our own business. The name of our store was the 'Hook and Line Sport Shop,' mainly a bait and tackle business.

The Department of Education for the state of Minnesota had established a new leave of absence for teachers. The leave would be handled on an annual basis, whereas the teacher involved could take advantage of it for up to five years; therefore, it became known as the "five year leave of absence." It allowed teachers to take a leave from their respective positions in order to refresh themselves educationally or by choosing some other career opportunity. There were some stipulations involved which required a teacher to have taught in the same district for eleven years. Other requirements included, letting the school district know of intentions to return or not to return each year during the month of February. It also allowed a teacher the privilege of remaining at the same level of status on the salary schedule without losing seniority during the time of leave. A request to obtain the leave had to be submitted to the education department of the state and accepted by them, before being considered by the local board of education. I applied for the leave and it was granted by both departments, which cleared the way for our upcoming move to Wisconsin. In order to obtain a small business loan here were many pages of papers to be filled out and sent to the SBA, which is the Small Business Administration, who acted on and approved our loan application. Everything was falling into place, and now all that was left, was to sell our home in Braham. My friend, Gene Okerlund, helped with the SBA papers and the sale of our home for which I am ever grateful. We also had a mobile home at Cass Lake to sell, and Rich Becker, the owner of Sah-Kah-Tay Resort purchased it to use as an added rental unit for the resort. During the spring months of 1979 we made numerous two hour trips to Hayward, from the opening fishing season in early May, until school was out the first of June. Those weekend trips were made to operate our new business, then we would return to Braham to teach, each following week. Finally the time had come to move into the fairly new house we had purchased in Hayward, close to a lake in its city limits by the same name. It took most of the summer for us to settle in, but neighbors and friends were very helpful in making our acquaintance and showing us the locale. There weren't a lot of fishing trips that summer because of the business and our attempt at keeping overhead costs to a minimum. I opened the store every morning at six o'clock and would close up shop at ten o'clock every evening. It was a different pace than I was used to, not because of the hours, they were about the same as when I had been guiding, but more for the reason of having more people in my life continually. I had fished with a lot of people over the years, but only at the rate of a few a day. Now I was seeing more like one hundred to two hundred people in an average day. I loved it, because I love meeting and talking with people, especially about fishing or hunting and carrying on conversations about new and different trends and methods. My wife Jan spent most of her time being a fulltime mom to our children and bringing noon lunches and dinner meals to me at the shop, as well as helping out in the shop and tending the bookkeeping end of the business. Chad and Cristi, our children, were in fifth and sixth grade when we moved to Hayward, but they caught on to the in- store salesmanship quickly and with ease. They were comfortable around people and enjoyed the chance to get to work at the shop to earn a little spending money. They have told me many times about what a great gift it was to learn to count money back to the customer in change. We did not have a new style computerized cash machine that tells you the amount of change, so the kids had to learn to count the change back for the customer. My daughter, Cristi, worked several jobs during college, and most of her employers commented to her, how they appreciated seeing her ability to make change for the customers. Chad also worked a convenience store job during his years in high school, and his employer commented to him about how good it was to see a young person like him counting back change for the customers. It was good for me to have Cristi and Chad in the shop because it allowed us the opportunity to have quality time together, something we didn't get much of when I was guiding. I did hire one man named Harold Dunn, who was retired, and he worked part time for us when we needed to be away or when business was more than usually heavy. Harold was a fun person to have around as he kept abreast of most of the fishing activity in the local area. If you ever wanted to know where the fish were biting, just ask Harold, and you usually got a straight answer.

As I stated earlier, there wasn't much time for fishing, but I did manage to fish eight different lakes near Hayward on eight different occasions that summer. Fortunately my success was overwhelming, because in those eight trips we caught an even dozen muskies. I say we, because I hardly ever fish alone, there is usually always someone who is willing to spend a few hours on the water if you only ask. Most of the time it was a customer friend or a possible relative who had come to see our new place of residence and the sport shop. One time in August, cousin Bob Moore and his family came to visit us and I just had to take him musky fishing. We took my boat and Harold Dunn accompanied us to the Chippewa Flowage on one particular evening. We had fished about three hours without any action and it was getting late as we drifted near a beach area of a resort. Harold said, "I think we might as well pack it in and head for home." My reply was, "Let's try along the shore here by the resort, because there are some good looking weeds down there." Harold kind of grumped a little as he murmured, "I've never caught a fish by a resort, there's too much activity around, drives the fish away." Jokingly, Bob chimed in, "Well, Harold, I catch most of my fish around the resorts, cause that's where nobody else wants to fish, thinking the fish are driven away by the noisy swimmers." Bob went on chiding Harold, "Heck, back in Minnesota, we go looking for resorts just so we can fish in front of them." With that Bob had a hit and set the hooks into a nice musky, directly in front of the main lodge of the resort. As he fought the fish around the boat, Harold kept repeating, "Well, I'll be darned! Well,

I'll be darned! Would you look at that!" It turned out to be a nice forty-three inch musky and was Bob's first ever musky. He said, "Looky there, I had to come all the way to Wisconsin to get my first musky." At that point Harold realized Bob had been teasing him about fishing near resorts and let out a throng of words not worth repeating. Bob and I just laughed and Harold looked at me and said, "You just let me go on believing him didn't you ?" I tried to hedge his question by changing the subject, but he insisted on an answer. So I said, "Harold, this is between you and Bob, all I'm doing is guiding." To that he replied, "You're no help at all." And he went back to casting. Bob and Harold hit it off pretty well and we had a lot of fun that evening, despite the constant kidding back and forth from one another.

That fall, Ron Lykins, a fellow teacher friend, Myron Barrie, his son, Mark and I fished the Twelfth Annual Muskies Inc. Tournament on Cass Lake again. We did catch two muskies just under the legal size limit, but not big enough to be entered in the contest. We had not fished Cass Lake that summer, so it was a bit different coming back to a lake that I had known so well and fished many years. The fact of knowing where to fish was not the problem as much as just getting re-acquainted with the locations and trying to locate some fish. It took some time to establish what areas to fish and just what kind of structure the fish were holding to at that time.

Later in the fall, Myron, his son Mark and I fished the Second Annual Hayward Lakes Muskies Inc. tourney with a bit more success than back in Minnesota. We spent the two and a half days on a lake known as Lac Court Oreilles, pronounced differently than it looks, 'La Coot O-ray' would be a close pronunciation as far as I can tell. The lake is located just to the south of the city of Hayward, off highway twenty-seven. It is a clear water lake, very similar to Cass Lake, but with less structure. I was fortunate enough to catch a forty-six inch musky the first day, and followed that with a thirty-one inch fish during the morning hours of the last day. I received a fourth place trophy, a fifty dollar cash prize and a St. Croix musky rod for my entries. I was also given the sportsmanship trophy for releasing the largest fish in the tournament. Since I had enough musky rods and reels, I gave the rod to Myron's son, Mark, and I understand he is still using it today. We had a great time and the weather co-operated fully. I ended that season with two more Lac Court Oreilles muskies, thirty-nine and thirty- four inches respectively. We ended the season with a total production of seventeen muskies, not bad for a newcomer to the area, not knowing any of the lakes very well.

The winter came and little did I realize the store suffered greatly, mainly because there was a lack of tourists at that time of year, or at least business was not as prosperous as it had been in the summer. Since hockey was a big sport in the Hayward area, I took on a line of equipment and did a fair amount of business for that sport during the winter months. With the equipment, I offered a skate sharpening service which kept me pretty busy through most of the season. My wife, Jan, was hired by the Hayward High School to teach girl's physical education, a job that lasted the three school years we were in Hayward.

The 1980 fishing season came to Wisconsin the first weekend in May, just one week prior to the Minnesota opener. Al and Ron Lindner stopped in my shop to buy bait on the Friday evening prior to opening fishing season on Saturday. They were a great team and seemed to be having fun preparing to fish on Grindstone Lake which is a clear water lake connected to Lac Court Oreilles. They did have differences of opinion as to what kind of minnows and what size to use, but beyond that it seemed they agreed on most everything used in their fishing methods and techniques. As I was told, the Lindners had grown up at their uncle and aunt's resort on Grindstone Lake and had fished the lake for many years. It was a neat experience getting to visit with them and talking about the lake and its structure, plus some of the methods they used in their fishing experiences.

Our bait shop prospered that summer as the tourist industry continued on a less even keel compared to the past few years. I make a point of this as reference to the price of fuel and supposed lack of it. Automobile gas prices in the Hayward area, had gone from about a dollar per gallon to a dollar and fifty cents. This seemed to happen over night and had a direct effect on the tourism at the time. It was a fact that fewer people were traveling because of this scare, and it showed, as some of the other businesses suffered financial losses more than usual. There were still a lot of people visiting the area, and it is said that the Hayward area doubled in population during the summer months. Many of these people had summer homes or property which they used, and the price of fuel didn't seem to deter their summer vacations.

I was able to fish once a week, as my wife would take my place every Wednesday evening so I could get away to enjoy some of the surrounding area lakes. My children usually accompanied me, along with some other customer or friend, which was always a joy for me. We caught eight muskies that summer, prior to the fall musky tourneys. During the Thirteenth Annual International Muskies Inc. tourney in Minnesota, Myron Barrie and I fished Cass Lake again. Myron caught a thirty-three inch musky during the three day event, but there were no prizes for him, because there were many other fish registered, and his name was not drawn for a prize.

Myron and my nephew, Lindsey Heitschmidt, came to Hayward in October to join me in fishing the Third Annual Hayward Lakes Muskies Inc. tourney. As it turned out, I only fished the second day with them, due to business at the shop which needed my attention. They saw a few nice fish on Lac Court Oreilles the first day, but there were no takers, so they came in empty handed. The second day was a rainy one, and even though the conditions were cold and windy, I did manage to boat a thirty-seven inch musky which earned a gift certificate worth fifty dollars at a local gift shop. I believe my wife got the benefit of that prize, but she deserved it for taking care of the sport shop in my absence. There were no post-tourney fishing trips that fall, and the boat was put in storage for the winter. We ended the season with fourteen total muskies.

At the time we had hired another retired fellow who worked part time for us in the shop, his name was Paul Seaback, and what a joy it was to have him around. He was a slim, gray haired man with a very big heart, and would do about anything for us if we asked. One day late in October, it was my wife's birthday, and she was teaching in the Stone Lake school during the morning hours. At lunch time, as she was on her way back to the Hayward High School, she would stop by the shop to have lunch with me each day. On this particular day, Paul was in the shop, and I had called the local radio station to request a birthday greeting and song by Ann Murray, 'May I Have This Dance,' to be broadcast at twelve o'clock noon. Jan arrived about five minutes before noon, and as we sat down to eat, the request came on the radio. Jan's mouth opened, and for once she was speechless. I took her hand and we danced to the song, as Paul watched, he had tears running down his cheeks and he said, "I've never seen anything so touching." I think we all had tears in our eyes, but to see the big hearted softness coming from Paul made that time all the more special. I think Paul told about that occasion to everyone who came in the shop for the next two weeks. He was a special man and we'll never forget him and the many memories he left in our minds.

A sad day came in November that year as our other employee, Harold Dunn was planning for his annual 'wild game dinner' which he hosted at his home, along with the help of his wife, Ollie. We had been invited, and the dinner was to take place that evening, but Harold was doing a few last minute errands for the occasion. He came into the shop to obtain some pictures of wild game animals off a calendar I had, which he would place on the table next to each platter of wild game he was serving. As he left, he told me he had to go home and cut down a birch tree behind his garage that needed to be removed. Then he would position each picture by its respective platter, and he would be ready for the dinner. About two hours later, Ollie called me with a voice that sounded desperate and really shaken. She told me Harold had been cutting down the birch tree behind the garage, which was about ten inches in diameter, and it had glanced off the corner of the garage roof, and fallen on him. She had called the ambulance and when they arrived, he had been pronounced dead at the scene. I was stunned and couldn't believe what she had told me, I didn't want to believe it. I asked if there was anything I could do, and she said she needed help to clean up the fallen tree and put the chainsaw away. I went to her house and she told me to go behind the garage and do what I could, she just couldn't bear going back there again. The chainsaw was sitting on the ground, away from the butt of the tree, and from the tracks in the snow, it looked like Harold had done everything right. It appeared he had made the undercut on the side to the direction he wanted the tree to fall, he had made the cut through the tree on the opposite side and had stepped away from the stump to position himself clear of the falling tree. The one thing he hadn't planned on was, the tree had fallen a little to one side and caught the corner of the garage, making it bounce up and rebound to where he was standing. The misdirected, falling tree knocked him down and had landed directly on his head. It was a difficult task, as I used his chainsaw to cut the tree into smaller two foot logs. There was blood on the white bark of the birch tree, and with every cut, I couldn't help but see the red stains, knowing full well I would never see Harold's smiling face enter the doors of my shop again. Ollie asked if I would remove the logs, and I did, but while carrying them from behind the garage to my car, I found Harold's glasses in the snow where they had been knocked from his head. It wasn't an ordeal I wish to experience again, but we shall always remember Harold's cheerful attitude and keep his memory with us for as long as we live. A few days later we attended Harold's funeral, and I had the honor of being one of the pallbearers. Ollie gave me Harold's musky rod and tackle box, and I still keep them as a reminder of a terrific gentleman.

The rest of the winter was cold and long, but with the changing season we did experience growth in our shop's sales, and business as a whole, was a big improvement over the past year.

The 1981 season opened with a better outlook as the tourism seemed to be making a rebound for the surrounding area. Our shop was doing well and we had taken on another line of clothing, to add to our inventory. Cristi and Chad were becoming more and more of a big help in our daily business matters, so we were basically a family owned and operated concern. The weekly fishing trips continued and things were going well. We had our usual visits from friends and relatives, so we were able to enjoy the city and surrounding area more as time went on. My cousin, Tom Horn, and his family from Tulsa, stayed with us for a week and we did some fishing, eating out, and sightseeing around Hayward. Cousin Bob Moore, his wife, Karen, their two boys, Scott and Brian visited us also, and one day our families took three canoes down the Namakogan River, starting in Hayward and continuing downstream about seven miles. It was a neat adventure as we saw lots of wildlife and had a picnic lunch along the way. Our friends, Ron and Mary Lykins came to visit us in Hayward also, and we a good time with them, keeping up on news from back home. We enjoyed eating out with them as Ron and I would make pigs of ourselves at some of the local 'all you can eat buffets,' especially with crab legs on the menu.

The summer seemed to go faster than normal and before we knew it, school was drawing near, which meant I would lose my good help, in Jan, Cristi and Chad. It had been a good summer and with all the fishing, including the two musky tournaments in Minnesota and Hayward, we had netted and boated another dozen legal sized muskies.

A school administrator had stopped in my shop several times, begging me to come to his school to teach English for the winter months, so I took the job, in a small village called New Post. It was a reservation school and I taught English in a classroom with seventh and eighth graders. It was an opportunity to help with living expenses, and since the winter months were slow for business, I decided to take advantage of the situation. New Post was located a good distance south and east of Hayward, on the banks of the famous Chippewa Flowage. The village had been moved some years before, because of a dam and flooding to a low area where the previous village of Post had been. The area where the site of the old village was located became the Chippewa Flowage. So when the village was moved they decided to call it New Post. During the months of teaching there I realized how much I had missed the students back in Braham. One evening during dinner, I casually mentioned to my family how I had come to realize I actually missed the students and teaching profession. At the time, my children were involved in 4-H, and my wife and I were helping with some club leadership duties. That along with the teaching I was doing at New Post had an affect on my attitude to go back to teaching full time. My wife asked, "What are you saying ? Do you want to go back to Braham ?" I remarked, "Let's just think about it, we'll talk later, after we've had time to process some ideas." She agreed, and that started the wheels turning with ideas about house, business, moving and what it would mean for our family. Later, came sooner than we had anticipated, and since I was to notify the school district back in Braham of my intentions for the following year, I wrote a letter stating I would like to return to my original teaching position. The response was gratifying as the Braham district welcomed me back for the school year beginning the fall of 1982. Our intentions were to keep the shop in Hayward, and operate it as strictly a summer business, then return to Braham for the school year. These plans were being made, but we still had to finish out the present school year and operate the bait shop through the summer of 1982. With that we also had to look for a home in the Braham area and sell our house in Hayward. The process began to take form and needless to say it was a fast winter which seemed to blend in with a busy summer in 1982.

My nephew, Lindsey, came to live with us in Hayward, for the summer, and work for us at the shop. He was a great help to us, as he knew the fishing industry quite well, and kept abreast of things going on in the area too. Lindsey was a Sophomore in college, back in Minnesota, so I could trust him with the shop, and feel comfortable with him running it, if I had to be gone from time to time. We practiced archery every morning behind the shop, and continued the Wednesday evening fishing trips throughout the summer. Our family accompanied by Lindsey, even took a two-day trip to Milwaukee, Wisconsin one time to see the Brewers play the Minnesota Twins. It was good for us to get away, and Paul Seaback took care of the shop for us. When late summer arrived, my wife, Jan, and I made a few trips to Braham in search of a home, as we had to move by the end of August. With the help of our old friend, Gene Okerlund, who still worked in the bank in Braham, we were able to find a nice home just outside of town about five miles to the south. An offer was made and accepted, and we had a place to move to before school started. We had a small auction before the move, which my brother Larry and his wife, Juanita plus my mom and dad helped with tremendously. The move came in late August, and nephew Lindsey, whose school didn't start until late September, lived in our house in Hayward and ran the shop during the week. I would join him on weekends until he had to go back to school, and then we closed the store for the winter months and continued to live and teach in Braham. Our home in Hayward sold shortly after that, and we were relieved, not to be having to make two house payments each month. A friend from Hayward wanted to buy the business from us as an opportunity for he and his wife. At first we were reluctant to even think about it, but as time went on and we saw the need to be near Braham more, we sold the bait shop to him. So now we were permanent residents of Minnesota again, and had separated ourselves from all ties to Hayward, except for friends we had established while living there for a little over three years. Who, by the way, after twenty some years, we still keep in contact with.

After all was said and done that summer, I had only fished a few times, because of all the time consuming events with the move, but we had caught a total nine legal sized muskies and several smaller ones which went quickly back to their mothers.

The experience of owning my own business was a good adventure in life, but I found out that teaching was my first love as far as occupations are concerned. Having students in my classroom, and seeing them accomplish goals in their lives, seems far more rewarding to me personally, than having to wipe the dust off a bunch of lures hanging on the wall in a sport shop. That isn't a very good comparison, I know, but it is a way for me to say, "I missed the kids!"

Al Linder, Merv and Chad posing for a picture in front of the "Hook & Line Sport Shop" in Hayward, Wis.

1983 - 1993

During this era my family and I were getting re-established in Minnesota and trying to develop at least one eventful trip during the summer each year. In August of 1983 our family made a two week trip to Ontario, Canada, where we vacationed at a well known lake called Eagle Lake. We were accompanied by our cousins from Kansas, Bob and Karen Moore, their boys, Scott and Brian plus Myron and Bev Barrie, our friends from Waseca, Minnesota. It was a great trip and there were many walleyes caught as well as a couple nice muskies. It was a long trip for our cousins and we decided to try some Minnesota fishing again the next summer, in order to reduce their driving time and allow for more visiting and fishing. With that in mind we made reservations for a cabin at Cass Lake Lodge for the following summer. Birch Villa Resort and Sah-Kah-Tay Resort were both filled during the time we wanted to vacation, so the next closest place was Cass Lake Lodge. My boat made twenty-one musky trips in 1983 and we recorded eleven legal muskies plus several releases, so the summer was rather uneventful as far as fish stories are concerned.

1984 brought new hope as the spring walleye season proved successful. Ron Lykins, a friend, joined me on an opening weekend walleye outing and together we caught limits of fish and practiced "catch and release" a lot. Ron landed a six pound walleye near the mouth of the Mississippi River which turned out to be our largest of the weekend. The walleye action held up and continued through May and right into mid-June with many limits being caught.

During the first week of August our family along with the Moore cousins from Kansas and the Barries from Waseca, Minnesota, made our week long stay at Cass Lake Lodge. We were joined by my nephew, Lindsey Heitschmidt, and he brought with him a lure, new to us, which turned out to be a great fish catching tool. The lure was a number seven, crawdad colored Rapala, Shad Rap. It was fairly new on the local market and Lindsey was the only one to have possession of one. We had all heard of Rapala before, but the Shad Rap was a newer model that dives when retrieved or trolled. Most of us were using the old stand-by "Beetle Spin" as we fished for late summer walleyes. Since we trolled the Beetle Spins fairly fast, Lindsey was a bit reluctant to tie on his Shad Rap. I told him I would slow the boat a little if he wanted to try this new lure, so he agreed, and we tried his Shad Rap, along with the Beetle Spins, which weren't producing very many walleyes. Lindsey would let out a short amount of line as the Shad Rap dove to a depth of about ten or twelve feet, until he felt the lure bump bottom, then he gave it a crank or two up and would wait for the bite. It didn't take long before he had the first walleye, a nice two pounder, and then another, and another. Within a few minutes Lindsey had four walleyes and he had the rest of us at his mercy, wishing we had one of these Shad Raps too. By the time we made our way back to the resort, Lindsey had convinced us all that we had better invest in one of these lures. We found no Shad Raps in the town of Cass Lake, so it was off to Walker, Minnesota, some twenty miles away, where we found them at Reeds Sporting Goods store. I believe everyone bought at least two or three of the lures and now we were set to show the world what great fishermen we were. That evening, the walleye fishing did turn out to be better than normal, as we came in with a total seventeen walleyes, plus a few nice jumbo perch. The rest of the week proved successful as well and the walleyes continued to take to the Shad Raps. Cousin Bob was sold on the lure and vowed to take his back to Kansas where he intended to clean up on the bass in some of his local farm ponds. Personally, I felt it was another of those many phases I had witnessed and experienced throughout my guiding career. I remembered having lived through the "June Bug Spinner" and "Strip- On Spinner" eras, as well as the Lazy Ike, Brooks Reefer, Flatfish, Shyster, and original Rapala eras. They all lasted for maybe a few summers until something new and different came along, but eventually were phased out, only to be left lying in many tackle boxes. Oh, they would be recalled to service a few times, but usually without much success. I didn't know how wrong I could be, because the Shad Rap is still going strong in Cass Lake, as it is I'm sure in many other lakes as well, all across this great country. Here we are, twenty years later, and the Shad Rap is still going strong! The Beetle Spin is the alternative to that situation as well, since it has been catching fish for many years, but I believe the Shad Rap has been more consistently successful in its lifetime. I would be remiss if I didn't pause here and say, "Thank You, Lindsey!" If it hadn't been for my nephew in the boat that day back in August of 1984, who knows how long it would have been before I was introduced to the infamous Shad Rap.

The fall of 1984 came and we had caught a total fourteen legal muskies in my boat that summer, none of which measured over forty-five inches, but we had released them all, along with several sub-legal sized fish.

The teaching continued during the winters and our families, the Heitschmidts, Moores and Barries continued to vacation at Cass Lake each summer during July or August. Most of those summers produced many walleyes and muskies, and more often than not, we usually came in with a large fish in the boat. Myron Barrie caught a

forty-eight inch musky trolling one time and I think the story is worth telling. Cousin Bob Moore was along and I was guiding. We were tired from casting all morning, so Cousin Bob suggested that we troll for awhile. Myron and I agreed and we were going to troll a long bar that stretched out over a mile. We asked Bob which side of the boat he wanted and he replied, "I want the side where the fish are!" Eventually he decided to put his line out the right side, which was also the deeper side of the drop-off we would be trolling parallel with. Myron put his line on the left and shallower side, so naturally I put my line out directly behind the boat. As we trolled along, Bob would occasionally ask if we ever caught a musky trolling. Myron assured him that it had been done on numerous occasions, but then after trolling a few yards, Bob would again ask, "Do you ever catch a musky trolling ?" After about the fifth or sixth repeat of the same question, Myron reared back and set the hooks on a hard hit. It was a nice musky, and a fierce fighter, but no match for Myron's expertise at catching these toothy critters for over twenty years. Needless to say, we never heard Bob's question again for quite some time, but even today, almost twenty years later, especially when we are trolling, he will chip in with, "Do you ever catch muskies trolling ?" We just chuckle and think back on the time when that question first became a reality for Cousin Bob. Bob tried to accuse us of setting him up when Myron caught the musky, but we reminded him that he had first choice of sides, and also that you don't stage musky catches very often.

Cousin Bob did manage to catch a few muskies, but we are still looking for that trophy fish, for him. At this point I believe his largest musky is forty-two and a half inches. That fish came in 1987 which was a great musky season for my boat, not to mention its occupants. About a week after Bob and his family went home, Myron and a friend of his, Al Sack, from Waseca, Minnesota joined me on a special musky fishing trip into Ontario, Canada. We spent five days on a chain of lakes known as the Indian Chain. The muskies were not large, but they were numerous, and most of them measured in the mid-thirty inch range. I believe the three of us caught and released thirty-nine muskies total in three days of fishing. Many of those fish were caught on the figure eight method after following the lure right to the boat. On one occasion I was kneeling on the floor of the boat with my six and a half foot musky rod entirely under water, doing the figure eight with the lure nearly at the end of the rod. The fish followed the figure eight about nine or ten times around and finally grabbed the bait. That was a tough battle as the fish was wild on a short line, but we managed to land it. The musky was a thirty-nine inch fish and gave me all I wanted in that situation. My total in that three day stretch was seventeen muskies with the thirty-nine incher being the largest. Myron came in with thirteen total fish and Al got the balance of our catch of thirty-nine muskies. All in all that year, my boat produced seventy-two muskies, and all but one were released. That one took the lure too deep into its throat, tore its gills in the fight to get free, and bled to death.

Myron, myself and our wives made that same trip to Canada a year later. We had about the same result as the previous year, but caught more walleyes and some larger muskies as well. On this particular trip, Myron and I boated thirty-two muskies in four days and each of us caught sixteen fish. One day we had a nice sized musky follow our lures to the boat about five or six times and we kept changing lures and going back to that spot. Time after time it followed, but would not hit, finally the big fish had probably seen enough and struck my lure. It hit close to the boat, and given its size, gave quite a fight. Myron netted the musky and before releasing it, we measured it at forty-six and a half inches. It was a fat fish and we estimated her weight at about twenty-eight or twenty-nine pounds. We decided this chain of lakes is an ideal spot to take a new or young musky fisherperson, as it would allow for some valuable practice and experience of musky fishing.

That fall we ended with sixty-seven legal sized muskies in my boat and several smaller fish we didn't bother to measure, so 1988 was not a bad year either.

1989 through 1992 we continued to vacation at Birch Villa Resort on Cass Lake, and after our week with Cousin Bob, Karen, Myron and Bev; Jan and I would stay another week with friends, Jim and Dorothy Ronning from Braham. The Shad Raps were still hot lures and the Ronnings loved to troll for walleyes in the evening. What's more, they also loved to eat fresh caught walleye, and we enjoyed many fish frys with them at the lake.

Those four years seemed to go fast and during that span of time we landed ninety-six legal muskies in my boat and released every fish alive to swim and fight another day. We had also boated and released forty-two sub-legal sized muskies.

Early in June, 1993, we made a forty day trip to Alaska, in a motor home! My brother Larry, his wife, Juanita, mom, dad, my wife, Jan and I, all traveled from Minnesota to the state of Washington first, to visit our daughter, Cristi, and her husband, Joel. From Washington we ventured north into Canada, through British Columbia, and on up the Alaskan Highway. The journey to Washington had taken almost three days, and then another five days found us in Alaska. We were in mountains continually from Washington on through the remainder of the trip, until we again reached eastern Montana, on the way home. It was a spectular adventure and we never tired of the awesome scenery. During our first few days in Alaska, we went to the city of Fairbanks, visited the pipeline, panned for gold on Pedro Creek, in the mountains just north of Fairbanks, spent a day in Denali National Park and Mount McKinley. From there we visited a small village named Talkeetna, the starting point for almost all the mountain climbers attempting Mt. McKinley. Then it was on to Anchorage and down past the Russian River to Soldotna, Alaska. My brother and I had the privilege of fishing the Kenai River near there, in an effort to catch a king salmon. The action was slow, as the first run of salmon had already passed that area on their way upstream to spawn. We did have some light action with the trout in that stream, because the Dolly Varden were present and hitting the flashy spoons we were using in the strong current. A gentleman at one of the local bait shops told us the second run of king salmon was making its way toward the Kenai River, up the coastal waters of the Cook Inlet. The Cook Inlet extends from the north side of Kodiak Island up to the city of Anchorage. It is a body of salt water which allows the salmon access to the many rivers and streams flowing into it from southern Alaska's mainland. This gentleman also told us to go down the coast to a little Russian village named Ninilchik, and try fishing for king salmon there. Since we had spent five days in Soldotna, camped on the Kenai River, we decided to take his advice and motor down the coast to this small fishing village. It was on the way to Homer, Alaska, which was on our itinerary as one of the places we wished to visit. There was a campground at the edge of the village where we found a site to rent for a few days. My brother, Larry and I were fortunate enough to get on a fishing charter the very next day which was June 30, 1993. Our fishing success that day was not too great, as we traveled much and caught very little. We had been fishing for salmon along the coast the first few hours, then made our way to the middle of the Cook Inlet, for the remainder of the trip, fishing for halibut, a very ugly fish, but delicious to eat. We would not be denied, so that evening while we were doing some gift and souvenir shopping in the village, we met another guide, and he was free the next day. His name was Joe Simpsen, and he agreed to take us out for what would probably be our last chance at salmon and halibut fishing this trip. The next morning, because of the tide, we were up early and loading into Joe's boat by six o'clock. It was July 1st, my brother Larry's birthday, number sixty! I hoped he would get a great big birthday present that day, but time would tell. We fished the shoreline first, trolling big, muskie-like spinner lures parallel with the beach. Larry was the first to get a hit and it seemed to be a nice sized fish as it made several, long, one hundred yard runs away from the boat. Each time he fought the fish to the boat, it would take off and run most of the line off the reel again. Finally he played the fish down and the guide managed to bring it aboard. What a pretty colored fish, a silvery side with seemingly iridescent blues, greens and pinks flickering on and off with the angles of sunlight glancing from its skin. The guide put it on the scale which read fifty-three pounds, and we were still in awe at the strong, almost stiff looking body, but powerful looking as well. We continued to fish and Larry caught his second salmon, a fifty-eight pound beauty that gave him an even greater battle than the first. It was happening, his birthday wish was coming true, what a day! To make a long story short, I did catch my limit of two king salmon that morning, but mine weighed fifty-five and forty-seven pounds, and fought long and hard. After about four hours of the salmon fishing and our limits now in the hold of the boat, we journeyed to deeper water some fifteen miles out in the middle of the Cook Inlet. We were going to fish in about two hundred feet of water, in what I am told is the world's second strongest tide change. We would fish on the bottom for halibut, using large circle hooks baited with pieces of squid meat. When the tide was changing, and the current at its strongest, we could barely keep the bait on the bottom with six pounds of lead weight used to take it down! As the tide subsided or changed to go back, we reduced the weight gradually, a pound at a time, until we were back to the normal two pounds of sinker needed to get and keep the bait on the bottom. I caught the first halibut, a small sixty pounder, which had me begging for help, before I got it to the boat. It was very tough, sustaining, strenuous work, trying to maintain a steady strain on the fish while trying to reel it up. I compared it to having my line tied to a big garage door and trying to pull it upstream against a strong current. It seemed that the pull on the other end was unforgiving, and my arms grew so tired, they felt like they were going to cramp. After about thirty-five minutes of this torture, I finally managed to bring the halibut to the boat. I had been begging my brother to take the rod and give me a rest, but he declined and said, "Nope, you hooked it, you catch it!" To that I replied, "OK, I'll remember that." Now the guide came to my rescue with a harpoon type spear gun and shot a short, barbed spear into the halibut on the end of my line. The fish went ballistic and took off away from the boat and sounding down to the depths it had just come from. The harpoon was attached to a strong nylon cord with an inflated twelve inch rubber ball on the end. As the fish, harpoon, cord, ball and my line all disappeared under the boat, all I could think was, I had to work at reeling it back in again. The guide said to bring the fish back up and I asked, "How soon?" My brother thought it was funny and laughed, but the guide didn't see the humor in it and said, "Right now!" I began reeling the fish back to the surface and it was a struggle, as the halibut was still very much alive and in control. This time the red ball came popping up first followed by the now tired halibut. As I pulled the fish near the boat, the guide, Captain Joe Simpsen, shot it in the head with a .410 shotgun and number four shot, at point blank range. The fish died and was brought on board to be taken home. Later I was told this process is the normal way most guides handle halibut, because of their excessive body strength, the fish is capable of doing considerable damage to equipment and bodily harm or injury to people. Every precaution is taken for the safety of all involved. No sooner than my fish was in the boat, Larry had one on! Before his forty-five minute fight was finished, he was begging me to take the rod and help him land this halibut. I said to him, "Nope, you hooked it, you catch it!" It was poetic justice in action as I watched him struggle with the fish, and I chuckled as he moaned and groaned his way through the ordeal. The halibut was handled in the same manner as mine and weighed seventy-one pounds. We returned to port that day with eight halibut and the four king salmon we had caught when the trip first started. Larry had countered with another ninety-one pound halibut and my largest weighed one hundred forty-nine pounds. We each had a couple smaller halibut too, but with the four king salmon, we had a very respectable catch. I remember thinking I had a really big fish, until we went into the village that evening to buy plastic bags for packing our fish. There on the wooden board sidewalk was a three hundred forty pound halibut that had been caught the same day! It made my fish look like a dwarf compared to its size. I asked the man who caught it, what kind of rod and reel he had used. He told me just an ordinary old rod and reel like everyone else was using. I couldn't imagine being able to pull a fish that size up, after having all the trouble with a fish one third the size. It was a great birthday for my brother and a great day for me as well, one we'll not likely ever forget. The remainder of our Alaskan experience took us back north from Anchorage through Palmer and Tok. Then over the "Top of the World" highway through Chicken, Alaska and back down over the Yukon River, by ferry, to Dawson, Yukon. We headed south from there to Whitehorse, Yukon and on down the Cassiar Highway through Prince George, British Columbia and over to Calgary, Alberta. After spending some time at each of these sites, we finally ventured back into the U.S. where we traveled through Glacier National Park, before turning the wheels of the motor home east toward Minnesota. As I stated earlier, it was an awesome trip which never got tiresome, because around every bend there were new scenes and adventures to experience. I would love to go back someday and take in many of the things I didn't see or do the first time.

In 1993, after returning to Minnesota, we made all the usual trips, except I took a friend of mine up to the Indian Chain of lakes in Ontario, Canada. Bill Coleman is from Braham, Minnesota, and works for the local electric company there known as ECE or East Central Energy. Bill was a new musky fisherman and I wanted to test my theory about trying this chain of lakes out on him. It didn't take long to prove the theory, as Bill not only caught his first legal musky, but several others too. In less than three full days of fishing, Bill caught seven muskies and left me with only five. We had a great time and I think it was even greater for me as I get much more satisfaction watching others catch fish than I do catching them myself. It was just fun seeing Bill get the hang of a newly developed fishing skill. Besides all that musky fishing, we caught our limits of walleye to bring home and even had a couple fish dinners up there. This was another good musky year as we boated fifty-four legal fish plus numerous smaller releases.

These years are difficult to write about without being too repetitive, because most fishing was done with many of the same people, and since I wasn't guiding any more, I had the freedom to fish for whatever I wanted. That turned out to be a lot more musky fishing than I had ever dreamed I would do.

The Alaska trip. Several halibut and king salmon. Guide
Joe Simpson, Merv & Larry Heitschmidt. July 1, 1993 –
Larry's 60th birthday.

Walleyes caught on Cass Lake by Merv and a friend from
Brainerd, MN.

1994 - 1999

In the last two chapters, the stories will involve new friends and some of the past friends and relatives I have already mentioned, but the tales will all be different. To close the last chapter I mentioned I was not guiding any longer, but actually I am still guiding in most respects. The fact is, I am not guiding professionally any more, just taking friends and relatives out fishing. I have grandchildren now, who like to fish, and you can bet I'm going to spend as much time as I can with them. My immediate family enjoys fishing, so they will receive a lot of my time as well. That leaves the many friends who I enjoy fishing with, and whenever my boat leaves the dock at Cass Lake, it usually has a full load of fisherpersons just as excited as I am to go fishing.

1994 was quite a memorable year for many reasons, one of which was a cold, windy, and snowy opening fishing season the second weekend in May. My brother Larry and I were camped in his motor home at Marclay Point on Cass Lake. On Saturday morning, the opening season had begun, and the fishing wasn't the only thing that opened. Apparently the wind gates had been opened, because we were faced with a thirty mile per hour northwest wind, and some biting sleet and occasional drizzle. The temperature was hovering around the thirty degree mark, and it was difficult to find a comfortable location to fish anywhere on the lake. We tried braving the open water as much as possible, but with the wind pushing us along too fast, all we could catch with our fast moving baits were the few northern pike that enjoyed chasing lively looking minnows. By about nine o'clock in the morning we found ourselves tucked in behind a point on the west side of Star Island, out of the wind's vicious and gusty attacks. My brother, Larry's nose was running and dripping from the cold and I knew he was not enjoying this moment anymore than I was. As I looked across the bay toward our campsite the snow was now falling and blowing so hard I couldn't see the shore. I thought to myself, "What are we doing out here ?" Then I said to Larry, "Let's go in for awhile and warm up!" I hardly got the words out when he was reeling up his line and saying, "I thought you'd never ask!" We went to shore to wait it out, but the weather remained relentless and didn't subside until the next morning. We did catch a few walleyes on Sunday afternoon, but after the weather had been so forceful the previous day, it was difficult to get into any kind of consistent pattern. Since my brother and I had both been guides, we used to have to go out during times of inclement weather, but now we were fishing for ourselves and didn't have to suffer those occasions. I think it took awhile for that thought to register and were probably reliving the past more than we actually realized, but not anymore. I made a couple more trips to Cass Lake in June, but the mayfly hatch had been in full swing, so we didn't do very well with the walleyes.

In July, our group consisting of Myron and Bev Barrie, Bob and Karen Moore, along with Jan and I, made our annual stay at Birch Villa Resort. It was filled with fishing, fun, food, and occasional shopping trips to the various towns around the area. The men would usually fish muskies all day while the women went garage sale shopping and making crafts back at the cabin. In the evening we would eat an early dinner and everyone would go walleye fishing in two boats from seven o'clock until dark, or when we felt like the walleyes had stopped biting. After our week at Birch Villa, everyone went home, but Jan and I stayed to join Jim and Dorothy Ronning in their motor home at Cass Lake Lodge. This particular year a man brought his family in an amphibian airplane to the resort for the week. We found out his name was Steve Remus, and he and his wife and two children had flown up from the Fairbault, Minnesota area, where he kept his plane. Their family was actually from Northfield, Minnesota, and they were friends of some other guests at the resort. During their week, Steve would give daily airplane rides to those wanting to get a view of the lake from above. One day I happened to be helping him dock the craft to let people out, and he asked if I wanted a ride. He said he needed gas and was going to fly to the Bemidji, Minnesota airport and land on the ground to fuel up, then return to Cass Lake in time for dinner. I ran to get Jim Ronning and tell our wives the plan, and in a few minutes we were taxiing off across the lake. Since the belly of the four-place plane sits right on the water, it was like riding in an aluminum boat during take-off. The water was slapping against the outside of the fuselage before the plane lifted off. The ride to Bemidji was fast and smooth, and before I knew it, we were making an approach to the landing strip for our final descent. We landed on wheels, taxied to the terminal, gassed up, checked the flotation tanks for water, and again taxied down the runway for take-off. On the flight back, Steve brought the plane down over Lake Andrusia and did a so called, "touch and go" maneuver which I thought was neat. He did it again on Cass Lake before we circled the lake and landed at Cass Lake Lodge. All this was done in a matter of less than one hour and we were back in time for dinner. The plane was called a SeaRay, I believe, and Steve told me it carried a two hundred fifty horsepower, pusher motor, located above and behind the cockpit and wings. It had lots of power and was a fun ride to take. Steve was a pilot for Northwest Airlines and I am sure he still is, but I haven't seen him for a couple years now. It was a highlight of the week and the Ronnings and us enjoyed more walleye fishing and fish frys before returning home to Braham, Minnesota.

During the month of August, my wife, Jan and I traveled to Kansas to visit some relatives. We stayed with our cousins, Bob and Karen Moore, who farm and raise beef cattle on about twenty-five hundred acres of land. One day, Bob and his son Scott, took me fishing for flathead catfish on a stream known as Elk Creek. There had been some earlier rains which brought the water levels up, and the run-off had eventually made its way down stream to the Delaware River and on into a reservoir called Lake Perry. As the water ran down toward the reservoir, the fish moved up river from the lake against the current, and into the tributaries, one of which was, Elk Creek. We were using heavy equipment, fishing the holes of deeper water left behind by the receding run-off. It was a spectacular afternoon, because in approximately three hours, we had caught five flatheads, weighing a total two hundred pounds. The largest fish tipped the scales at fifty-two pounds, and the smallest weighed in at thirty-one pounds. I had caught big catfish before, but not quite as large as these big hawgs. The fish did not go to waste, as we skinned and cleaned them. There is a lot of darker, brownish meat on a large fish, such as this, that has a very strong taste most people don't enjoy. We cut away all the brown colored meat and kept only the pure white steak-like fillets for a big fish fry. All the meat we kept from those five fish filled a fifty-five quart cooler, plus another small eight quart cooler. Needless to say there was enough fish to feed an army or more. Bob and Karen invited many of their friends, neighbors and close relatives over the next evening, and we devoured most of the fish caught the day before. It was a fun time and as we shared the pictures of our catch, most couldn't believe the size, from such a small stream. It's one of those situations where you have to catch the water at the right level.

Later that year, at Labor Day time, we found ourselves at Cass Lake Lodge again, enjoying more friends for one last outing of the camping season. The group included the Steve Johnson family of five, the Bill Coleman family of four, Pastor Dan Brodin, his wife, Petra, and their daughter, Brittany, plus my wife Jan and I. This annual weekend adventure had become an outing we all looked forward to, and of course, it was inclusive of morning and evening fishing trips. The idea was to catch enough walleyes to have a fish fry while we were enjoying each other's company and the great fall weekend. Over the years I had reserved at least one evening during that weekend, in my boat, for the ladies to enjoy a nice fishing excursion. Usually this evening occurred a night or two before the end of our stay. It got to be a kind of joke as I was given the nickname of, 'the moonlight guide' and we had a lot of fun with the teasing and joking about it. I was the one who got most of the teasing from the ladies in the group. On one occasion, there were four women in my boat for "ladies night," and the group included my wife, Jan, Carlyn Johnson, Debbie Karnos, and Brittany Brodin. Carlyn was the "cut-up" of the bunch, and she always took a book along which she pretended to read. I would usually put her line out for her and place the fish pole in a rod holder near her place in the boat. She would pretend to read, but all the while, would be telling jokes and poking fun at other people in boats nearby, usually her husband and sons. After a while she would have the other ladies laughing and responding with jokes of their own. I have been told by others that everyone knew where my boat was on the lake, especially after dark, because of the noisy laughter which was being emitted from within its gunnels. Only Carlyn was capable of such contagious laughter while we were on the water, and her laugh carried a long way over the water, as others will attest. That same evening, there was a full moon and everyone was feeling particularly spunky, especially Carlyn. She had caught most of the walleyes that evening, only after I had told her that she had a fish on her line, and she would put her book down and proceed to reel it in. I believe it was more the lucky seat than her expertise at fishing, but she and Brittany caught a good majority on the walleyes. Anyway, darkness had set in, the walleyes had stopped biting, and we were on our way back to the resort. Carlyn's husband, Steve, and their boys were going in at the same time. As we passed by their boat, Carlyn did the unthinkable, she mooned her husband and sons. Everyone's jaws dropped and then we all burst into laughter at what we had just seen. I had tears in my eyes the rest of the way in and it was difficult to navigate, trying to look through watery eyes, but when we reached the dock, Steve said, "I can't believe you did that!" To which Carlyn responded, "Believe it!" Like I said, "There was more than one full moon out that night!" That was the joke of the camp for the remainder of the weekend and for some years to come, and the story is usually told to newcomers to our group, as we sit around the campfire each night before turning in. The very next evening, I took Pastor Dan Brodin, his son, Chris, and daughter Brittany out again. Brittany liked the way Carlyn's seat had produced so many walleyes the night before, so she took up occupancy there for her evening of fishing. We fished an area of the lake east of Star Island known as Pagoda Bar. From the first pass along the drop-off until we quit fishing that night, it seemed like Brittany's rod was always bending under the strain of a walleye. She had the hot Shad Rap that time and caught her limit of nice keeper walleyes, while brother Chris, her dad, Dan and I barely caught six walleyes between us. It was a fun evening and the wind had come up a bit, so on the way back to the dock we had to take some one to two foot waves, straight on. Brittany loved it as she bounced up and down in her seat as we hit each wave head on. There were times I could see daylight, or actually moonlight, under her as she left the seat from the bounce. I stopped the boat once to see if she wanted to relocate closer to the back, where the ride wasn't quite so rough. She informed me she was having fun and enjoying the bouncy ride, so I left her to her place and continued back to the dock, watching her leave the seat with the thrust of each wave. When we arrived at the resort, all Brittany could talk about for a while was the fun, bumpy ride she had in the front of the boat. It actually made my body ache just to see her bouncing up and down with each jolting wave.

The last day of our stay was actually Labor Day, John Karnos, Bill Coleman and I went musky fishing one last time before packing up to go home. Bill was in the front of the boat, John in the middle, and I was guiding from the stern. We had fished a couple areas in Allen's Bay and had moved on to the West Potato Island, after having not had action elsewhere. Near a tip of bull rushes, I pointed out that this is where I had caught my first musky. On the very next cast, right near the bull rushes, Bill had a strike and set the hooks on a very lively musky. It didn't take him long to restrain the fish and we netted it and brought it aboard. I think it was Bill's first Minnesota musky and measured forty-six inches, then was released and Bill went home a happy man.

During that year we landed forty-three legal sized muskies in my boat, and there were no post season tournaments. A few trips were made to Rush Lake, near Braham, but only a few small muskies were caught and released before the season came to a close.

From the late eighties up to present time, Ron Lykins and I have opened the Minnesota walleye fishing season each year on Cass Lake. My brother Larry, his son, Lindsey, and others have joined us from time to time, but most consistently, Ron and I have continued our tradition each year. Some years are better than others for various reasons, but we usually manage to get limits of walleyes. Our best method of taking walleyes in early season cold water, is to anchor on or near the edge of a drop off, cast a jig tipped with a shiner minnow combination into deeper water and pull the bait up the bar in slow deliberate movements. Patience is the key to this process, and if you can wait it out, the result is usually successful. I once heard that, "patience is a virtue, but it never helped a rooster to lay an egg!" That's not the type of patience I'm referring to in this case, but being able to play the waiting game, can sometimes prove fruitful. While we are on sayings, I also heard this one, "Give a man a fish, he eats for a day; teach him to fish, and he may never come home!" I'm sure some wives feel that way once in a while, but I enjoying eating and getting my rest, so my wife never had to worry too much about my not showing up. During the summer of 1995 we made the same usual trips to Cass Lake with friends and family, but most were without any uncommon occurrences. I believe Bob Moore caught another forty inch musky that summer and we registered another thirty fish in my logbook. 1996 and 1997 were less fruitful, as far as fishing is concerned, we did the usual trips to Cass Lake again, catching lots of walleyes and a few muskies, but nothing out of the ordinary worthy of mentioning. Our total take of legal muskies for those two years was twenty-one and eighteen respectively, and they were all released.

In July of 1996, my dad and mom came to Birch Villa Resort, as they usually did, but dad wasn't feeling his best and was having trouble walking and getting around. He had been on dialysis for almost a year, due to having only one kidney after surgery to remove the other, some nine years earlier. Now the one and only kidney was failing him, forcing the dialysis. After about a year, dad decided to go for a method called, 'peritoneal dialysis,' a form of dialysis a person can administer to themselves. Dad was doing OK with it, but his health was slowly fading from a combination of other system breakdowns in the body too. Our daughter Cristi and her husband, Joel, visited us at the lake while mom and dad were there. When they said good-bye before they left, my dad broke down and cried, as if he knew maybe he wouldn't be seeing them again. It was quite emotional as he gave them each a hug that seemed to want to linger, giving the message, "I don't want to let go." Then as they left, I said something to Cristi like, "You may not see grandpa alive again." She shook her head as though she knew it too.

In December of 1996, we said a final good-bye to my dad, Alfred Heitschmidt. He went to be with his father in heaven, but he left behind a legacy for us all to be proud of. My dad only had an eighth grade education, but he was much wiser than many people I have known with numerous college degrees to their credit. He had that extra pound of "common sense" that many wish they could possess, and he used it in his everyday life. He was a genuine role model for my brother and I, as well as being our best friend, especially when we needed one. Thanks, dad, for all the times you took me hunting and fishing, and for all those times you allowed me to go do it on my own. Cristi and Joel flew back from the state of Washington for grandpa's funeral and we had a wonderful celebration together with our son, Chad, his wife Regina, and the grandkids, Colton and Ashley. I don't think "gramps" would have wanted it any other way. Christmas wasn't the same that year, but we were confident dad, and grandad, was in a much better place.

One of the few highlights in 1997 was a second trip in as many years to the White River in Arkansas. The year before, my brother, Larry and I had traveled to an area near Flippin, Arkansas, to meet our first cousins, Tom and Jerry Horn. It was the first time the four of us had been together in thirty-one years. They had both been living in Oklahoma, mostly in and around the Tulsa area, and Tom Horn had been our dock boy at the resort in Minnesota for four summers. Now that we were finally back together in this trout fishing reunion, we had opportunities to renew our old memories from growing up in Kansas and visiting each other's families almost on a weekly basis. About the time my family moved from Kansas to Minnesota, their family had moved in the opposite direction, from Kansas to Oklahoma. That put us so many miles apart, we seldom had opportunity to visit or see them for many years. This reunion was special for several reasons, but I believe the most important was the fact that we had now started an annual trend which would allow us more visits and more time together with close relative relationships. We fished in two separate boats on the White River, located below the huge Bull Shoals power dam. It gave us a lot of individual time and attention to learn about what each had been doing and planning in their lives. Plus, we got trout!

In 1998 my brother Larry, his wife, Juanita, my wife, Jan and I, took a trip to Yellowstone National Park in early June. We both had campers and planned to spend about two weeks there in an effort to meet our daughter Cristi, and her husband, Joel. Our plans also included meeting up with a first cousin of Larry's and mine, after we had been settled a day or two. The cousin was from our mother's side of the family and his name was Earl LaOrange. Hc and his wife Joan lived in Pocatello, Idaho, which wasn't too far from the west gate of Yellowstone. After Cristi and Joel arrived, we all ventured to Old Faithful the next day, where we met our cousins for the first time in about thirty-one years. It was a great reunion and we spent most of the day together, visiting, catching up on old times, exchanging address, having lunch, and sight seeing. Before departing, Earl and Joan invited us to come visit them at their coastal summer home in Oregon. We vowed that we would and then went our separate ways, cherishing those precious moments together with loved ones. Most of those two weeks were spent traveling around the park sight seeing, but we did manage to get in a few mornings and evenings of trout fishing. Yellowstone Lake is a fun lake to fish, and you can easily find accesses to the water. All you need is a spinning rod and reel, plus a light flashy spoon. Cast the spoon out as far as you can and count to ten, letting it settle in the deeper water. Then begin your slow steady retrieve and wait for a hit. Usually you don't have to wait too long or make too many casts before a trout takes the bait. Most of the time you'll catch a nice sized cut-throat trout. It's a lot of fun and takes very little effort. Crist and Joel had to leave for their home in Tumwater, Washington the day after Father's Day. We were sad to see them go and it meant that our vacation was almost over and we would be heading back to Minnesota, to our homes and families.

The summer continued with our usual trips to Cass Lake, but nothing much out of the ordinary took place. We caught our usual share of walleyes and a few muskies, and so it went, quite naturally uneventful, but interesting. We finished the summer with twenty-six legal muskies in my boat and a few more than that in the sub-legal size.

That fall, my brother Larry and I took our annual trip again to Arkansas, where we met our cousins, Tom and Jerry Horn from Tulsa. This time we took our sons, Chad and Lindsey Heitschmidt, and our cousins, Tom and Jerry brought their nephew, Bob Horn. It was another grand reunion as some of the cousins had never met, and it gave everyone a chance to learn more about each other. The trout fishing was spectacular and fun, as we caught and boated our limits to take home, plus enough to have two delicious fish frys. We caught mostly rainbow trout, but an occasional brown trout or cut-throat would take the bait. Most of the fish measured about thirteen to fifteen inches on the average, but once in a while someone would pull in a seventeen or maybe even a twenty-two inch trout. We usually kept the boats close together on the river in order to communicate with each other, and to make sure everyone was enjoying themselves beyond reason. There was much joking and kidding between the two boats, and because we traded boats and fishing partners each day, there were no one-sided arguments. Each person received his fair share of the teasing, but it was all in fun, and we had a great time.

The summer of 1999 was much more eventful as I will explain throughout this segment of the chapter. First Ron Lykins and I had a very, very cold and windy opening fishing season. The wind was relentless again from the northwest at about thirty miles per hour. It even snowed and sleeted at times, and we wore gloves, but still had to sit on our hands occasionally in order to keep them from getting so stiff we couldn't bait our hooks. It blew all day Saturday and Sunday until about four o'clock in the afternoon. Then we made our move out to a sand bar where we fished and caught our limits of walleye in about an hour. It was still cold, but the wind had subsided, and conditions felt much more favorable than they had for the past two days.

Later that spring, just after school was out, Ron and I began another annual retreat to his mother's home on Lake Minnewaska, in west central Minnesota. Margaret Lykins enjoys quilting, cooking, entertaining guests, visiting and traveling. She lives in a nice lake home on the southwest shore of Lake Minnewaska, and has a convenient access to good highways and towns in the surrounding area. We arrived at her house sometime in the afternoon, and Margaret had a list of things for us to do, so we would immediately set to the task of reducing the items on the list. There was a water pump to be taken to the dock, mounted, primed, and made to operate for the summer season. A hose had to be taken from the storage room under the house and hooked up to the pump on the dock. Salt needed to be added to the water softener, windows needed to be washed, air conditioner installed, and the cover for the boat lift had to be put on and secured. When the list was mostly eliminated, Ron and I would take the boat out for an evening of pan-fish and bass fishing. Early in the season like that, the sunfish were eager to take the small Beetle Spins, and with ultra light equipment, made the catching a joy to experience. The bass fishing was even more enjoyable. I recall the first time Ron told me that we would probably catch forty largemouth bass in an evening, I thought he was stretching the numbers a bit, but we came in that first evening after having caught and released forty-seven bass! I have never been a bass fisherman, and I don't profess to be a good one, but when the fish are cooperative, even a novice can be successful. We caught all the bass on top water baits, and that made it even more exciting. When a bass hits a top water bait, you can see the water erupt where the bait is lying. A person has to be quick to set the hook, because the bass is capable of spitting the bait as fast as it took the lure in. It was a good introduction to bass fishing for me, as I had never experienced bass in those quantities before. We would fish until dark and then go back to Margaret's house, where we visited until bedtime and usually would have pie and coffee or popcorn. The next morning it was up and at the list of chores again, until everything on the list was completed. Margaret always took us out for lunch at least one time during our stay, and after two or three days, it was always difficult to leave the serene beauty of the lake, and the warm hospitality of a great cook and caring person.

In early June, my brother, Larry, his wife, Juanita, my wife, Jan and I took my mom, Alyce Heitschmidt, on an Amtrack trip from Minnesota to the west coast. The entire trip lasted about two weeks, as we journeyed first to Tumwater, Washington, where we spent a week with our daughter, Cristi and her husband, Joel. The time went fast as we became tourists and took in all the wonderful sights around the western part of Washington. We visited Mt. St. Helens, Mt. Rainier, the west coast, the Olympic Mountains, Puget Sound, San Juan and Orcas Islands, plus many attractions along the way. After the first week, Cristi and Joel joined our family group, and we all went to the coast of west Oregon, where we spent the second week with our cousins, Earl and Joan LaOrange. Their home was located in Lincoln Beach, Oregon, about a two hour drive south and west of Portland. Our time was spent visiting, sight seeing up and down the coast, flying kites on the beach, and even a fishing trip for sea bass. The fishing trip found cousin Earl, Larry and I on a charter boat, and the sea bass were average five pound fish. We started fishing on the bottom, but as the morning progressed, the bass would follow our bait and the other hooked fish to the surface. Gradually we had to keep letting our bait down less and less, and by the end of the trip, we were casting the baits out on the surface and catching bass near the top of the water. The three of us caught fifty-four bass that day and released them back to the coastal waters from where they came. We had enjoyed a great two-week vacation by rail and it was time to return home. After saying our good-byes, Cristi and Joel went back to Washington, and the remainder of our family boarded the Amtrack in Portland and began the journey to Minnesota. The return trip took us east along the Columbia River and then eventually north through orchard country and on to Spokane, Washington. From there we headed east through the northern panhandle of Idaho and on into Montana through Glacier National Park. It was nice to see Glacier National Park going out to the west coast and also on the return trip, once during the evening hours and again in the morning. The train traveled slowly through the park, so everyone could get a fantastic view of the different areas that aren't usually seen from a car. Then it was on through Montana and across North Dakota to Minnesota and home from another great experience.

Our usual Cass Lake vacation took place in July that summer and along with Bob and Karen Moore, Myron and Bev Barrie, Jan and I, we had visits from another cousin, Dean Heitschmidt and his son, Josh and daughter, Chelsa. Bob Moore's brother, Lowell came to spend a few days with us at Birch Villa and he caught a musky one day trolling for walleyes. We were in my boat, and Bob wanted to go to one of his favorite spots, the North Cedar Bar. As we trolled our Shad Raps up the drop-off, Lowell felt a tug on his line and set the hook. At first he didn't say too much about the weight or fight of the fish, but after a few cranks of the reel, he was convinced the fish was not just an ordinary catch. I stopped the boat and had everyone reel in, so we wouldn't have any trouble with tangles. I was thinking the fish was probably just a decent northern pike or possibly a nice walleye. As we waited for Lowell to play the fish toward the boat, it surfaced, showing us its silvery side dotted with dark tell-tale musky spots. I yelled, "He's got a musky!" Lowell just kept cranking and said, "A what?" I then explained to him the fish was a musky and all he had to do was let it run when it wanted to, and play it in when he could. With six pound test monofilament you don't try to overpower or horse a fish if you don't want to lose it. Lowell played the fish to the boat and eventually I netted and measured it in the water. The musky was forty-one inches long and we estimated it at about twenty pounds. A couple pictures were snapped and the fish was released. It was Lowell's first musky and he is to be commended for releasing it back to the water. Myron Barrie caught a nice forty-six inch musky that week and released it and another forty incher that had a nice girth and some beautiful distinct spots.

Later that summer, I guided some friends on Cass Lake during mid-August. Gene Mattson, Mike Peterson, Ski, Little Ski, Joel Antil, and Ross Johnson all worked at a business in the Blaine, Minnesota area called General Pattern. They wanted to fish Cass Lake, and this was actually our third annual trip to Cass Lake with their group. Mike Peterson was fortunate enough to catch his first musky, a forty inch beauty that he released after a few pictures were taken. He caught his fish on one of my black bucktails, so I gave him the lure to keep as a souvenir. We caught several walleyes and some northern pike that week and had a huge fish fry one evening before we had to leave.

Our usual group outing came during Labor Day weekend and the fishing was a little slower than it normally had been in previous years. The group had to do some very serious fishing in order to come up with enough to have a fish fry. Everyone came through and contributed an adequate amount, so the shore lunch was a huge success again, as usual. Steve Johnson and I did some pre-tournament musky fishing during the Labor Day weekend, and we felt ready to enter the First Annual Minnesota Musky Tourney to be held later in September. It was to be a large tournament worth thousands of dollars in prize money, so we wanted to be ready for the big event. The weekend came to a close and everyone returned home ready for the new school year to begin.

In late September, Steve Johnson and I returned to Cass Lake for the big musky tournament, in which we were confident for our chances. We had been given the number forty-nine, which meant our boat would be the forty-ninth boat to be given the green light to begin the tournament. We had our boat inspected before the departure time and waited for the signal of number forty-nine to be called. There were about one hundred boats in the tourney and they were all waiting with us for the event to begin. A thunder storm had moved through during the early morning hours and some lightning was still a factor, causing a slight delay in the start time. The temperature was about forty-seven degrees with a southeast breeze, and a few lingering showers. Steve and I were dressed in our long underwear, extra flannel shirts and sweatshirts, plus warm coats and two- piece rain suits over that. We each had our boots on and in an effort to wear our life- jackets, found that we were too bulky to get into them. The life jackets were placed on our boat seats in order for us to have quick and easy access to them. It was a little after seven o'clock in the morning, still basically dark, due to the clouds, rain and some-what early hour of the day. Finally the judge started to let the boats go, one at a time, in order of their number, and the tournament was underway. Steve and I waited through the first forty or so numbers, and then began to inch our way to the front, so we could be ready when our number was called. We had decided to fish in my sixteen foot Lund boat, equipped with a forty horsepower Johnson outboard plus a four horsepower kicker motor used for trolling. This decision was made because Steve's boat with steering consol, was giving him trouble and wouldn't shift into gear without shutting down and having to be restarted numerous times. The time came for our number to be called and we were off, heading east across the lake. I had allowed for the boat to plane off level and then eased back on the throttle to maintain a sort of cruise mode. We were traveling at about fifteen or sixteen miles per hour, and I noticed two separate wakes ahead in front of us, mov-ing in opposite directions, causing a wavelike "V" to form on the water. Apparently the wakes were formed by boats having gone in the same general direction previous to our passing this way. I judged the distance between the two and decided to split the difference and take them directly in the center, where they met or came together. As we approached the two-foot high wakes, the one on my right lifted the stern part of my boat up at such an angle, that the left bow of the boat dipped down into the opposite wake, causing the bow of the boat to act as a rudder. The boat dove to the right with such momentum, I was forced out in a cata-pult-like maneuver. The right stern was still being lifted, while the left bow went down and into the wave causing the boat to do an immediate ninety degree right turn, and almost flipping the boat upside down. Steve was in the second swivel seat from the front of the boat, facing me, and he said he remembers seeing me fly over and past him. I went into the water head first and immediately felt the boat's motor with my left leg. Kicking to get clear of the motor, I drove myself further down into the water, to a depth that made my ears pain from the pressure. I don't think I was more than twelve or thirteen feet below the surface, but as I began to right myself in the underwater fury, it was becoming evident to me that I was indeed in a serious situation. I knew if I reached the surface, Steve would bring the boat around and pick me up, but reaching the surface was more difficult than I could imagine. Running out of air and wanting to gasp for another breath, I began to kick harder and paddle with my hands in an effort to get to the surface. I remember getting the feeling that I was sinking or going down rather than up, and that caused me to kick and paddle even harder. At one point during this frantic effort to survive, I saw my dad's face looking at me, he had a smile that seemed to calm me and let me know everything was going to be alright. I continued to kick with those heavy boots and all that bulky clothing, and suddenly I felt my head above water as I took a long gasp of breath, and another, and another. It was then I heard Steve, loudly calling my name, over and over, and then I realized, he was in the water too, and the boat was drifting away. Steve had tumbled out of the boat backward when it had almost tipped over, and in doing so, had managed to trap some air inside his rain suit, which helped keep him afloat. During my time back on the surface, I counted at least four boats going by, two of which, looked at us and continued on. I really never could understand the reason for that to have happened, but it actually did. Fortunately a man and his daughter, fishing the tournament, happened to come by and see us in the water, and they stopped to help. First they threw me a floatation cushion from their boat and along with that I was able to swim to Steve and grab the hood of his rain gear to keep him from going under for the third time. He had lost the air that had been trapped in his rain suit and was struggling to keep himself afloat. We both clung to the floatation devise until the man brought his boat to us then Steve got hold of the trolling motor shaft and held on until a second boat stopped to help. There were two men in the second boat and together they literally pulled Steve into their boat. I grabbed the side of the first boat and hung on until they could help me out of the water and into it. As I looked up before being helped out of the water, I was looking into the face of a beautiful young lady, I told the girl that she was the prettiest rescuer I had ever seen. With wet heavy, soggy clothing, it is very difficult to maneuver or swim, even in the best conditions, but this was a test we never hope to have to endure again. The two men who picked up Steve also rounded up my boat and pulled it back to me. As we assured the occupants of the other boats that we were alright, I looked around to see if everything was still in tact. The cast iron steering handle on the forty horse Johnson was broken off entirely and hung by the control wires leading to the tip of the handle. That had caused the engine to shut down, a fact I wasn't aware of until after I surfaced. The LCD graph depth finder was still running, and I noticed we were in fifty feet of water and the surface temperature was fifty degrees. We radioed to shore for permission to go in and change into some dry clothes, and they granted us that privilege. There were several tournament judges standing by to meet us, and told us we could dry off and do whatever we needed, but to let them know if we were going back out. As I stepped from the boat, my left leg hurt with each step. I stopped to examine the shin area of my left leg, only to find the flesh peeled back exposing the shin bone. That's not saying much, because that area of the shin doesn't have much more than a couple layers of skin covering it anyway. I limped back to the motor home where Steve and I changed into some dry clothes, turned up the furnace to get warm, and laid all documents from our wallets out to dry. Steve tried calling his son back in Braham to see if he could bring the other boat to us, since mine was broke down and could not be repaired without ordering parts. Unfortunately Steve's cell phone was ruined from the dunking it received while in his jacket pocket during the accident. It literally fried the internal wiring of his phone. With that, Steve used the resort telephone to reach his son, Brant, and request the delivery of his boat to Cass Lake. That phone call took place at about nine o'clock in the morning, and Brant went to town to tell his mom (Steve's wife) about what had happened and what he was doing. The boat arrived in Cass Lake at noon, and by one o'clock, Brant was on his way home with my boat and Steve and I were fishing in the tournament again. I don't know if we were trying to be "macho men" or whether we were still in shock, but the remainder of that weekend tourney seems like a blur. We fished, but our hearts were not in it a hundred percent, I don't think my heart was in it even fifty percent. My leg began to throb and hurt worse, and up to that point I had only covered it with gauze and pulled my sock up over it. We attended the banquet after the first day of fishing, and even though we were not the center of attention, we did become the source of a newly established rule to the tournament. 'Everyone in the tournament will be required to wear a life jacket while their boat is under way to or from any location.' I think it is a very good rule, because Steve and I are living proof that you never know what circumstances you might encounter. I had been fishing and guiding in a boat for over forty years and will say that I never experienced anything remotely close to this accident. On Sunday morning we were back on the water, trying to endure a situation that probably each of us would rather have done without, but the end of the tourney was so close, we decide to stay. We did see some muskies following our lures that morning, but no takers, and so a trophy or place or prize money wasn't to be, at least for us. The tourney was to end at two o'clock Sunday afternoon, and by one thirty, Steve and I had decided to quit fishing and go in. We had been babying his outboard motor, as it kept stopping on us every time Steve tried shifting it into gear. After two or three tries, Steve managed to keep the motor running and we were on our way back to the resort dock. His boat had a sixty horse Johnson outboard and it moved the boat across the water quite well. We were at full speed as we approached the harbor entrance and Steve pulled back on the throttle control. Nothing happened, there was no response, Steve tried again, and again, quickly, still no response and the harbor was getting closer. At the last second Steve turned the key in the ignition off, and the motor stopped. The boat slid forward, slowed itself in the shallow water, and crunched against the rocks at the edge of the harbor entrance. As Steve and I sat there speechless, we thought, "What else could go wrong?" I stepped to the back of the boat and held onto the throttle control wire that fed into the motor and asked Steve to work the handle. As he pushed and pulled the throttle handle I could feel the broken wire moving inside the cable covering, but nothing was causing the motor's throttle control to respond. We were still in a second and seemingly delayed state of shock, not yet entirely over the first incident of the weekend. Steve pushed the boat back from the rocks and let the small electric trolling motor down so we could finish this trip and get the boat on the trailer, ready to take home. We quietly went about packing and loading up and checked out of the campground, happy to be leaving, but counting our blessings that everything had turned out fair, especially after the two close calls with dangerous odds. We stopped in town for the awards ceremony, but I don't remember too much about it. My leg was still throbbing and all I wanted to do was get home safely and chalk this weekend up to experience. An experience I shall never forget. Upon arriving at Steve's house, his wife, Carlyn, took one look at my leg and told me I should see a doctor. I said it hurt a little and after I got home and elevated it, I thought it would be better. That's exactly what I did and the pain seemed to subside. The next day, Monday, I was back in the classroom, but by the end of the day I couldn't stand or put weight on my foot. I went directly from the school to the clinic and the doctor took one look and said I had some infection in the left leg, so he prescribed some antibiotics. He also told me to stay off the leg for a day or two and keep it elevated. I did that and had a substitute teacher in my place at school, but the pain got worse and my leg wasn't getting any better. The doctor sent me to a specialist, and he said the infection was spreading, and that I had to maintain complete bed rest with the leg elevated for two weeks. He also prescribed a stronger antibiotic, and after two weeks of lying around and reading and getting bored, my leg began to heal, and I was able to stand and put weight on it again. There was another month of physical therapy and whirlpool baths, but the healing took place and I regained full normal use of the left leg. Needless to say, there was no more fishing for me that fall and my boat was repaired and put in storage for another season.

The total musky count for my boat that year was twenty-two legal sized fish and fourteen sub-legal, all which were released.

The annual October trout trip to the White River in Arkansas was on again, and Larry and I were accompanied by his son, Lindsey, and son-in-law, Dave Anderson, from Isle, Minnesota. We met our cousins, Tom and Jerry Horn for another round of searching for that elusive, "Big Boy Brown," in a place known as the "White Hole," but we never boated such a creature. There was, however; a poem written by yours truly, about the group, and their escapades on the White River, in search of that big trout. The poem's pattern of rhythm was a take-off of the classic narrative poem written by Robert W. Service years ago, called "The Cremation of Sam McGee." I have included it in this chapter, if you care to indulge yourself in someone else's humor.

BALLAD OF THE WHITE
(with apologies to Robert W. Service)

*There are strange things done 'neath the Midwest sun by the men
    who fish for trout.
To watch them cast as the hours crawl past could make your hair fall
    out.
And many a rise comes to their flies until the sun goes down.
They can steam and sweat, but they'll never get that trout called
    Big Boy Brown.*

*Now you should know the name, and honor the fame, of the stream
    called the LaFave.
The Taneycomo has had its fill of romanticizing rave.
The Strawberry, the Cache and the Buffalo are names that set our
    jaws tight.
But the most renown, know the world around, is the great stream
    called the White.*

*It rises ice-cold from a big black hole at the bottom of a dam in the
    hills.
It splashes and spits and spills in fits through riffles and runs and
    rills.
It rages and roars and down it pours, and it settles in pools so
    profound.
That men still relate, right up to this date, that the bottoms can easily
    be found.*

Now in such a good brook, any child with a hook can't help but
    catch a good trout.
He can throw in his bait, and he barely needs wait, before he pulls
    one out.
There are cutthroats galore, and rainbows for sure, and browns both
    wiley and fat.
And even at worst (when your tackle seems cursed) they will strike at
    the drop of a hat.

But there is one fish that is every man's wish to hook but once in his
    life.
Out on the White in hours of plight, the situation rife.
For in one of its holes, the story is told, is a mammoth and ancient
    brown.
That elusive beast, at the very least, weighs almost seventy pounds.

For ages, it seems, both awake and in dreams, that fish has been the
    bane-
Of men who have cast with both graphite and glass and with bamboo
    of Tonkin cane.
Yet not one soul who's sought that goal with patterns of feathers and
    furs.
Has ever come near that stream so dear—regardless of what he
    avers.

Then came a platoon, to the White so soon, of anglers fine and fair.
They came to the land near Big Boy's stand and stayed at the White
    Hole there.
And they made a pact upon that tract that—come whatever might-
To the very last gent, their time would be spent in getting that fish to
    bite.

Now Tom, if he can, was a streamer man, and rarely fished anything
    else.
Over the years, in the eyes of his peers, he'd made quite a name for
    himself.
So he took up a post with his trusty "Grey Ghost" and he cast both
    up stream and down.
Two years there he spent, til his heart finally went, but he never did
    outsmart 'ol Brown.

Then another club guy went to give it a try, a fisherman mainly of
    nymphs.
He also fished wets both in singles and sets, and occasionally tied on
    some flymphs.

His name was Larry, and he stayed with his quarry for seven days
    short of three years.
Then a cramp in his hand put an end to his stand, and we saw him
    retire in tears.

Then next to lay claim to a shot at the fame of taking that brown,
    speckled prize-
Was a man named Ol' Jerry who held to the theory of fishing the
    tiniest flies.
Every fly in the box of that wiley old fox was a midge of minutest
    invention
And no spider could spin a line quite as thin as his tippet's exquisite
    dimension.

But even Ol' Jerry admitted it eerie that nothing could get Brown to
    rise.
And after a time—from fishing so fine—he finally lost use of his eyes.
He'd been on that brook with a twenty-eight hook for five years, two
    months and a day.
And sad though it be, we all went to see when they led poor Ol' Jerry
    away.

Then came along Lindsey with experience quite flimsy.
He fished for Ol' Brown 'neath the ripples.
Often he tried and more often he plied-his hackle upon the riffles.
As a fisherman he was dandy, he seemed extra handy at sidearm and
    casting around trees.

But to his surprise Ol' Brown opened his eyes and brought Lindsey
    down to his knees.
Now he's walking quite bent cause his lower back went.
And his wrecked lumbar proves he is hurting.
He did come and try, but we cannot deny, that with Big Boy he had
    to stop flirting.

Now another guy came, he was new to the game, but he thought he'd
    give it a try.
But Old Dave was aghast after that blast when Big Boy hit his fly.
He headed for land with his rod in his hand, fearing it was too late.
Dave dreaded the end and the fate Brown would send, so he took
    himself out of the race.

And last we observe, an angler named Merv, who was given to
    fishing at night.
He had eyes like a cat and could hear like a bat, with instincts tuned
    drum-head tight.

He would go out at ten and was not seen again until dawn lit the sky
    rosy red.
Then in he would steel with a full heavy creel, say "Good morning"
    and head off to bed.

Though the rest of his crew were defeated and blue, Merv still had a
    plan up his sleeve.
And he told his old chums that no matter what comes there'd be no
    reason to grieve.
For he had a suspicion that on his next mission he'd hook that great
    prize they all sought.
And by dawn's early light, they'd see he was right, and Big Boy
    Brown would be caught.

So they all wished him luck when ten o'clock struck, and Merv
    headed out to the pool.
Where the monster fish lay that—until that day—not an angler was
    able to fool.
Then Merv took a stand with his boots in the sand, and he stretched
    his leader taut.
And he tied on a yellowish, pinkish affair on a hook size number 1/0.

Merv stood in the water four hours and a quarter, his wristwatch
    read twenty of three.
He made darn sure that the darkness was pure; not a glimmer of
    light could he see.
And then at last, the fly was cast into that dark inky air.
The line swished out to find the trout that Mervie knew was there.

The fly hit "splat" and hearing that, Merv stripped his line in fast.
He wanted to make one heck of a wake that a fish would hit with a
    blast.
And on the next tug something hit that big bug with a wallop that felt
    like a ship.
Merv had no doubt he'd nailed that trout, and the hook was in
    Big Boy's lip.

Then the fight was on from then 'til dawn and from dawn 'til dark
    again.
And from dark 'til dawn again they'd gone—eight days, nine days,
    ten.
In another week the battle peaked and both were wearing out.
But it looked as though, in a day or so, Merv would have his trout.

But as Big Boy Brown was wearing down, he got his second wind.
While Merv was beat—had cramped his feet—and both his hands
    were skinned.

Brown saw his chance, resumed his dance, and carried Merv away.
And by the full moonlight, out in the White, you can still see Merv
*   today.*

Just gaze down there in the pool so clear in the spot they'll all point
*   out.*
It's the living room, in the White Hole Flume, of Big Boy Brown the
*   trout.*
And on the wall (you can see it all) mounted and stuffed in a curve-
With his rod in his grip and his fly in his lip, hangs that erstwhile
*   angler, Merv.*

There are strange things done 'neath the midwest sun by the men
*   who fish for trout.*
To watch them cast as the hours crawl past could make your hair fall
*   out.*
And many a rise comes to their flies until the sun goes down.
They can steam and sweat, but they'll never get that trout called
*   Big Boy Brown.*

The amphibian plane owned and piloted by Steve Remus.

Kansas Catfish. Merv, Scott and Bob Moore of Holton, KS. Caught on Elk Creek near the Delaware River.

The Historic "Pagoda" House on Star Island. A fishing bar located east of Star Island was named after it.

Dorothy and Jim Ronning flank Jan Heitschmidt with a stringer of walleyes caught in Cass Lake.

46" musky held and caught by Bill Colman. Merv is in the background. It was Bill's first Minnesota musky.

Sunrise over the SE point of Star Island and Cass Lake.
Looking east from Birch Villa harbor.

Merv and Ron Lykins with limits of opening day walleyes.

A 48" musky caught and released by Merv.

L-R: Bill Coleman, Dennis Nilsen, Merv, Joel Komschlies, (Merv's son-in-law) and John Karnos with some of the late evening walleyes.

Merv with a rainbow trout caught in the White River.

On the White River in Arkansas. Cousin Jerry Horn, Merv, brother Larry and Tom Horn. First time together in thirty-one years.

Dock at the White Hole Resort on the White River.

Myron Barrie, Merv and cousin Bob Moore with a couple of northerns they caught on Cass Lake.

Merv's grandson, Colton, his son, Chad, and his granddaughter, Ashley, with some late evening walleyes the kids caught.

Jan Heitschmidt, Myron and Bev Barrie and Merv with some late evening walleyes caught on Cass Lake.

Merv's grandson, Colton Heitschmidt, with his first walleye at the age of five years.

Grandkids, Colton and Ashley, in Gramps' boat.

Cousin Lowell with a 41" musky he caught and released.
His brother, Bob Moore, is in the background.

Some late evening walleyes caught on Cass Lake by the
"General Pattern" crew. Ski, Little Ski and Merv with the fish.

Mike Peterson with his first Musky. Caught and released
on Cass Lake. Gene Mattson is in the background.

Gene Mattson of "General Pattern" holding a stringer of his limit of walleyes caught on a late evening outing on Cass Lake.

Merv holding a 46" musky he caught and released on Cass Lake.

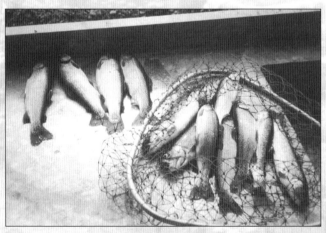

Rainbow trout ready for cleaning and eating. On the White River in Arkansas.

Chad, Regina and Colton Heitschmidt posing by one of the family's sand castles made annually on the beach at Sah-Kah-Tay Resort on Cass Lake.

The trout fishermen the poem was written about.
L-R: Larry and Lindsey Heitschmidt, Tom Horn, Merv, Dave Anderson and Jerry Horn.

2000 - 2003

The summer of 2000 was a normal year, Ron Lykins and I opened the season on Cass Lake, and caught limits of walleye again, with the old jig and minnow method. Then we made the annual trip to Lake Minnewaska, to help his mom prepare for the upcoming summer, plus catching our share of sunnies and bass. June found us making a couple trips to Cass Lake, fishing for walleyes. The first trip proved successful, as a quarter ounce weight on a long leader and number four hook tipped with a minnow, produced limits of walleye for four of us. The second trip allowed a few scattered walleyes, but the mayfly hatch was on and the catching was more difficult. We did not succeed with limits, but we managed enough jumbo perch and walleyes to have a delicious meal or two.

Our July vacation rolled around and the highlight of that trip found cousin Bob Moore, Myron Barrie and I fishing muskies on July twenty-fourth in an open area of Cass Lake. We were drifting along a drop-off, casting spinner bait type bucktails over shallower water, six to eight feet deep. The morning had been interrupted with occasional follows by a few smaller muskies, but nothing to get us excited enough to pound them harder with our baits. It was about ten o'clock in the morning, when out of nowhere, beside the boat, a nice sized musky attacked my black bucktail lure. It was a close-in battle for a short period of time, but I was able to give the fish a little line and let it do the fighting out away from the boat. The big fish went around the boat, jumped on both sides and returned to the side where it had first taken the bait. I thought the battle was over, for the most part, but I was wrong. The fish made a lunge and a run under the boat to the other side, leaving me with the rod tip in the water, trying to look over my shoulder to watch its next move. The musky jumped again, and all I could do was keep a tight line and hope the fish didn't get any slack. At that point the fish began to play itself down, seeming to be physically spent after the three attempted jumps, and was lead back to the original side of the boat. Cousin Bob put the net under the fish and she was brought aboard for measuring and pictures. In about thirty or forty seconds time, the fifty-one and a half inch musky was swimming free, on its own, in the lake again! It was my first fifty inch plus fish of the season, and I caught some teasing, as usual, from my companions, about my placement of the boat in relationship to the drop-off. We continued to fish, and for some reason, my bait had that special touch, because there were three more muskies that took a pass it before the noon lunch break. I told Myron and Bob that I felt sorry for them, so I pulled the lure away from the muskies at the last second, in order to give them a chance at catching one. They didn't believe me and went on joking about my having all the action and not letting them in on the fun.

In August our family spent a week together at Cass Lake and the grandkids were the center of our attention. We enjoyed fishing together, but also games, taking turns cooking or preparing meals, swimming and sunbathing, visiting animal farms like: Deerland and Moondance, but most of all, the all day building of our annual sand castle. We get together each year with our immediate family and what a blessing it has been, especially for grandma and grandpa!

Later in August, another week was spent at Cass Lake with Gene Mattson,

Mike Peterson, Ski, Little Ski, Duc Fortado and a few other boys from the General Pattern plant in Blaine, Minnesota. We caught numerous walleyes in the late evenings, trolling Shad Raps over the shallow flats, in about ten feet of water. There were also a couple northern pike trips which proved successful, as Ski and Duc each caught an eleven and seven pound northern respectively. That is always a great August trip, and the friendships that have grown out of it are genuine, almost brotherly, as there isn't anything those men wouldn't do for a person.

There was the late September musky tournament, Steve Johnson and I were back, hoping for a better time this year than the previous, accident prone tourney of 1999. As it turned out, we fished the entire tournament free of any accidents, and unfortunately, free of any boated muskies. We did have several nice fish follow our lures but we could not entice one to eat the bait. There was this one musky we saw late Saturday afternoon that seemed to be aggressive, but wouldn't take the bait. It followed Steve's lure first and seemed interested enough, although it wouldn't go for the figure eight movement Steve presented at the end of his retrieve. The fish turned and swam back in the direction it had come from, so I cast my lure in that direction, to the spot where I thought the fish might be. Steve reached for his second rod, in an effort to present the fish with yet another lure of different character. On my retrieve the musky followed again, only to turn and swim back, not paying any attention to my figure eight either. Steve tossed his next lure to the fish and again it followed aggressively, this time chasing the figure eight, and seeming to want to eat the bait, but turning away to swim away for the third time. I had picked up my bucktail rod and placed a cast ahead of where the musky was retreating, we could see the fish do an about face and swim after my lure. I thought it was going to finally inhale my lure, but all it did was follow to the boat and swim off to its lair hidden somewhere in the heavy weed cover. We kept working the fish until tournament time rules forced us to give it up and try the next day. The next morning we were back at it, only to find the spot vacant and seemingly void of fish. I think we hit that area, casting our baits to the specific spot four different times, but the musky never showed up after that first evening. We estimated the size of this fish to be forty-eight plus inches, and it would have more than likely put us in the running for some pretty good prize money. I think we were just happy to have been able to compete again and not have any more bad experiences like in the past year.

The total number of muskies landed in my boat that summer was thirty-one, four of which were under the legal size limit, but all were released.

Our annual reunion and trout fishing trip to the White River in Arkansas took place again in mid-October. This time my brother, Larry, my son, Chad and I met our cousin Tom Horn on the river and spent the better part of the week catching and releasing many trout. We had our limit to take home by the end of the second day, but we kept eating them and having fish dinners, so we kept fishing and enjoying the beautiful Ozark scenery. There were many fifteen to seventeen inch rainbow trout caught, as well as an occasional brown or cut-throat trout. We always have a good time and enjoy each other's company. Some of the others of our regular group couldn't come because of other conflicts, but I'm sure they will return again to fight the spunky trout of the White River.

2001 brought some new adventures and friends and proved to be an exciting summer filled with fun and enjoyable times. Late in April, before the regular fishing season opener in Minnesota, our Fishers of Men group traveled to Woman Lake in the north central part of the state. We were fishing crappies on a small bay, near a brush pile located on a drop-off next to the shore. It was a fun group and we enjoyed catching thirty-two or thirty-three crappies, cleaning them and telling stories about who was the best crappie fisherman. We enjoyed some fine food, good fellowship, and lots of kidding to and from everyone in the group. The best part of the outing was, most of us got to fish together on a pontoon boat, so we kept the competitive spirit close. I know that I look forward to these outings and try to attend as many as I can. It's a great bunch of men and you can't beat the fun and fellowship we have when we all get together.

Ron Lykins and I made our usual annual trip to Cass Lake and caught limits of walleyes again, in our favorite spot. The weather cooperated a little better than in years past, so we were able to anchor the boat near the middle of the lake. The old jig and minnow method worked again, so we had our limits by the end of the first day. We gave our spot to some other fishermen and found out later, they limited out too. This place had been good to us and we agreed that the old method along with a little time and patience were the answers to this consistent, but effective success. I suppose you'll find us in that same spot each year because of its location and convenience. I don't think we used more than a gallon of gas on this opening weekend, compared to all the other years we spent much of the weekend running from place to place in search of walleyes.

The first of June, Ron and I traveled again to Lake Minnewaska, where we helped his mom get her lake home ready for the upcoming summer. We also caught lots of bass and sunfish again, and released them all to fight again another day. The surface lures were still working for the bass, and the sunnies loved the small Beetle Spins, especially the sixteenth ounce size. We use ultra light equipment on these fish and that makes for some fun and exciting action. I have come to realize that the main reason for going to Margaret Lykins' house on Lake Minnewaska, is to get to taste her sweet rolls! She bakes the most delicious sweet rolls, they seem to melt in your mouth, and she usually serves them warm, like right out of the oven. I always enjoy getting spoiled by her cooking and will never get tired of her to-do lists as long as she keeps those sweet rolls around. I think Ron and I averaged forty some bass each two or three hour trip and probably as many sunfish. It's a great lake and holds many fish that are basically easy to find and catch.

In mid-June, John Karnos, a friend from Braham, and I fished a musky tournament on Rush Lake close to our hometown. The tourney was sponsored by the North Metro Muskies, Inc. group and has become an annual event enjoyed by as many as fifty or sixty musky fisherpersons each year. It is a one day contest, usually held on a Saturday, with an awards ceremony after the tournament closes in the late afternoon. John and I started at six o'clock in the morning, throwing larger musky jerk baits and crank baits. We allowed the boat to drift along a drop-off or over the edge of weedy areas, casting our lures out and retrieving them back to the boat. By ten o'clock we were getting hungry, so we ate a sandwich and planned some different strategy. I told John that I was getting tired of tossing those heavy baits and thought I would go to my bucktail rod with a small spinner bait, for a different kind of presentation. He said he was thinking of doing the same thing, so we both switched. I was throwing a perch colored , Fudally's Musky Candy bait and it seemed like casting a feather compared to the heavier lures I was using earlier. John went to a black in-line bucktail and within two casts, had caught a nice northern, which he released. Within about two more casts I felt a tug and set the hooks on what I thought was a northern, but the fish took line and made the drag work under its steady powerful run. At that point I told John I thought it might be a musky, and he reeled in and got the net ready. Sure enough as the fish came to the surface in an attempt to jump, we could see its silvery side with dark spots, and knew right away it was a musky. It was a long fish with a small girth, but it still packed plenty of power as it made three or four good runs. It did manage to jump once, but by then it was tired and playing itself down. After a few minutes I brought the musky by the boat and John got it in the net, where we kept it until a witness boat could be summoned by radio. In a minute or two the witness boat came along side our boat and together we measured the musky at forty-nine and a half inches. Its girth was a mere twenty-one inches and the fish weighed only thirty pounds. We released the fish alive and it swam under the boat and back to the cover of weeds from where it had come. The two witnesses signed my release form and left, so we were off again to see if we could be lucky enough to find another one. It was only ten thirty and John indicated that he was still hungry, so we ate another sandwich on our way to a new location. I learned by use of the two-way radio there had been several other muskies reportedly caught, but we didn't know the size of those other fish. We did think that we might possibly be in the running for a prize though and continued to fish even harder. We had fished for another two hours with no result and I thought of changing back to my original baits that I had used earlier that morning, but decided against it for no reason. The weather began to change from a bright sunny sky to a partly cloudy one, with the possibility of what looked like rain in the distance. The wind began to blow a little harder from the west and for a short time I thought we may have to go in. As it turned out, we positioned ourselves behind a point and out of the wind, but still in a good musky producing area. There was a man in a boat fishing panfish in the weeds and lilly pads near shore, so I tried to keep the boat at a distance trying not to interfere with his fishing privacy. As the boat floated around him I made my first cast with the small spinner bait and before I turned the crank three times, there was a huge crashing impact on the end of my line. Instinctively, I set the hooks, and it felt like a live cement block at the other end. I wasn't sure what the fish was, but I had a pretty good idea it must be a musky. It made a long powerful run for deep water, and I told John that it had to be a huge fish, because I had never had a fish so powerful as that on my line before. The fish then charged the surface with fury, in an attempt to jump and free itself from the hooks. When John saw it, he gasped, "That is a big fish!" I replied, "It certainly is!" The huge musky made three more long, solid, powerful runs, and tried to jump after each one. By this time there were a half dozen boats gathered around us and the musky began to lose strength and play itself out. Only a couple more short runs and John had it in the net! There were cheers and shouts as the occupants in other boats got to witness the catch. Fortunately, one of the boats was fishing the tournament and witnessed the fish almost as soon as it was in the net. We measured it at fifty-one and a half inches, with a girth of twenty-six inches. It was a beautifully proportioned fish and tipped the scales at forty-four and a half pounds. A quick picture and then a live release and the fish was free and swimming again. The witnesses signed the release form and continued on their way as we continued to fish for another musky. After all these years, I finally had my lifelong goal of a forty pound musky! My record of thirty- nine pounds, fifteen ounces, had been shattered by almost five pounds! What a day! Two huge fish in a tournament and friends around to witness the big event, it was great! That fish was caught at two thirty in the afternoon with an hour and a half to fish before we went in. The minutes seemed to go fast, because before I knew it, it was time to load the boat and get to the resort for the awards ceremony. I believe there were fifty-three fisherpersons in the contest and fourteen muskies were caught, ten of which were forty inches or over. Three people caught two muskies, and needless to say, my two held up to take the first place trophy. The story made the local papers and it became quite a notable event, as I received many letters congratulating me on the fantastic catch. One letter I received, was from a Minnesota State Representative, congratulating me for catching two muskies for a combined length of one hundred inches and weighing a total of seventy-five pounds. It was a great feeling and a memory I'll remember for the rest of my life.

Early in July I was blessed to take another fishing trip with the Fishers of Men group. It was to a fly-in resort located on Atikwa Lake in west central Ontario. We made the week long outing with twenty total people in our group. Atikwa Lodge is the only resort on the thirty-five mile long lake, and is only accessible by air. The fishing there consists mainly of trolling for lake trout or northern pike, but walleyes, muskies and small mouth bass can be caught if a person wants to take a short portage over land to another lake. There were several large northern caught that week running from ten to fifteen pounds, and many nice lake trout in the average five pound range. We had some delicious meals at the main lodge and everyone made new friends within the group. There were a couple shore lunches, a few fish were kept, but most were released as we didn't want to bother with the transporting of a few fillets, because of the ice supply being in short demand. It was a great trip and I especially enjoyed the plane rides in and out from the resort.

In July we made our regular trip to Cass Lake again and one of the highlights of the trip was a fifty inch musky caught by my friend, Myron Barrie, trolling! We had been casting all morning and it was hot and still, so Myron suggested that we troll some crank baits down the sand bar to the next weed bed, almost a half mile away. We rigged up the crank baits and started trolling, trying to keep the boat positioned above the break line where the fish might likely be. I don't think we had gone more than fifty yards when Myron set the hooks on a powerful strike. Immediately we could see the fish on the surface, fighting to get free. Myron fought the musky around the boat several times letting it run and keeping a tight line when needed. He did a great job of fighting the fish and several times we commented on the fact that it would go an easy fifty inches. I even guessed it at thirty-five pounds. When the fish played down a bit more, Myron brought it along side the boat, and the net man, (that's me) asked if he was ready. He said he was, so the net man (that's me) put the net under the musky and just happened to get one of the hooks caught in the mesh, before the musky was completely in the net! Now the net man (that's me) had a big problem! The musky gained new life and thrashed and tore the hook out of its mouth, while the net man (that's me) stood there dumbfounded and watched the big fish swim away. It's one of those times when you wish you could crawl in a crack and not come out for a month or so. There is no excuse except to say, "I goofed!" Oh well, I think Myron has forgiven me and we still fish together and he has even allowed me to net some muskies for him since that little incident back in July of 2001. The remainder of the July trip went well, as usual, we caught lots of walleyes during our evening trips and Bob Moore caught another forty inch musky. My big fish for that week was a thirty-one inch musky, which I released before anyone could snap my picture. The week went too fast as usual and we found ourselves packing to go home long before we were ready to.

A week later, the first of August, our family enjoyed the vacation we had been taking annually now for a few years. Our niece, Denise Vandeloo, her husband, Shawn, and their daughter, Taylor, joined our family and we all had a terrific time. Our son, Chad, his wife Regina, their children, Colton and Ashley and our daughter Cristi, her husband, Joel, Jan and I all took up housekeeping in one of the larger five bedroom cabins at Sah-Kah-Tay Resort. The cabin sleeps thirteen people comfortably, so the eleven of us got along quite well. We did the usual things, shopping, eating, fishing, swimming, sunbathing, sight seeing, jet skiing, hunting arrowheads, and most importantly, working on and building the all day sand castle. Our fishing was done mostly in the evenings, and everyone caught walleyes on the ever famous Shad Raps, which continued to be the hot lure again. Shawn enjoyed fishing probably more than anyone else, so he and I would get up in the early morning and go musky fishing while everyone else slept. The first time out, he caught a forty-two inch musky on a large crank bait and he was hooked on muskies. A short time later I landed a forty-six inch musky which turned out to be my largest of the season. Shawn is an avid catfish fisherman, and he and Denise live in Atchinson, Kansas, located on the west banks of the Missouri River. He has caught many big flathead catfish and promised to take me river fishing the next time I came to Kansas. Again our week was much too short and ended before we were ready to leave.

I had planned to make the annual trip to Cass Lake with the General Pattern group again, but because of the death of my wife's mother, we traveled to Kansas for her funeral in mid-August. I got to go fishing with Shawn sooner than I had anticipated. My wife had to meet with her brother and sister to tie up some estate details, so upon Shawn's invite to go fishing on the big Missouri River, I jumped at the chance. We spent the better part of one morning down river from Atchison, and caught a few small channel catfish, two large carp, and had one of those big head European carp jump into our boat. It is a different strain of carp, brought here to eat and clean up the zebra muscles that seem to be taking over our waterways. Something happened in Louisiana or Mississippi, where some of these carp accidentally were lost in a flood near some fishery operation, or so the story is told. Now this species has made its way up rivers and streams to many points in Illinois, Missouri, Kansas, and even Iowa and Wisconsin. The species is a very nervous type fish that will jump, dart, and go crazy as a boat approaches or when something disrupts its habitat, namely the water it is swimming in. The river trip was both educational and enjoyable, because I had never fished like that before, and it is always a neat experience to navigate new and different waters.

During the Labor Day weekend, our same group enjoyed the trip back to Cass Lake, and this time many walleyes were caught in the late evening hours. The "ladies night" fishing party showed up the men again, as they brought in more walleyes than the other boats. One night, while everyone had returned to the resort early to get a good seat around the campfire. Bill and Josh Coleman accompanied by Tory Auger, had stayed well beyond the walleye bite, and to their surprise the bite continued. They came in just before midnight with fourteen really nice walleyes, a very credible stringer, but they missed the campfire and the jokes and stories being told by the group, in general. Jerry and Beth Johnson caught the three nicest walleyes of the weekend, all three pounders, and they fished an area of shallow water where hardly anyone ever goes. We all took a lesson from that experience, but it didn't do anyone else any good, because they tried in that spot again and didn't have success. The weekend passed and we found ourselves back in school or on the job, tending to our responsibilities at home.

Later in September, our Fishers of Men group had another outing on Boy Lake, located just east of Leech Lake. We experienced a cold, windy, wet weekend, one with many games, laughs and enjoyable discussions, despite the weather.

We ended the season with twenty-one legal muskies and fourteen under the legal size.

That fall, in mid-October, we made our trout trip south, but not all the way to the White River. My brother, Larry and his wife, my cousin, Tom Horn and his wife, my wife, Jan and I had all invested in a time-share in Branson, Missouri. Branson is located in the southern part of the state, almost on the state line, separating it from Arkansas, where the White River is nestled in the Ozarks of the northern part of that state. Our three families met in Branson for a five day break, taking in a few shows, sight seeing, and fishing. We fished Lake Tanneycomo, actually a river below the Table Rock Lake dam, and caught many rainbow trout. It was very similar to the White River in Arkansas, especially since it is the same river system. Tom and Jodee Horn, Jan and I went to the White River one day for a scenic boat ride and accidentally on purpose, Tom and I had brought the fishing tackle along! We fished for almost half a day, catching more trout than we could eat, so many of them were released. Upon returning to Lake Tanneycomo, we decided fishing was just as good in Branson as it was in Arkansas, and we caught more brown trout in the Tanney. There are several public fishing piers located in and near Branson, so it's easy to access the lake and enjoy the fishing and scenery. There are also plenty of marine facilities up and down the lake where a person can rent a boat to take sightseeing or fishing. It's a beautiful area all year long, and offers plenty of diverse entertainment, plus good, clean, wholesome fun for the entire family.

Back home and near the end of October, I took a big step in the direction of a new boat. Actually, it was a used boat, but new to me, a 1998 model Warrior. The price was right and I had been looking at newer boats for a couple years, waiting for the appropriate one and the right time. The Warrior is built locally in Maple Lake, Minnesota, and this particular model is eighteen and a half feet long, powered by a ninety horse Mercury outboard motor. A very comfortable fishing boat, as well as providing a smooth, dry ride, even in bigger, rough water. The problem was, I had to wait about six months before getting to use it on Minnesota waters. I considered towing it south in February or March, but decided against that idea, thinking the wait would make it all worthwhile. The sixteen foot Lund, which I had been using the past few years, was in very good condition and a friend, Gene Mattson, spoke for it soon after I had purchased the Warrior, so I knew the Lund would be getting a good owner as well as a nice home.

In early May, 2002, Ron Lykins and I took my newly acquired Warrior to Cass Lake for our annual fishing opener. We initiated the boat in grand fashion with two limits of walleyes the first morning out. The electric trolling motor allowed us to move slowly enough to entice the cold water walleyes into biting. We also anchored for a short time, in the favorite old spot, using our favorite old method, a jig and minnow combination. It proved successful again, as usual, and before long the live well was filled with our twelve walleyes. During that weekend we ate a dozen walleyes, caught a dozen more to take home, gave a dozen to some other less fortunate fishermen, and released another two dozen that we couldn't legally keep. We were both impressed with the comfort the Warrior awarded us and the smooth ride across rather wavy waters we enjoyed.

Our fifth annual trip to Lake Minnewaska, was again pleasing as in years before. The bass were cooperative, as they literally attacked our surface baits and gave us plenty competition, using the heavy weed cover to attempt to run to, after being hooked. Ron and I always practice as much "catch and release" as we can. This was no exception as we actually tallied an average forty-five bass per every two hour trip, and never kept one fish. The sunfish were just as aggressive and provided lots of entertainment on the ultra light equipment we used. Once again, all the jobs on Margaret Lykin's to-do list were taken care of, the fishing was great, and the food was super. It seems like those two and three day weekends always go by too quickly, but the nice thing about it is, we get to go back, year after year.

In June, the North Metro Muskies, Inc., Rush Lake Challenge was into its fifth annual event. John Karnos and I fished the tourney again as we had the past year, when we won the first place trophy. This year proved to be a different story, as John was the only one to register a musky in my boat, a thirty-nine inch fish that didn't earn enough points to place in the contest. We had spent most of the day casting, trolling, and searching the various areas of the lake in an effort to land another big musky, but it didn't happen. The tournament is always a joy to fish, and there is always a great group of people involved, both in participation and organization.

As July rolled around, we found ourselves getting prepared to take our annual trip to Cass Lake, with friends and family. Our usual venture to the lake takes the better part of a day, where an actual three hour trip really ends up taking us about six or seven hours. Mainly because we like to stop for breakfast, antique shops, garage sales, and lunch, before arriving at the resort mid-afternoon. Another reason is, the resort needs time to clean the cabins after each party has checked out, and before the next party is to arrive. It is only common courtesy to make sure we arrive sometime around one or two o'clock in the afternoon, just to give the owners a chance to make adequate adjustments to their cleaning schedule. The day came for us to make our way north, and after our arrival the usual plans were to unload all the luggage, food, and miscellaneous items first. Then Myron and I would launch our boats and make them ready, while our wives, Jan and Bev arranged everything in the cabin. Sometimes, if the women felt like they wanted to fish, we would all go out for a trial walleye run, but this particular evening they chose to relax at the cabin. Myron and I went musky fishing in my newly acquired Warrior. I was anxious to have Myron fish from my boat, and I think he was anticipating being able to. We were only going out for a short time and then return to have dinner with our wives. We made a quick stop by an area called the "Kettle" with only a small northern pike taking Myron's lure. Then it was on to Cedar Island, to an area that was sparsely populated with under water vegetation, where we drifted and cast crank baits over a gradual drop-off. I guess we were about one hundred yards into our drift when Myron set the hooks on a fish. It was a musky, as it surfaced immediately, and we could see the tell-tale dark spots on a silvery side. At the time, I wasn't sure which lure Myron was using, but as the lengthy fish swam past the boat, I could see this bright pink bodied bait hanging out the side of its mouth. I exclaimed, "What is that!" Myron questioned, "What ?" I re-phrased my question saying, "What is that pink conglomeration in the muskies' mouth?" Myron chuckled and replied, "Oh that, that's my secret bait!" I'm still not sure what the lure is called, but it looks like a pink squid with a plastic lip molded into the front body of the lure, which causes it to dive and wobble. The back two thirds of the lure is all rubber, with tiny finger-like projections that seem to flutter as it is pulled through the water. This was a nice musky, so I wasn't about to distract Myron's efforts to bring the fish to the net, so for the time being, I dropped the subject of "pink." I managed to snap a few pictures of Myron fighting the fish and when the time came to net it, I was there with the net and scooped the musky up and into the boat. We quickly measured the fish at forty-nine inches and estimated its weight at about thirty pounds. After taking pictures of the fish and Myron releasing it, I began to question again, "Pink ?" Myron just laughed and answered, "It worked, didn't it?" I agreed to that, but I also told him the fish must have been sick or something and thought it was getting a dose of Pepto-Bismol! He still hasn't heard the end of that story, as I tease him every chance I get, but I have to admit, you don't argue with success. We fished a while longer and it was time to go in, the women were surprised to hear that we had landed a nice musky the first two hours into our trip. After cousin, Bob Moore arrived, the three of us fished the remainder of the week, and Bob was the only lucky one, catching and releasing another forty-two inch musky. Bob had asked me on the way out, what color bait he should use, I advised him to use a black bucktail spinner with a gold blade, since it was a cloudy day. He followed my advise and caught the nice forty-two inch fish on the first weed patch we hit. He wouldn't give me any credit though, as he thought it was just a lucky guess. We had fun teasing him about it anyway.

The first week of August, there were a couple highlights to our stay at the resort. This was our week with family, and Scott, Lisa, MacKenzie, and Lauren Moore joined us at Cass Lake. Scott is the son of cousins, Bob and Karen Moore from Kansas, his wife is Lisa, and their two daughters are, MacKenzie and Lauren. Our son, Chad, his wife, Regina, their children, Colton and Ashley and our daughter Cristi, her husband, Joel, my wife, Jan and I had reserved the big cabin at Sah-Kah-Tay Resort for that week. We spent most of the week, entertaining the kids and keeping them busy, which included a few short fishing trips. MacKenzie caught some perch and had a great time getting her picture taken along with Colton and Ashley with their catches. During mid-week, Scott, Chad and I were supposed to go musky fishing early one morning, but Chad had a hard time waking up and didn't make the trip. Scott and I boated across the lake to some musky areas near the east shore to begin our morning of casting. As we put the slight breeze to our backs, drifted the drop-off, and cast our lures, I concentrated the boat so that Scott would be fishing over the best musky water. It was a sharp drop and in the back of the boat, I was fishing over about fifteen to twenty feet of water. Scott, in the bow of the boat, was directly over the prime depth of the break, eight to twelve feet deep. I assumed he would probably have the action and I was attempting to run a deep diving Cisco Kid crank bait down in hopes of attracting the attention of a deeper fish. My theory for Scott didn't work out, as I had a terrific hit in the deep water. Immediately after setting the hooks on what felt like a hefty fish, it broke the surface in an attempted jump, shaking and thrusting its head and body, trying to eject the lure from its mouth. There were three short runs around the boat and another attempted jump, but the lengthy musky was losing ground, and exhausting itself with each futile try. Scott had the net ready, and when I gave the signal, he put it under the fish and scooped it up. We quickly brought the fish into the boat, took pictures, measured and released it within a matter of about a minute. The musky swam away, looking healthy, heading for the deep water and probably wanting to rest from its hard fight. The measure read forty-nine and a half inches and we guessed the girthy fish to have weighed thirty-two pounds, give or take a pound or two. I was disappointed that Scott hadn't been able to enjoy the catch, but I guess that is what happens when you try to plan the outcome that you don't have too much control over. We caught some walleyes that week, but as a whole, the fishing was slower than normal, except for that one nice musky. Near the end of the week, Chad, Scott and I were fishing muskies along the south shore near Norway Beach. Scott spotted something in the water between us and the south side of Cedar Island. It was a small dot of something swimming, and after observing it for awhile, Scott and Chad decided it was a deer. The animal must have been in the water for some thirty or forty minutes when we first saw it, judging from its location and distance from any shore. As boats were coming and going across the lake and around the point of the island, the deer would become more and more confused, changing its direction each time. I paid little attention to it, as I had seen deer swim across the lake many times from one point of land to another. Scott and Chad were more interested in the animal, because it wasn't getting any closer to shore, and it had to be getting tired. I continued to cast for muskies as they became more interested in the reactions of the deer to the several boats causing it to become still more confused. Finally we reached the end of our fishing area and I sat down to observe the animal a bit more closely, noticing it was swimming parallel to the south side of Cedar Island, but not attempting to head toward shore. After it had passed the point off the southeast corner of the island and headed toward the east shore, which was a mile away, we decided that maybe we should intervene. We headed to a location just in front of the deer, which we could now see was a rather large doe. It was afraid of our boat and changed direction, heading back toward the island. It took some time and herding, as the seemingly exhausted animal kept turning and swimming. After about twenty minutes we had the deer close to shore and now it wanted to escape our pursuit. All the time, Chad was in the bow, taking pictures of the doe as she made her way to land and what would probably be a long rest, once she hid herself in the underbrush, away from all this activity. When her hooves touched upon some solid underfooting, she staggered out of the water, stood wobbling back and forth, and shook herself off. Then she staggered a few more steps, stopped, turned to give us a last look, and bounded into the dense wooded area of the island. I am not certain the deer had enough energy to swim to that far shore, but I am glad we were able to help it to shore, knowing it would be safe and able to rest before making its way on across. The week ended and we all went home with much to talk about and retain those memories to tell about later.

The month of August was finished out with a trip to Cass Lake again with the General Pattern crew. Fishing in general was still a bit slow, but we managed to catch enough walleyes to have a nice fish fry and a few of the boys even took some fish home. The northern fishing was good during that week, as we "soaked some suckers," and caught a few impressive eight, ten and twelve pound fish. The use of a bobber is always fun if you don't mind anchoring and playing the waiting game with the northern pike.

In September, there were a few muskie trips to Rush Lake, near Braham, where we caught and released several average sized fish. Then in late September, we made our annual trip with the Fishers of Men group to Boy Lake again. That year we received a tip that the walleyes and crappies were hitting on Cut Foot Sioux and Little Cut Foot Lake. We trailered our boats to those lakes and enjoyed two fun-filled days of crappies and walleyes. Those fish were kept and used for an inner-city fish fry to feed many needy people and bring the message of God's love to them. The weekend was spent in fun, fishing and fellowship, plus having Ron Linder being our guest and key speaker for the weekend.

The fall weather turned cold early that year and my thoughts turned to hunting, so the boat was winterized and put into storage for another season. The problem with that is, when the hunters are picking up their guns, we should be going fishing, but I enjoy hunting too, so some choices must be made, and I usually choose to go hunting.

In late November, about Thanksgiving time, Jan and I purchased a twenty-four foot travel trailer. We secured a seasonal site for it at Sah-Kah-Tay Resort on Cass Lake, and planned to move it there the following spring. It was an exciting time for us, as we would now have a place to stay, anytime we wanted to go to

Cass Lake, without making previous reservations.

2003 brought several exciting experiences and some new adventures which proved to be both exciting and enjoyable. Since we had purchased a trailer, and had a site to place it on, that was one of the first orders of business. Ron Lykins and I had reservations in a cabin at Birch Villa Resort for the opening fishing season, so we traveled there and enjoyed a cool, rather slow opener, as far as fishing goes. It was slow going at first, but as I mentioned before, patience paid off for us before the weekend came to a close. We took our limits of walleye home and had a nice fish dinner while spending most of the weekend in the boat.

The following weekend, my nephew, Lindsey, pulled my trailer to Cass Lake for me, while my brother pulled his trailer to the same area where we had sites side by side. I had brought my boat, so the three of us set the trailers on blocks for the summer, and then went fishing. It was a beautiful weekend, weather-wise, and we enjoyed the warmth of the sun over the cool water. Surface temperatures varied from forty-two degrees up to forty-six that weekend, and we presented a very slow moving bait for the walleyes. It paid off, but we had to move around the lake a lot, trying many different spots, and catching maybe only two or three walleyes at each location. We managed to get our limits to take home, and had a beautiful day on Sunday to enjoy a fish dinner outside, on the picnic table. Most of these fish were caught on jig and minnow rigs, but a few were taken on a leech set-up, with presentation in or near the weeds along a sharp drop-off. It turned out to be a very nice weekend and before we left, the trailers were secure and all the water and electrical hook-ups had been connected. All we had to do now, was come to the lake and enjoy our new little summer home away from home. The very next weekend happened to be Memorial Day. Jan and I journeyed to Cass Lake to give our trailer its first try-out, and for the first time that I can remember, the weather was beautiful all weekend. I commented that it must have been too nice, because the fishing was terrible. We fished the entire three-day weekend, and Jan caught the only keeper walleye, which turned out to be only a sixteen incher. The sun was warm, the sky was continually bright, and the lake stayed calm for the entire three days. I concluded that since the water was still very cold, the fish must be in shallower areas, and with those weather conditions, it was difficult to get them to bite. The eight fish we caught, including Jan's keeper, all came from four to six foot depths. We tried the ten to twenty foot depths, but to no avail, as most of the fish were in the shallows. It was frustrating, because we were enjoying the beautiful weather and scenery, but the walleyes were not cooperating. We even tried our old late summer stand-bys, the Shad Raps and Beetle Spins, but nothing seemed to work for us. I guess you can't always have everything the way you want it, and we did enjoy the great boat rides around the lake and all the extras that go with it, namely the eagles, the early loons, and all of nature's beauty. There was one other factor that probably played a major role in this fishless outcome, and that was the fact there had been a huge insect hatch at the time. Jan and I noticed the large areas of dead insects and insect carcasses floating on the calm water as we boated around the lake each day. It looked like large areas of oil slicks on the surface, but was actually the buoyant remains of the insects. These were present almost everywhere we went on the lake, and that was pretty much over the entire body of water. You can see we were disappointed in the fishing, but considering the fortunate luck we had the two preceding weekends, it was not a big issue with us, as the weather made up for the lack of fish.

One week later, Ron Lykins and I made our annual trip to Lake Minnewaska again to help his mother, Margaret, get the spring chores done for the summer, at her lake home. Can you imagine, I'm retired, and now experiencing the fourth fishing trip of this young season, in as many weeks ? It was like a little taste of heaven, as I was being able to live a dream that I had dreamed about over the years. Ron and I enjoyed the bass fishing and the panfish, but only after we had completed the chores on Margaret's to-do list. We also enjoyed the food and sweet rolls she had for us at each meal. It's always a joy to spend some time at her home.

Later in June, I had promised three friends I would take them musky fishing on Rush Lake, near our home. These were each different trips, so my first guests were to be, Michele and Tim Kleven, and we were going to fish the second Wednesday in June. As it turned out, Tim had to work that day, so I took Michele and headed for Rush Lake. I met and worked with her at several NWTF meetings over the past few years. That is an organization called National Wild Turkey Federation, which supports the preservation and conservation of wild turkeys over the United States and elsewhere. We were on the water by nine o'clock that morning and fished until about two in the afternoon. Michele had one nice musky follow her perch colored crank bait to the boat, which got her a little excited, and later caught a fair sized northern. I didn't have much luck that day, and was a little disappointed we hadn't seen more action than we did. Michele was happy to have seen a musky follow and said she enjoyed the time on the water, just getting away for a few hours, so the day wasn't a complete wash. The next day, June twelfth, I took Keith Petersen and a friend, Mark Larson, back out to Rush Lake. Keith is also an NWTF member, and chairman of our local organization in Cambridge, MN. The weather was almost perfect, partly cloudy, threatening rain, a slight breeze from the south, and cool enough so that a light jacket felt good. Keith was the first to connect on a musky, and a good one it was, too. The fish had followed a Pflueger Muskil bucktail out of some heavy weed cover and took the bait halfway to the boat. Keith did a great job, playing the big musky out and away from the thick vegetation, and after a short fight, he brought the fish along side the boat and I netted it for him and scooped it into the boat. We quickly took some pictures and measured the forty-six inch musky before releasing it back into the water unharmed. It swam away almost instantly, and we said our congratulations to Keith, then prepared to continue fishing. In less than five minutes, Mark hooked into another fish and was playing it, as a light mist had set in. Keith and I donned our rain gear while Mark played the fish around the boat, in an effort to bring it to the net. It was a smaller fish than Keith's, but it still had the power of a nice sized musky. Finally, Mark won the battle and I netted the fish for him, we measured it at forty inches, took pictures and released it. Everything worked out the way I would have wanted it, two guests and each with a musky, but the trip wasn't over. When Mark finally put his rain gear on, it had stopped misting and we continued our task. Within the next five minutes, both Keith and Mark each had another musky on and lost it. Shortly after that, we all had other follows to the boat. This all took place in about a twenty or thirty minute span of time, which I believe, explains those short windows of chance we get every now and then. If we are on the water at the time, it's important to keep doing what we are doing, and hope the situation favors our odds. I have seen so many of these "active times" while fishing, that it has made a believer of me, and I try to stay with the task until I feel it is more than likely over. Usually it has paid off and the result is a successful fishing trip. We fished the remainder of the day, having our lunch in the boat, eating on the run, and trying to make a great day of musky fishing, a little greater. It ended up being one of the best trips of the summer in my boat, as the musky fishing seemed to get a lot tougher after that. Keith and Mark were pleased and that made me feel good, as I still maintain a lot of the old guide spirit within my heart. I enjoy seeing others catch fish as much, if not more, than I enjoy catching them myself. We ended a fun day on a positive note, despite having lost a couple nice fish, and always remembering the two muskies we did get into the boat.

The very next day, June thirteenth, another friend, Jim Haga and I returned to Rush Lake. It seemed as if someone had turned everything off from the day before, as we fished all morning with only one small musky follow. It was a nice day with bright sun, clear skies, and very little wind, and the muskies must have been enjoying the weather someplace else as the activity was nil. Regardless of having caught no fish, it's always fun to fish with Jim, we have made two or three trips together on Rush Lake and one of these times, he is going to connect on a big musky. I can feel it in my bones.

A week later, Jan and I took our grandchildren, Colton and Ashley out to Rush Lake for a day of fishing for whatever would bite. We try to do that at least once during the summer and the kids enjoy catching panfish and having lunch in the boat. Ashley caught a nice twelve inch bluegill and Colton hauled in a hefty four pound northern pike. Grandpa caught a little bitty northern on a musky surface lure, and we all had to laugh, because the lure was almost as big as the fish. Sometimes those pesky little fish attack things twice their size, it makes you wonder what they are thinking or if they are thinking. It's always fun with the grandkids no matter how many fish we catch.

In mid-June I arrived at Cass Lake a day earlier than the General Pattern crew from Blaine, Minnesota, so I thought I'd do a little scouting, before the group arrived. I had done a little visiting with friends in the area during the middle of the day, but when six o'clock had rolled around, I had eaten supper and was in my boat headed out to one of my favorite walleye spots, the West Cedar Bar. I fished from six to eight that evening without a bite, covering the entire length of the half mile long bar at least three times. I had used minnows, leaches, and Shad Raps with only an occasional perch insisting on having its interruption of my valuable time noted. I was about to give up when I decided to make one last effort to catch a walleye by switching to a lime green colored Beetle Spin, and troll it down the West Cedar Bar. I cast the small quarter ounce lure behind the boat and began to troll, moving along at three miles per hour. I had no more than relaxed to prepare for the wait when, bang, something hit the lure with avengence. It was a nice two pound walleye! The fish went into my live well and I continued on, within a minute, another nice seventeen inch walleye! This action continued for about an hour, after which time I took stock of what I had in the live well. There were five walleyes, one short of my limit, the time was eight forty-five, and I had decided to go in at nine o'clock, for no apparent reason other than it was getting dark. I thought I would troll for about another five minutes to see if I could fill my limit and then go in. It didn't take five minutes, and the last walleye was a twenty-three inch, chunky fish that weighed a little over four and a half pounds. Now my evening was complete, so I headed to the dock to put the boat away and clean my fish before going up to my trailer. The twenty-three inch walleye was the largest, along with an eighteen inch, two seventeen inch, and two sixteen inchers that rounded out a very nice stringer. I had released seven or eight other small walleyes that didn't make the fifteen inch mark, a standard rule in my boat, for keeper walleyes. If it doesn't measure fifteen inches, it goes back, unless my wife catches it and gives me that "hungry for walleye look," then I usually get soft and let her bend my rule a bit. She is usually pretty good about releasing the smaller ones, but still gives me some teasing grief about my rule. The next day the General Pattern crew showed up and we began a seven day fishing outing that allowed us the privilege of some fish, but the ones we caught, we worked for. We had enough for a nice fish fry, and a few to take home, but not our limits. I guess I was the only one with my limit, thanks to the success of the Beetle Spin from that first night, and that one hour window of time between eight and nine o'clock, when the fish hit. The group is always a thrill to be with and I enjoy their company on these trips we take every year.

In mid-July, our friends, Myron and Bev Barrie accompanied Jan and I to Cass Lake for the first week of a two week vacation. We caught a few walleyes during that week, and Myron and I did a lot of musky fishing, catching many northern, but not too many muskies. During the evening hours of our fifth day there, Myron was using a surface bait, and a forty-one inch musky took it. He had a dandy fight with it and after a few minutes, brought it along side the boat where I was able to net it for him. The fish was measured, pictures were taken, and it was released within a minute, healthy and eagerly swimming away. During the second week of our stay, cousins Bob and Karen Moore joined us at Birch Villa Resort, and we continued the week with the men fishing muskies during the day, while the women shopped or worked on crafts. Then after an early evening meal, we would all go walleye fishing, trying to get enough fish for a fish fry and some to take home. Limits of walleye were taken by everyone in our group, but no more muskies were caught that week. It was time to pack up and leave again before we were ready, but I guess that's what keeps us coming back.

During the first week of August, our family enjoyed the week long vacation at Sah-Kah-Tay Resort, but the fishing had all but died, for some reason. I managed to catch a small thirty-nine inch musky, but the walleyes were getting hard to catch. It wasn't until the last two evenings that we located and caught decent catches of fish. They were all caught on Beetle Spins before dark and Shad Raps after dark. My grandson, Colton, caught his limit of walleyes and a nice thirty inch northern pike. The big event, "sand castle construction," took place our last day, and what a fun time we had, all working on some part of its completion. That is probably the highlight of our stay, along with getting to visit with old friends like the Hintzsche family and the Merv Michalyshens. The time spent there would be perfect if we could bottle it and save some of it for the winter months, but I guess that's why God gave us a memory, so we can savor those precious moments.

A few more trips to our trailer followed in August, and the walleye fishing got progressively better. I was able to catch one more Cass Lake musky, a forty inch fish that was released. Between the Cass Lake trips, I made frequent visits to Rush Lake, where I landed three more muskies, including a forty-six inch fish with a girth of twenty-two inches. The other two were thirty-eight and forty-one inches respectively.

Our Labor Day group outing took place again with the Steve Johnson family, Dave Youngbauer family, Vern Fix family, Tammy Engberg and my wife and I. Fishing was fair, but I was still in somewhat of a Cass Lake musky drought for the summer, only two small fish from this lake. Steve Johnson had several follows, including a fifty inch fish, which is a lot more than I can brag about. We had our "ladies night" in my boat again, as my wife, Jan, Carlyn Johnson, Jeanine Youngbauer and Lynn Fix all enjoyed catching their share of the walleyes. They caught twenty-six walleyes in three and a half hours, but wc kcpt only seven, as most did not pass my fifteen inch rule. There were several fourteen inch fish that were released, and I heard about it all night from this bunch of women. It was a fun time in the boat, as it always is, and we look forward to coming in to a nice campfire visit before retiring for the night. Dave Youngbauer and Vern Fix had the fire going and ready for a great evening as we told stories on each other and a few jokes, as well. Oh yes, and the story of Carlyn's "full moon" escapades from a few years earlier, surfaced again for the newcomers to our group.

Later in September, we made the Fishers of Men's fall outing on Boy Lake once again. Mike Cummins was my fishing partner for the weekend and once we located the fish, "It was a piece of cake," as Mike put it. I tell him he had a good guide, but really, he had the hot spinner bait, as we combined for a total of twenty bass and fifteen northern on Friday, and another eighteen bass and fifteen northern on Saturday. Mike caught two limits of bass and northern both days, including a twenty inch bass weighing in excess of five pounds. I followed with a limit of bass and two limits of northern each day, including a nineteen inch, four pound bass. It was a fun group and we were joined by Wally Hilgenberg, who fished with us all day Saturday and was our keynote speaker for the evening fellowship. Wally is a past Minnesota Viking, and a very personable man to get to know. It is an event I will always look forward to in the fall of the year.

The first weekend of October, found a friend, Bill Coleman and I back on Cass Lake for one last, late fall fling at fishing. We found the fishing in general to be difficult to say the least, as the walleyes would not cooperate with any type of bait, method or presentation. We fished hard for both walleye and muskies and never even saw one musky follow our lures. I believe we caught one keeper walleye, but it was late in the weekend and we decided to release it. Other than a few short trips to Rush Lake, that was the end of the fishing for my boat, as hunting season was upon us, and it was time to pick up the shotgun and go looking for birds.

I have come to the end of my book, except for a few brief author's notes, I only hope you enjoy reading it as much as I have enjoyed writing about these many fishing memoirs.

Ron Lykins and Merv with opening morning walleyes. Standing on the Birch Villa dock.

Ron Lykins with a large mouth bass from Lake Minnewaska, MN.

Merv holding a large mouth bass from Lake Minnewaska, MN. One of 47 caught that evening.

Merv holding a 51¹/₂" musky he caught and released while fishing with cousin Bob Moore and Myron Barrie.

Merv holding a 41" musky he caught and released in Cass Lake.

A 45¹/₂" musky Merv caught and released in Cass Lake.

A 45" musky Merv caught and released in Cass Lake.

Merv's daughter and son-in-law, Cristi and Joel, fishing for muskies at sundown on Cass Lake.

Regina and Chad Heitschmidt with some walleyes they caught on Cass Lake.

The family out looking for arrowheads.

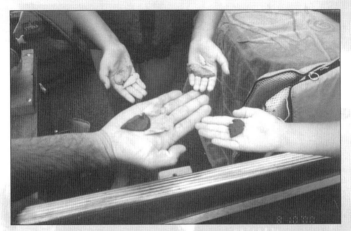

Some arrowheads found along the lake shore – another family outing.

More arrowheads found along the shoreline.

Merv with a 49½" musky he caught on Rush Lake in Chisago County, MN. This was one of two he relased in the tourney.

A 51½" musky. The second to be caught by Merv that day in the Rush Lake Tourney. This was Merv's 1st 40 pound musky. The girth was 26" and the fish weighed 44½"#.

Part of the "Fishers of Men" group enjoying some scenery along the way to the fly-in trip to Atikwa Lake Lodge in Ontario, Canada.

Some of the "Fishers of Men" & wives boarding the plane which took us to Atikwa Lake Lodge.

Beautiful scenery from plane flying in to Atikwa Lake Lodge.

Owners of Atikwa Lake Lodge, Renee and Frank Evans, greeting us as we arrived at the dock by float plane.

"Fishers of Men" enjoying a shore lunch on Atikwa Lake.

"Fishers of Men", Jack DeOtis and Mike Cummins, relaxing after a shore lunch.

"Fishers of Men", and wives enjoying an evening movie and popcorn in the Atikwa Lake Lodge.

Merv holding one of many nice lake trout caught on Atikwa Lake.

Part of the group of "Fishers of Men," hamming it up before the
float plane departure from Atikwa Lake Lodge.

Merv's wife, Jan, with a nice walleye she caught doing some late
evening fishing on Cass Lake.

Myron Barrie holding a 49" musky he caught and released in Cass Lake. Merv didn't get this one tangled up in the net.

Merv's granddaughter, Ashley, with a rock bass she caught during a family outing at Cass Lake.

Merv, son-in-law, Joel, and daughter, Cristi, with some walleyes caught in Cass Lake.

Cristi and dad, Merv, fishing for muskies on a beautiful August evening.

Merv with some of his fresh walleye being prepared for eating.

A Cass Lake musky caught by Merv in August. The fish was 46" long and was released.

Merv's nephew, Shawn Vandeloo, from Atchison, KS. It was Shawn's 1st musky and measured 42" before being released.

A twelve pound northern caught by Merv on Cass Lake.

Merv with his newly purchased Warrior boat manufactured in Maple Lake, Minnesota.

Merv with a 45" musky he caught and released in Cass Lake.

A 41" musky caught and released by Merv in Cass Lake.

Merv holding a 49½" musky he caught and released in Cass Lake during an early August trip.

The deer that Scott Moore, Chad Heitschmidt and Merv herded to shore on Cedar Island in Cass Lake.

Merv getting ready to release a 40" Cass Lake musky.

An early June limit of walleyes caught by Merv while fishing alone in Cass Lake. Ready to be cleaned and eaten.

A 42" musky caught on a surface lure and released by Myron Barrie.

A 10# northern caught and released by Merv on Cass Lake.

A 15# northern caught by Merv on Cass Lake.

Merv's grandson, Colton, with a northern he caught.

Merv's wife, Jan, with a large mouth bass she caught on a musky lure.

Keith Peterson with a 46" musky he caught and released on Rush Lake fishing with Merv in June, 2003.

Mark Larson with a 42" musky he caught fishing with Merv in June, 2003 on Rush Lake.

Author's Note

First let me say, I found it very difficult writing in first person, as I do not enjoy drawing attention to myself as much as I felt I did in this book. Having been a part of each situation was not only rewarding, but tremendously gratifying, because if it had not been for the many other people, my book would not have become a reality. I owe all these people a great deal of respect and appreciation for being a very important part of my life. The difficulty was, that since I was a part of each story, there are a lot of "me's," "I's," "us's," and "we's" included in each segment. I was always taught not to use those personal pronouns too much in my writing, but that ideal suggestion went "out the window," so to speak, with almost every tale that was told. I apologize for that, and hope you were not too bored by those numerous instances.

Every effort was made to write each story as if I were speaking it from my lips. There are many grammatical errors, I realize that, but the main goal was to deliver my information simply and understandably, and communicate the result in my words. For that reason I wrote it like I would casually and comfortably speak it.

This was my first attempt at writing a book, and I must acknowledge the fact that it was one of the most rewarding tasks I have accomplished. It was very time consuming, two years worth of a lot of writing and re-writing, and yet it seemed that time went very quickly. The note taking and log books started way back in 1957, and little did I know then, that it would become a book someday. The serious part of organizing and compiling much of the material has been in the making for probably the past ten or twelve years. Since retiring from teaching in January, 2002, much of my time has been devoted to finishing the book. I will forever be indebted to many of the students I have had in recent years, because they kept me accountable, by always asking, "How is your book coming?" There were many close friends and relatives who asked the same question, and that is what kept me on task and committed to completion of these many memoirs.

There are many more of these little stories which did not make the pages of the book for various reasons. Some of them were very minor in interest or content, while others were merely general in significance, and still, others would offer too much repetition. The book would have been much longer than it is, and probably would have taken another year to complete.

One more person who I am dearly indebted to is, Della Theis, she edited the book for me, and for that I am very appreciative. Della and I taught English next door to each other for many years in the Braham School system. Thank you, Della!

Without all the notes and logbooks over the years, it would have been next to impossible for me to accurately document and list names and statistics for all the entries covered. My advice to any young writers would be to keep logs, records and documentations of your activities, especially those of major interest in your lives. I can only wish I would have documented more experiences from my thirty-five years of teaching, because there were some golden moments that have been long since forgotten. Good luck, God bless you, and thanks for reading my book.

Merv Heitschmidt

The author, Merv, at his computer work station where this book was finished.